A FIELD OF DREAMS

A FIELD OF DREAMS
*Independent Writing Programs and
the Future of Composition Studies*

Edited by

PEGGY O'NEILL
ANGELA CROW
LARRY W. BURTON

UTAH STATE
UNIVERSITY PRESS
Logan, Utah

Utah State University Press
Logan, Utah 84322-7800

Manufactured in the United States of America.

Cover design by Barbara Yale-Read.

Library of Congress Cataloging-in-Publication Data

A field of dreams : independent writing programs and the future of composition studies / edited by
Peggy O'Neill, Angela Crow, Larry W. Burton.
    p. cm.
Includes bibliographical references and index.
    ISBN 0-87421-440-8 (alk. paper)
    1. English language—Rhetoric—Study and teaching. 2. English department administration
(Higher) 3. Independent writing programs. I. O'Neill, Peggy A., 1963– II. Crow, Angela, 1965– III.
Burton, Larry W.
   PE1404 .F45 2002
   808'.042'071–dc21

CONTENTS

INTRODUCTION
Cautionary Tales about Change

Angela Crow
Peggy O'Neill

This volume, like so many texts, grew out of lived experiences. When the idea for this book took hold, the three of us were working in a newly constructed writing and linguistics department at Georgia Southern University (see Agnew and Dallas, this volume, for more information). Larry was chair of the department (after serving as acting chair), and Angela and Peggy were assistant professors fresh from graduate school. Like the rest of the department, we didn't have any experience working in a freestanding writing unit—most of us had come through English departments and expected to spend our professional lives in English departments—but we were committed to the possibilities we envisioned in a writing department separated from traditions of literature scholarship. As the three of us struggled—along with the rest of the department—to figure out life in a writing department, we looked to the literature about the formation of writing as an academic field to help us define and legitimize ourselves in the campus community. We found a selection of scholarly texts on the disciplinary formation of English and the history and formation of composition studies; however, we didn't find much discussion about stand-alone—i.e., independent—writing departments.

We knew, though, about several stand-alones through informal sources such as conferences, listservs, or an occasional article, but we needed scholarly work. We wanted to learn from others, to resist making the same mistakes others may have made, and to situate our department in the disciplinary field of composition and rhetoric; but it was difficult to find resources—especially scholarly publications, the form of research most valued by the larger campus community. So in the midst of working to build a viable department, we decided to create a book that would collect stories of the formation of independent writing programs—writing programs or departments that are institutionally separated from literary studies and English departments—not only to document various institutional changes related to composition but also to provide information to others who may find themselves in similar circumstances.

The focus on independent writing programs and departments highlights trends that are distinctly different from other configurations the discipline has taken or might take. A variety of types of institutions—four-year public comprehensive universities, smaller regional colleges, private liberal arts schools, Research I universities—are included. These institutions, in most cases, have only one thing in common: a writing program that is not part of a department but rather stands apart as an independent program or department. Because of this focus, we haven't included stories of writing housed in multidisciplinary departments such as humanities or communications departments, structures not unusual at two-year schools, technical colleges, even small private institutions. While the discoveries and experiences of such multidiscipline departments are also important, we wanted a book that would speak to the unique issues facing composition and rhetoric specialists working in a separate (usually newly formed) disciplinary space devoted exclusively to writing. And we wanted essays that would address the conversations compositionists often hear, even participate in–conversations that are often framed by "what-ifs" and "if-onlys,"in which compositionists imagine professional lives institutionally separate from an English department.

Debates about composition studies' disciplinarity and institutional positioning have long preoccupied composition scholars, whether through conference presentations, scholarly publications, or more informal venues. These conversations can take different forms and draw on different analogies, but all seem to recognize at some level the wrenching apart or the dissolution that separation requires. For example, in the past two years' discussions on Victor Vitanza's moderated *Pre/Text* listserv, some participants have suggested that composition and rhetoric "divorce" from literature departments. The suggestion is by no means new and certainly has legitimate cause in the view of many compositionists. After all, in the early twentieth century Fred Newton Scott formed a separate rhetoric department at the University of Michigan, which was dissolved and absorbed back into the English department upon his retirement. In more recent history, Maxine Hairston, in her 1985 Conference on College Composition and Communication (CCCC) Chair's Address, called for composition and rhetoric to "establish our psychological and intellectual independence from literary critics who are at the center of power in most English departments" (179). While

Hairston called for intellectual independence only, many writing professionals have found that without structurally separating from English it is
impossible to realize the independence that Hairston and others have
called for. The decision to relocate, away from literature, has often been
seen as an option because of the historical relationship between composition and rhetoric faculty and their English department colleagues. As
Theresa Enos has argued, "Survey comments, narratives, and conversations made it clear that we in composition and rhetoric studies face a
number of problems that seem unique to our position in English departments" (38). And this position is rooted in the traditions of English
departments and in our field's history with them:

> Lower division writing courses in colleges and universities are staffed primar-
> ily by women who receive low pay, low prestige, and lessened job security in
> comparison to their male counterparts. Male writing faculty, however, are
> affected by factors like salary compression and the undervaluation of a field
> now considered "feminized." (vii)

Stories of these conflicts are chronicled in a variety of texts (for
example, Haswell and Lu; Roen, Brown, and Enos), and these tensions
are also present in the experiences of composition specialists and writing program directors. In the *Pre/Text* discussion (fall 2001), using the
metaphor of divorce, participants argued about whether we should split
with English or opt for marriage counseling, but as readers of that discussion, we three had a much thicker sense of how complicated the
move can be. In such discussions, we as a field need a fuller understanding of what happens when literature and rhetoric and composition are
housed in two separate departments.

From our experience in compiling this book and developing a
department, we would argue that any "divorce" requires a certain attentiveness, rhetorical savvy, counseling, and models for "how to" avoid simply shacking up with another "oppressor." Our experiences, and the
experiences gathered here, tell us that it's a matter of family systems, of
the local situation, of the institutional system in which one attempts a
shift. For example, at Georgia Southern University, the main difficulties
emerged in the politics of gaining approval for a major; in hiring,
staffing, and other personnel decisions; and in the unique hierarchies
and structures of the new department. At other institutions, as readers
will see in this text, other concerns have been central. This collection of
essays reveals the complications involved in figuring out how to move

towards the possibilities for change. We have learned much in backward glances, in rethinking, in analyzing structures, in deciding which academic structures we wanted to replicate, in figuring out ways around structures we cannot yet replicate; and we have learned from working with other independent writing programs. The labor on this book allowed us to mark our other work and also enabled us to be more thoughtful in our negotiations at the local setting.

But this book also raises important issues that have yet to be settled. In many ways, the independent writing department becomes extremely careful, even conservative, in order to gain acceptance within the larger institution. As many in independent writing departments would like to be creating the department of the future, these moves towards independence often feel like a catch-22 situation. In order to separate and gather creative momentum, independence is necessary; however, independence within the university is illusory; thus the independence requires a caution contradictory to the initial ideals.

Independence, of course, is an ideal that North Americans have often championed; but independence, particularly within the traditional institution of the university, is perhaps a fantasy, as we always function in dependent ways within institutional systems. The concept of independence from literary studies, of somehow emerging out from under the auspices of English studies or literature, demands a discussion about how change occurs. Whether one follows the traditions of English departments and tries to change from within or one ventures outside that particular paradigm, other traditions are often adopted. An independent writing department moves away from literature traditions and then aligns itself with communications, which calls forth another set of traditions; or, an independent writing program announces itself and evokes the traditions of programs and disciplines in formation, such as women's studies programs. If astute, we learn from the experiences of others as we work to form new structures, new traditions, and new identities; but often, having the time and distance necessary for such reflection and research eludes us as we are caught up in immediate events, daily obligations. The essays collected here, then, are not only narratives of change, but also an opportunity for the contributors to reflect and inquire into their local circumstances and to situate the local within a larger community.

The essays, as well as the larger discussion of university-wide change, demand that we ask ourselves hard questions: How should we as writing professionals—with specialties such as professional writing, technical writing, composition, rhetoric, creative writing, writing center, and writing in the disciplines—respond to and create change in the shifting landscape of the university? How do we define our discipline? How are we positioned in relation to other academic scholars, departments, disciplines? What are our values, our traditions? What do we want for the future? These questions are difficult for any field to address, but our responses seem complicated by our differences. For example, composition and rhetoric professionals have different positions on first-year composition. Some believe it should remain a universal requirement; others campaign for making it an elective. Some believe only trained compositionists should teach it; others argue that the pool of qualified composition teachers should include those from other disciplines. Some believe that first-year composition should introduce students to academic discourse; some argue that it should focus on broader texts; and others think it should be an introductory course to writing in the disciplines. And, of course, in all of these discussions (and more) there are interested, informed compositionists representing a spectrum of positions. As a field, we even debate issues such as the relationship between rhetoric and composition, between literary theory and composition, between "applied" specialties (such as technical and professional writing) and more "theoretical" work (for example, cultural studies). We even disagree on what to call our discipline: composition studies, composition and rhetoric, or rhetoric and composition. We argue about how we should articulate our relations to corporations, which increasingly donate the necessary funds for research and resources. These debates influence others, such as discussions of tenure and how best to create the conditions in which qualified, talented composition and rhetoric scholars routinely gain tenure. All of these differences, however, seem to stem from a desire to create reasonable working conditions as well as the best learning experiences for our students. We have a fundamental hope that our contribution to the university will be valued, that our labor will extend beyond limited and constrained definitions of service. While differences and debates are not new or necessarily bad, they are complicated by the changing nature of the university and higher education, changes that are most noticeably manifest through funding and decision making.

As a field, we are inundated by difficult issues that require action. Identifying these issues is a first step, and readers will see all of these issues surface throughout the essays collected here. The impetus for change, however, occurs locally, often resulting from institutional crises or conflicts over issues such as funding, staffing, tenure and promotion, curriculum, or administration. How best to address change, how best to act, how best to confront the issues that we face as composition and rhetoric scholars—these procedures remain unclear, as the essays here confirm. Choosing to develop an independent program, instead of a department, can be a matter of local context. In elite institutions, the separation of writing "programs" from literature has a certain agenda that seems different from the formation of separate writing departments (see O'Neill and Schendel). Departments can typically be found at regional institutions or at research institutions where the strategies for staffing first-year composition courses aren't exclusively controlled by the English department through the funding of English graduate students (for example, see Royer and Gilles; Agnew and Dallas). There are exceptions, however, and we have a small sampling of these types of independent units represented. These programs and departments have much to teach us about the complex issues involved in attempting change, but also, more specifically, about our field's location within academe and the department's location within its institution.

Some moves toward independence set in motion a repetition of the familiar structures in the traditional English department, where a few composition specialists oversee a large pool of contingent labor, where only the few senior faculty teach upper-division and graduate courses exclusively. Some programs exist within English departments that have such skewed power relations that the composition and rhetoric professionals have little or no control over administrative, pedagogical, and staffing issues—a situation that compromises the ability to create a viable writing program. To avoid re-creating the dynamics of this type of English department, skillful negotiations are needed among all stakeholders—upper administration, chairs, faculty members—if a full-fledged, freestanding writing department is to emerge. However, the hierarchical structures in the university often limit what can be accomplished when a new group of colleagues is brought in to shape a department or when established faculty have to create new identities outside of English.

Because the formation of independent writing departments is one possibility in the movement toward change, these departments become rich sites for analysis. For example, the essays in this volume demonstrate multiple responses to a need for change: Should the decree come from upper administration as it did at Georgia Southern (Agnew and

Dallas)? Should the movement be one of consensus by both the literature faculty and the writing faculty as it was at Grand Valley State
University (Royer and Gilles)? Should we start as a small program and
move toward departmental status gradually (Turner and Kearns) or
remain a program focused on a limited mission (Rehling)? In institutions just getting established, is it possible to create the ideal (Maid)?
Although we want easy answers to how to begin, the situations are complicated and are determined by local variables.

In places such as Hampden-Sydney and Harvard, where programs
exist, one sees the complexities of opting for program instead of department status. Harvard's program seems to come from a compromise—no
tenure, few permanent positions, limited course offerings (O'Neill and
Schendel). Although Harvard's program appears to thrive and Elizabeth
Deis, Lowell Frye and Kathy Weese argue that Hampden-Sydney's program fits within the local institutional culture, these programs raise
important questions about the decision to split off the core writing
courses. Do they thrive because of or despite their marginal status? Only
with expertise and financial support present in programs such as
Harvard's is it possible to shape a writing curriculum founded on the
required first-year course. However, the working conditions at Harvard
are troubling. Placed within the institution but not within the familiar
framework of tenure, independent writing programs such as Harvard's
face complicated issues. Given the limited and constrained histories of
composition and the accompanying assumptions about service, this
move toward program—rather than departmental—status doesn't seem
a change for which to advocate.

In responding to local conditions, then, composition and rhetoric
scholars can learn from the experiences chronicled here. If the option is
to create an independent program founded on providing the first-year
required course, we should consider issues of staffing, workload, promotion and tenure, administration, and institutional support. However, if the
option is to create a department, one that can function within the existing
structures of the university system, we need to consider not only these
same issues but also the ability to develop a vertical curriculum, an undergraduate major or graduate program, as well as the institutional location
of the department. Given typical university structures, a department seems
to be the better option, but creating a viable department requires the ability to gain administrative support and an awareness of the work required
to make change happen in positive and productive ways. Faculty also need

to be realistic about the time line for implementing change and for determining success. Syracuse University's Writing Program has been developing into a full-fledged department since the late 1980s, the University of
Arkansas at Little Rock's Department of Rhetoric and Writing, which split
from English in 1993, already has strong undergraduate and graduate programs in place, while San Diego State University's Department of Rhetoric
and Writing Studies seems to be still under construction after seven years.
Each of these departments had different beginnings determined by the
local conditions. However, their experiences, as well as others', highlight
several issues that affect the ability of the department to function: the
number of faculty who are on tenure tracks and can be promoted to asso-
ciate/full professors; the number of existing faculty at senior levels; the
local institutional culture; and the degree to which upper administration
gives concrete support. Complicating the situation even more is the fact
that change occurs for most state and private institutions in the midst of
shifting finances, goals, or opportunities. Funding and personnel are
always in flux; upper-level administration changes; budget priorities vary;
and multiple uncontrollable local factors—enrollment, state mandates,
and capital projects—fluctuate.

In the midst of such flux, the actual work of creating a department
with a major becomes challenging, as questions about curricula can
emphasize disciplinary differences among composition and rhetoric specialists. But change can be accomplished and can be positive. The possibilities for community, for new kinds of collaborations, for radical
changes in writing instruction, for rearticulations of disciplinary boundaries emerge. New opportunities for research, especially regarding the
effect on curricula, pedagogy, and student writing, also surface and can
contribute to our disciplinary knowledge. The essays included here also
raise powerful questions about where community happens, how it happens, what the boundaries of our field actually are, and how one sets up
the situation so that the politics, the financial support, can best address
the students' and the faculty's needs. The difficulty, throughout, is figuring a way through the inclinations to replicate the "family systems," the
histories established in the traditional literature department, where most
composition and rhetoric specialists received their educations. In the
midst of disciplinary debates about fundamental concerns, attempting a
move away from literature doesn't necessarily create the panacea for
which writing specialists long. Nonetheless, the creation of stand-alone
writing units—whether programs or departments—provides us with an

opportunity to define ourselves in new ways instead of against literature and literary scholarship. It is a chance to begin new and better academic traditions where we can enact what we value instead of spending our energy defending it.

CONTENTS

This volume, then, is part of the larger discussion about where writing programs—as well as the composition and rhetoric professionals that staff them—belong in postsecondary institutions. It collects stories and discussions about what happens when a writing faculty or an administration decides to separate from the field of literature or from the English department. While the content includes diverse voices and experiences (from research I and comprehensive state universities and from a Canadian university), we recognize that it is a limited sample of postsecondary institutions. Many different kinds of configurations for departments exist, but we are primarily interested in writing departments that have split off from their English departments and formed some semblance of independence, either as a program or as a department invested in a four-year degree and graduate programs. This kind of focus provides very different information than if we were to look, for example, at two-year colleges, which have very different agendas. Two-year schools, such as community colleges, prepare students to matriculate to a four-year school, and thus the majority of their course and programs focus on general education. Or, two-year schools offer technical training and certification programs that have more narrowly specified curricula. In either case, departments usually offer only lower-level undergraduate courses, and multidisciplinary units are common. Besides the absence of two-year schools, institutions that define themselves as serving the needs of underrepresented groups or minorities, such as historically Black colleges and universities, are also missing from this volume. This is not surprising, however, since we found no stand-alone writing departments in reviewing material from scores of historically Black, Native American, and Hispanic colleges.

While more independent writing programs exist than are represented in this collection, the twelve different institutions described here offer a look at the multifarious routes available. Although many of the essays tell local stories of independent writing programs and departments, we have divided them into three sections: Section I, "Local Scenes: Stories of Independent Writing Programs"; Section II, "Beyond the Local: Connections among Communities"; and Section III, "The Big Picture: Implications for Composition, English Studies, and Literacy Education." The first section tells six stories of departments or programs that are independent of literature departments. We decided to start with descriptions from independent writing programs and departments in order to emphasize the differences among institutions and their strategies for gaining independent status. Interestingly, in this first section, we were struck, as we read through the stories, by the enthusiasm and optimism of the authors, even when the situation, as viewed by an outsider, does not seem to warrant such a response. We do not know exactly why the authors opt for this type of spin to their story but there could be many reasons: because they are still at the institution and have a real investment in the program/department, because of the politics of revealing ugly details, or because the experience was actually positive. However, we read this section with an attentiveness to what remains unspoken. For example, the emotional toll—especially to those whose voices aren't included—may be hard to convey.

The section opens with Dan Royer and Roger Gilles of Grand Valley State University, who use discussions and decisions made in faculty meetings to tell the story of the transformation from a literature-focused department to a separate writing department. They describe a composition community that came to realize the positive implications of staffing composition courses with faculty who wanted to teach and share the labor of writing-intensive classes. While they emphasize the connections they see between their literary and speech communications roots, they also articulate the distinct difference they perceive between their function and English studies traditionally based in literature: "Obviously, writing studies and traditional English studies share quite a bit of common ground. But unlike those in literary studies, who use writing as a way to deepen their primary art of reading, those in writing studies use reading to deepen their primary art of writing." Their story includes strategies they used to negotiate the changes. In contrast to Royer and Gilles's story of almost a bottom-up transformation, with faculty making significant moves to establish a separate stand-alone department, Eleanor Agnew and Phyllis Dallas, at Georgia Southern University, explore the consequences when upper administration determines the division between literature and composition faculty. According to Agnew and Dallas, the upper administrators concluded that the Department of Writing and Linguistics would be a welcome addition, and faculty were placed in the department. Although both Grand Valley and Georgia Southern share similar characteristics in terms of size and population of students and the location of the university within the state system, the local traditions and the participants involved create important contrasts for how independent writing departments can come into being.

The first two stories contribute "start-up" processes, while the third essay, the Metropolitan State University narrative, indicates what can happen once the split has occurred. As Anne Aronson and Craig Hansen suggest, a department separate from literature can imagine and establish alternate interdisciplinary arrangements. Metropolitan State has aligned more with communication studies than with English. While the article discusses the positives, it also raises the larger and important question of how writing is viewed across departments and suggests issues for tenure and promotion. Similar to Metropolitan State, which established a program that emphasizes professional writing, in the next essay Louise Rehling describes the Technical and Professional Writing Program at San Francisco State University, how it emerged separately from the English department, how it handled its initial struggles, and how it currently functions. Questions of tenure and funding become the underlying text within Rehling's story. She not only tells the history of how the department came into being, but also discusses the economic issues at stake in keeping such a program afloat. A certain number of large courses, taught primarily by adjuncts, affords the hiring of one full-time faculty member, who must also negotiate a department—in which she is the only full-time tenure track member—with the dean's office. From such a precarious place, Rehling celebrates the successes of the program and raises key concerns.

According to Rehling, her program thrives because it makes its way under the radar, while the rhetoric program at Hampden-Sydney College, described in the essay that follows Rehling's, succeeds because of its high profile and ubiquity. In this unique program, the experts on writing seem to emerge from every field, with the program administered by the composition faculty, but with input from many departments. Interestingly, Hampden-Sydney's story articulates some of the tensions that emerge when many voices have input into the program. Service remains the mark of distinction for composition within this program, but service is expanded from preparing students for literature courses to preparing students for a multitude of majors and for writing beyond the academy. Like Hampden-Sydney, the University of Winnipeg has an

independent program, not a department. Brian Turner and Judith
Kearns, whose essay closes the section, explicitly discuss the means by
which they have moved their colleagues' perceptions away from service
and technicians into a broader understanding of the potential for composition and rhetoric studies. They explore the tenure and promotion
consequences of participating in a new writing program, and they discuss
the pros and cons of program versus department.

Each of these stories in Section I tells of the problems and possibilities
for composition studies if we pursue "independence" including the successes and difficulties involved in attempting to create a space in which
the full possibilities of the field may emerge, outside the service mentality
and the shadow of the literature department. Independence takes on
multiple meanings, none of which may accurately reflect individuals'
ideals and all of which demonstrate the complexities of attempting to
establish a department or program. What these first stories indicate is that
change can take multiple routes, and much is dependent on the local traditions, histories, and systems. Authors in the second section, "Beyond the
Local: Connections among Communities," contribute their stories as well,
creating the opportunity for readers to see seven additional institutions.
Besides describing particular stories, authors in this section make a more
explicit move to connect their local experiences to larger issues in the
field. They contribute theories about what makes for successful moves to
independence, what complications arise in those moves, and the difficulties encountered in desiring to mark independence.

The second section opens with Jane Hindman, who describes the
move to independence at San Diego State University and reminds ideal-
ists who might long for independence of the real dangers of working
within the frameworks of late capitalism, where independence is used as
a ruse for more labor. Her story reminds us of the tenuous relation faculty have to administrative decisions and of the role established power
plays in negotiation within late capitalist cultures. By delineating the
enormous work involved in creating an independent writing department (work which, by the way, is typically unfamiliar to tenure and promotion committees), Hindman's essay explores the consequences of
signing on to an independent writing structure.

After Hindman brings us into the labor dilemmas, Barry Maid's and
Chris Anson's pieces discuss the complications of establishing independence within larger universities. Maid considers the challenges he faced
at the University of Arkansas at Little Rock and how, in his current post,

he is using those experiences to establish an independent writing department from the ground up. His advice provides us with the kinds of cautionary tales that make us think twice about the desire for independence but that also offer hope as he theorizes about how independence can be shaped. Anson's story also sounds a cautionary note. He describes the fate of the composition and communication program at the University of Minnesota and reminds readers that funding often shapes how learning occurs. In corporate university systems, in which access to institutionalized support depends on numbers of students served, the bread and butter courses of composition are up for contestation. And as a result, the curriculum is also driven by those who gain the power. Anson's story warns us that we should be careful, when creating independent departments, to play within the system in such a way that we establish access to power for those in the writing department/program. He reminds us to be careful about establishing the kinds of structures that fit within the university system.

Anson's tale also acknowledges the profound consequences these power struggles have on students; but Jessica Yood, who earned her Ph.D. from the State University of New York (SUNY) Stony Brook when the writing program was splitting from English, tells the story of her own experience. Her experience emphasizes the effects such splits can have on graduate students who learn in the midst of these turf battles, for they are often the most profoundly affected. For Yood, the battle is marked in her thinking, in her peers' writing, in her sense of "work." Through her experience and research, we discover the effects of shifting values and structures. While there are positive spins, the more troubling consequence of this kind of disruption is that graduate students lose their ability to participate, they hear schizophrenic messages, or they understand that the family system is in disrepair and decide not to contribute their important voices to our discussion.

From San Diego State University, the University of Arkansas, Arizona State University East, the University of Minnesota, and SUNY Stony Brook, we learn about the independence movements at larger—or more comprehensive—institutions from those personally involved in the movement. Peggy O'Neill and Ellen Schendel, on the other hand, add information about an established program (Harvard University) and department (Syracuse University) from an outsider's point of view. After documenting the increase in the number of independent programs in institutions that belong to the Association of American Universities

(AAU), O'Neill and Schendel explore two different manifestations of independence at two universities—Harvard and Syracuse. Each suggests the complications of playing within the university structure and the consequences of choosing the route of program versus department. Where Maid, Hindman, and Yood tell us about the formation of departments, O'Neill and Schendel discuss well established programs and think out the implications of following either model.

Many of the articles address tenure and promotion concerns, and the section ends with Angela Crow's discussion of these issues, especially in deciding to participate in an independent writing program. While all composition faculty need to consider general climate questions, labor issues, and the means of evaluation, scholars who work within independent writing programs, particularly in their infancy, must understand how the general climate may affect the department's or program's ability to meet its goals and support newly hired faculty. In addition, much of the labor that is required to start a program is often not recognized in ways that make it possible for junior and senior faculty to be compared to colleagues across the college and the university, so each department/program must establish the means by which it can protect its faculty.

From reports and discussions of writing units at particular places, the third section turns to a larger discussion of composition and rhetoric's location within the university, with an eye toward the future of the discipline. This section raises questions about the viability of independence as a response to current tensions in the field. Are we, as participants within the university, inevitably doomed to "making theoretical sophistication, specialized expertise, and sheer scholarly output the prime criteria of success" (Connors 1999, 19)? Is an independent writing program simply, to quote Richard E. Miller, "preparing itself only to live in some bygone era" (1999, 103)? Is the move to independence on par with Andrea Lunsford's notion of interdisciplinary centers (Strain 65–66), or is it simply a replication of tired disciplinarity? In other words, is this change foolish for the ways that it inevitably replicates the traditions of the university? Or are independent writing departments more able to address changing conceptions of disciplinarity because they are separated from English departments? Is it possible to create more radical change than we would have heretofore imagined because we are situated outside English departments?

Connors's image of "scholars who embrace their teaching and service as indispensable parts of the world of their research, and [put] scholarly research in the service of action in colleges and universities" (1999, 20) raises the debates within the field regarding service, teaching, and research. In independent departments, the question remains: what should we be trying to create? The first two sections of this book explore the issues at stake in establishing independent writing departments, the tensions that make for some conservative proposals of identity. While these sections may create a sense of caution in readers, they also may aid them in examining the possibilities for and the consequences of independence by gathering together the voices of different communities and revealing different choices and situations. The third section moves from examining local situations and discussions grounded in particular institutions or issues to looking at the future of composition and rhetoric. Respondents take up the issues, patterns, and questions echoed throughout the first two sections and put them in dialogue with larger concerns of the field. In constructing this section, we deliberately sought scholars who came from varied experiences and specialties but who have established a record of scholarly work in the field. None of them currently work in a stand-alone department, however, and we didn't know when we invited them if they favored independent writing programs or not. We didn't want them to champion the independence movement, but rather to offer a critical, thoughtful response to it, not a detailed critique of the individual stories. What we found was that they gave thoughtful advice about how to further shape independent writing programs. We anticipate that programs deciding on independent status might gather the stories, the cautions, and the enthusiasms and integrate the critiques and suggestions of the respondents to create new models of independent writing programs or departments.

One of the issues for a remodeling is the relationship to service. Wendy Bishop, whose essay opens this section, begins by evoking this familiar conversation about divorcing from English by admitting the following: "I was always (and in one chamber of my heart still am) unable to imagine divorce, no matter how hard the marriage so far had been. Finally, I can imagine it—change, separation, divorce," but then she goes on to raise very important questions that she gathers by comparing her situation to those in the collection. She reminds us that compositionists—and composition programs—are a tricky lot and that uniting "all writing instruction" is extremely complicated. We don't necessarily make good bedfellows on our own, separated from the literature people. The question of what is lost, what is gained, in the move away leaves us much as many divorces would, entangled with few easy answers. The move to autonomy threatens issues of tenure, but the decision to stay in English departments also threatens tenure. The impact of a split on adjuncts and graduate students (or the faculty who predominantly teach composition courses) can be devastating, but remaining in an English department can be as well. Despite the worries and hopes, Bishop reminds us that we play within corporate management structures that threaten our ability to pursue the ideals Connors advocates: "scholars who embrace their teaching and service as indispensable parts of the world of their research, and [put] scholarly research in the service of action in colleges and universities" (1999, 20). In the midst of a corporate university climate not prone to rewarding the intertwining of service, research, and teaching, Bishop concludes by suggesting that a knowledge of independent writing department/program experiences gives her fodder for arguing for her own agendas within a structure that as yet has not proven to be sympathetic or adequately supportive of composition and rhetoric. If nothing else, independent writing programs—because they make the very threat of divorce a very real possibility—might be useful to improving the lives of those who live within English departments that are frequently fueled by the first-year composition program. The high cost of divorce might be the only language this corporate partner could understand.

Like Wendy Bishop, Theresa Enos questions the value of splitting from English, and also worries over the role of service. If she were to embrace an independent writing department, one would imagine that it would need to create a different relation to rhetoric than she finds in the descriptions given here. Bishop points out that we have among ourselves adequate diversity that translates into our own conflicts, and Enos highlights one of those areas. The role of rhetoric—a heavier emphasis on theory—she sees as slipping away as the field emphasizes composition and, by extension, for her, service. She sees what is happening to the field at large as replicated in the stories told within this collection of essays: the loss of an emphasis on rhetoric, the needed emphasis on "history, theory, research, and pedagogy—not just text production." She also worries about the issues that have always concerned her: what our jobs look like (what kind of curriculum); what kind of funding we can gain, particularly if the emphasis remains on service, a traditionally underfunded aspect of universities; what work load senior faculty are assigned; what numbers of senior faculty exist (which help to enable the gaining of funds/resources for a department); what role the independent status has in an individual's ability to gain tenure; what impact, on the field at large, these independent writing programs make when they are housed in a particular sector of universities; and finally what impact these independent writing programs will have on graduate study, particularly on the study of rhetoric.

Enos and Bishop raise a mighty voice of concern over changes—in terms of corporate evaluations and in terms of directions the discipline takes. Enos suggests an important cautionary note; if we are not careful in our enthusiasm to build a major, create a viable department, we will lose the very history that makes our research and study possible. To lose rhetoric, in her opinion, is to lose our theories. As if hearing Enos's concerns, Thomas Miller suggests that independent writing programs not lose sight of rhetoric as a means of bringing together the trinity of research, teaching, and service: "Rhetoric's traditional concern for the situated, purposeful, and dialectical dynamics of communication maps out a field of study that can help us reorient ourselves as we move beyond the traditional boundaries of English departments." The study of rhetoric, the tradition of our teaching ("learning by doing"), has the power, according to Miller, to present "a potentially radical critique of the scientism that has dominated higher education in the modern period." The challenge for independent writing departments is to attempt to address the needs of teachers and students in their institutions while at the same time drawing on "the disciplinary trends that are transforming literacy studies." Miller calls for grounding our research in other areas—labor organizing, social movements, state educational systems, and institutional reforms—to help us improve the experiences of faculty and students.

Miller's emphasis on rhetoric, on the work of literacy and learning, and his call to rhetoric become even more challenging if seen through the recommendations of Cynthia Selfe, Gail Hawisher, and Patricia Ericsson. They imagine a model of independence that allows for a radical reorientation to alphabet literacy in the midst of always evolving technologies. If Miller sees the answer in rhetoric, Selfe, Hawisher, and Ericsson remind us to look steadfastly at the future and to create, in the independent writing department, a different relation to print and alphabet literacy. Selfe, Hawisher, and Ericsson begin by suggesting that a "rapid pace of change has been driven—at least in part—by the rise of computers and the linking of institutions, groups, and individuals through an interconnected network of communication technologies." Our emphasis on alphabet literacy, our reticence to address the role of the visual, has meant that our conceptions of composition have remained narrow and, more troubling, may not actually address the kinds of "writing" our students will need to create. Our inability to accumulate the necessary literacies, they argue, may well result in our inability to be responsive to the needs of the changing audience. How change occurs and how radically we can transform ourselves may have something to do with our traditions; and Selfe, Hawisher, and Ericsson suggest that in the independent writing department, we might just have the location needed to respond more quickly, more fully, to the shifting nature of necessary literacies. They emphasize the future and the role of the visual and the necessity of understanding multimedia contributions to shifting definitions of literacy.

In the midst of these stories of migration out of literature departments, with conventional allegiances established to communications departments and with emphases on technical and professional writing, the respondents in the third section challenge composition and rhetoric theorists to actually imagine independence, to move further outside the traditions, to find other means of hybridity in department formation. Is it possible for independent writing departments to play a more significant role? Could these departments lead the humanities and the discipline in terms of rearticulating what it means to participate in composition and rhetoric? Kurt Spellmeyer believes that they should. According to him, we need more public voices, to connect ourselves with the powerful not the powerless. We need to address change instead of slowing it down, and our knowledge base should be relevant to public situations. "What this means for us as compositionists is that the teaching of writing unconditionally demands a working knowledge of economics, science, politics, history, and any other disciplines impinging on matters of broad public concern." Spellmeyer, then closes the third section with a notion that separating from English isn't enough; he challenges us to do more, to break free from the confines of the academy and its traditions.

Selfe, Hawisher, and Ericsson, together with Miller and with Spellmeyer, urge us to move further outside the frames under which we were trained, to expand our imaginary domain so that we participate in the communication age that is already evolving. Our ability to contribute requires even larger leaps away from our traditions, requires new ways of listening, seeing, and writing, new literacies that allow us to do more than participate in the antiquated structures of the university but that demands we contribute to the inevitable shifts already occurring within it. Can we, as independent writing programs, shift our gaze toward the future in such a way that we are able to participate in the university that is emerging?

I

Local Scenes

STORIES OF INDEPENDENT
WRITING PROGRAMS

1

THE ORIGINS OF THE DEPARTMENT OF ACADEMIC, CREATIVE, AND PROFESSIONAL WRITING AT GRAND VALLEY STATE UNIVERSITY

Daniel J. Royer
Roger Gilles

There has been a great deal of discussion recently about the decline and fall of literature, about the lost agenda and corruption of the humanities, about our embattled profession. Andrew Delbanco opens a November 1999 article in the *New York Review of Books* with a stinging anecdote meant to explain something about how funds are allocated for faculty positions. He tells about a Berkeley provost who warns, "On every campus there is one department whose name need only be mentioned to make people laugh; you don't want that department to be yours" (32). Delbanco insists that we all know which department that is these days.

What can make one department a laughingstock involves a nest of complexities. As the list of seven books under Delbanco's review might indicate, the debate is not just about the discipline of English, but about social agendas, the humanities, the unity of a discipline, literature itself, and jobs. The "rise and fall of English," as Robert Scholes describes it, has occurred over the last century, but of course the antecedents of some of these conflicts are found even among the debates of ancient thinkers. Delbanco's point, and the point of Scholes and perhaps others whose books he reviews, is that the time has come to restructure a discipline that has for too long taken itself for granted and lost touch with viable purposes and social commitments.

The formation of a separate department of academic, creative, and professional writing at Grand Valley State University (GVSU) reflects much of this current discussion—as well as its history. Our narrative affirms and broadly illuminates many of the general themes present in Scholes and other accounts of the conflicted state of affairs in the humanities and in English. However, our discussion also shines a directed light on three disciplinary functions that mark off contended boundaries in this ongoing conversation about English studies in general—and the viability of separate departments of writing in particular. These three functions—academic, creative, and professional writing—represent curriculum and activities within a department, but they also stand for larger purposes within the university, disciplinary activities, and social commitments beyond the campus boundaries.

ACADEMIC WRITING: SHOULD WE? WOULD WE?

It's largely with issues related to academic writing where the bid for a separate department of writing at GVSU began. First it's important to understand how much things had changed in the English department during the decade leading up to final approval of the new department. Back in 1990, the department, like many other English departments around the country, prepared for its first hire of a rhetoric/composition specialist. Certainly the department had its share of faculty interested in composition; such faculty had created both a writing center and a writing-across-the-curriculum (WAC) program in the mid-1970s, and by the late 1980s several faculty regularly attended and presented at the Conference on College Composition and Communication (CCCC) and other professional conferences. Everyone in the department taught composition, usually every semester. But the university was growing rapidly; the department began hiring three to five new tenure-track faculty a year; more and more part-timers needed to be hired; and the composition directorship was no longer a simple job that could be passed casually from colleague to colleague. Soon these versatile English faculty—who still considered their main job to be teaching literature—took stock and decided to draw on the emerging pool of new rhetoric/composition Ph.D.'s. As in many English departments around the country, the initial thought was simply to hire one or two composition specialists who could direct the program and keep the other faculty abreast of the latest developments in the field.

The first hire lasted only two years. After being asked to take over the campuswide WAC program during her second semester, she simply burned out—a fate shared by many lone compositionists. Roger was hired in 1992, and he fared better. He became composition director in 1993 and was promptly asked to restructure the program. The administration—does this sound familiar?—had heard too many complaints about low standards and inconsistency across sections of first-year composition.

Over the next two years the first-year composition courses were refocused, and a junior-level writing-in-the-disciplines (WID) course was added. Together with several colleagues, Roger initiated team-graded course portfolios and published a formal student guide, featuring course goals, sample assignments, grading criteria, and student papers. The department faculty started to see that having a "specialist" around meant a couple of things: one, they didn't really have to think about the composition program much anymore because Roger ran it—which was good; and two, the course wasn't much fun to teach anymore because now they had portfolio groups and grading guidelines and brown-bag lunches and all sorts of other things they hadn't had before that seemed to interfere with what they had been doing—which was bad.

Several of the faculty who'd been interested in composition during the 1970s and 80s remained interested and active in the program. But others lost interest; and as the university continued to grow, their teaching load moved more and more toward literature, linguistics, and English education courses anyway. The department continued to hire rapidly, two or three faculty a year, and most years one of those faculty was a rhetoric/composition person. Dan came along in 1995, when the new program that Roger and others had created went into effect. By this time some faculty had become openly resistant to the portfolio groups, and the chair of the department found it much easier simply not to assign such faculty to composition. In fact, in one faculty meeting Roger made his own position clear: he really didn't want faculty to teach composition who didn't *want* to teach composition. He'd much rather work with the adjunct faculty who, despite their low wages—or perhaps because of their low wages—seemed perfectly willing to work together as members of a program.

This was an important turning point. Before then, composition was a necessary chore, made more palatable simply by its being a required part of the job. As one literature faculty member later described it, teaching composition was like cleaning the toilet. No one liked doing it, but knowing that everyone in the house had to do it made it seem okay. But surely no one wanted to be the *only* one who had to do it. It had to be everyone—or no one.

Now Roger and Dan were running the composition program and saying they didn't mind if people chose not to teach it. Portfolio-group grading became a required part of the course, computer classrooms were being used for all three of the composition courses, a new writing center director had come along, and now writing center tutors were a required part of every class. In 1996, Roger and Dan instituted directed self-placement. That same year the program created a new position, a full-time "composition fellow," designed more like a postdoctoral program in teaching writing than a dead-end visiting position. By 2000, they had filled nine such positions—and these composition fellows were moving on to solid tenure-track jobs at other institutions. It was a non-tenure-track position that really seemed to work. In the meantime, ever since the 1995 revision of the program, Roger, and later Dan, made it a point to report annually to the university curriculum committee and the vice provost. Things were going well, the reports said. Very well. More rhetoric/composition folks were hired—one each in 1996, 1997, 1998, 1999, and 2000.

In the ten years since 1990, the look and feel of the composition program had changed utterly. Now there were *eight* rhetoric/composition specialists teaching and working in the program, and there really was something that could rightly be called a *program*. The program offered nearly 150 sections a year, taught almost exclusively by rhetoric/composition faculty, full-time composition fellows, and part-time adjuncts.

That was the upside. The downside was that almost none of the other thirty-five or so English faculty chose to teach composition. Some did, either out of a lingering sense of duty or continued interest—or perhaps simply because of a canceled literature seminar. But from the administration's point of view, not enough tenure-track faculty were teaching composition to justify the steady stream of hires that had been given to the English department over the years. It appeared that composition was very low on the department's priority list, and by the spring of 1998 the administration made it clear to the English chair that in order for the department to continue receiving those new positions, the tenure-track faculty had better start teaching more composition.

At this point, the department held two meetings devoted to the twin issues of growth and composition staffing, and these meetings evolved into a summer task force charged with investigating various options for restructuring the English department, which in turn evolved into a proposal to form a separate department of writing. But even at that first meeting, the issues seemed clear enough. There were only three ways to increase the percentage of tenure-track faculty teaching composition: insist that more faculty teach it, hire new faculty to teach it, and/or reduce the number of sections we offer. The first two options meant increasing the size of an already large department—forty tenure-track faculty, twelve full-time visitors, and twenty-five to thirty part-time adjuncts—so the department also had to discuss ways of administering a department that had grown well beyond what any faculty could have imagined only ten or twelve years earlier.

Most of the literature faculty resisted the first option. They were teaching what they were best at—literature—and, after all, the department now had *specialists* around who could and should teach most of the composition. Best to have the compositionists teach two or even three sections a term and hire a few more to join them. Option three also made sense: perhaps we could eliminate the basic writing class or attach it to the writing center somehow and grant composition waivers to some of our brighter students, and pretty soon we'd have a healthy percentage of first-year composition courses being taught by tenure-track faculty, and we wouldn't even have to add many faculty to the ranks. Smiles and backslapping all around.

Not surprisingly, eliminating courses and granting waivers didn't seem like the best answer to us rhetoric/composition faculty. We resisted the idea of changing the foundation of a program that had actually begun to work. Even at this first meeting, the rhetoric/composition faculty argued from the basis of creating a writing-oriented *community* of teachers, either inside or outside the English department. We could support going back to insisting that all English faculty teach composition, but we'd expect all of the faculty to participate in the program and community that we had begun to build up. Nobody could slip back into the old "Intro to Lit" composition course. Composition—and writing in general—would have to be recentered in a department of faculty who increasingly defined themselves according to specialty area. The department offered more sections of composition than any other kind of course, so in a literal sense composition already was at the center of the department's work. Certainly the administration viewed us that way. But there would have to be a rather radical adjustment in the minds of the majority of English faculty for this recentering to occur.

On the other hand, the rhetoric/composition faculty wouldn't mind teaching more composition ourselves and hiring more new faculty to join us, but we wanted to do so within the context of a whole department that was behind it, in an academic culture that was supportive. If the English department didn't want to make composition a central part of its identity, it would be a never-ending source of tension, and it would be difficult to develop writing as a central, departmental focus. We knew that composition deserved to be at the center of some department on campus; if not English, then perhaps a new department—a department of writing.

It is important to keep in mind that after our programmatic successes of the 1990s, the rhetoric/composition faculty felt very good about our relationship with the rest of the campus community, particularly the administration. Our association with the composition program benefitted us in that larger community. The English chair understood this, and during this first season of departmental discussions she discouraged the notion of dividing the department. Much of the department's budget, and many of the new faculty positions, could be traced to the composition program, which was the economic center, if not the curricular center, of the department. English was one of the two or three largest departments on campus, in large part due to the 150 sections of composition printed in the schedule book every year; and though the size of the department made it increasingly difficult to manage, the chair understood that removing composition from the department would dramatically reduce the department's overall presence on campus.

Despite her resistance to the idea of splitting the department, the English chair did want everyone to understand the implications of whatever decisions were made; and at the end of the 1997–98 academic year she circulated a document that ended up turning the tide toward the formation of a separate department. In order to highlight the implications of sharing the responsibility for composition instruction, she reworked the fall 1998 schedule, for illustration only, with everyone in the department teaching at least one composition course. What would a schedule look like where everyone taught one section? But this was after the fall 1998 faculty schedule had been fully arranged and printed, so to virtually all of the faculty the mock schedule represented a loss of some plum class, or at least a class in their specialty area. The faculty were horrified. Since we normally don't offer contracts to adjuncts until shortly before each term, the fall schedule gets printed with "Staff" typed in next to most of the composition classes. Now, in this illustration schedule, "Staff" had been typed in next to British literature surveys and linguistics classes—even modernism seminars and the capstone course! The faculty were aghast.

The talk turned to faculty specialties and the principle of staffing classes with the most qualified people. Clearly, argued the British literature, linguistics, modernism, and capstone faculty, we best serve our students by staffing classes with faculty with the most training in the course material. And surely we owe it to our English majors to staff our own English *electives* with tenure-track faculty, not adjuncts.

Nearly everyone agreed that in this age of increasing specialization, the sensible thing to do was to staff classes according to specialty. Someone asked the chair if she'd really make us follow this revised schedule. No, she assured us, it was just an illustration. Relief spread through the room like a cool breeze. In that one moment, as faculty members relaxed their shoulders for the first time in days, the main issue was clearly settled: the majority of the English faculty would *not* support any plan requiring the universal teaching of composition.

WHAT IS THE JOB OF A RHETORIC/COMPOSITION PH.D.?

But then the department returned to the issue of composition staffing. On the same principle of staffing courses by specialty, was it not best to staff composition classes with compositionists? If we had unstaffed sections of Shakespeare, surely we'd hire more Shakespeareans. So since we had unstaffed sections of composition, the argument went, we should obviously hire more compositionists. This line of reasoning held some appeal to us all, and we compositionists could well imagine a much different department of the near future, one with fifteen or twenty rhetoric/composition specialists in a department grown to fifty-five or sixty tenure-track faculty. Given the administrative mandate for more tenure-track faculty in composition classes and the generally favorable regard in which we were held around the campus, moving toward such an English department certainly seemed a possibility.

As unexpected and tantalizing as this possibility was, we weren't sure that it was exactly what we wanted. Really we thought of ourselves as *writing* specialists, or rhetoric and composition specialists, as opposed simply to *composition* specialists. First-year composition was a part of what we did and was a central part of our identity, but it was not *all* that we did. Indeed, many of us had extensive graduate preparation in creative writing, business writing, and technical writing, as well as in the history and theory of rhetoric. To define our hiring so narrowly around composition seemed somehow to play too neatly into the needs and desires of those faculty who had already washed their hands of the work we hoped to elevate into something more than a mere chore.

We also believed, just as we would have a hard time drawing top job candidates to teach exclusively "Intro to Shakespeare," we would likely have a hard time drawing top candidates to teach exclusively first-year composition. And we wondered if such candidates would be eager to join a department that so clearly cordoned off the "chore" of composition teaching and left it to the minority of faculty willing to teach it. Would such a department be a healthy one? Even comprising a third of the department, would the rhetoric/composition faculty play a prominent role in the academic and intellectual life of the department, or would we form a kind of large ghetto at the center of a happily thriving suburban literary landscape? Would it be too easy at some point to simply section us off and staff us as a service unit?

It was not an easy issue to resolve. On the one hand we wanted to embrace the teaching of composition as the center of our work, but we still wanted more than anything to place it at the center of our *department's* work—not just at the center of *some* of the faculty's work. Even if we did find tenure-track faculty to teach almost exclusively composition and even if we agreed to do so ourselves, we finally decided we weren't much interested in doing it within a department that had so clearly rejected the teaching of composition. At one point Dan said to the department that if everyone agreed to teach one composition section a year—which would have doubled our overall tenure-track presence in the composition classroom and pleased the administration—he'd be delighted. But as a member of that community of faculty, he'd want to teach only one section a year as well. At the same time, he said, he'd be perfectly willing to teach two or even three composition sections a *semester* in a separate department—as long as the community in such a department supported doing the same. The point was about the value of composition within the academic unit. If the department reluctantly valued composition at the rate of one course a year, then to teach three or four courses a year would be a way of devaluing oneself and one's work vis-á-vis what the departmental community claims, in practice, is important.

"But wait," protested the mythology teacher. "I often teach two or three sections of mythology a term, and I don't feel devalued!" That's because mythology is not a devalued course, we explained, and no one argues in meetings about how many sections a term of mythology everyone *has* to teach. And of course we were not proposing to hire faculty for the express purpose of teaching mythology for two or three sections a term.

Indeed, the issue of teaching first-year composition is very much a cultural value, as commentary in the field has been claiming since composition's reemergence in the 1960s. The confidence we had developed by making our work and program more visible to the university community, more responsible to the values of that community, gave us much psychological and practical leverage as we discussed these matters within the smaller community of our department. By the late 1990s there was a core of composition specialists at GVSU that was developing a clear sense of community, value, and voice. It had become obvious that our literature colleagues valued first-year writing much less than we felt was needed to make it the centerpiece of a scholarly community, even less than many of our colleagues outside of the department. We wanted to find our own voice and work within the larger academic community and not be marginalized within our own departmental structure.

We needed to define, for ourselves, what our advanced degrees in rhetoric and composition prepared us to do. A Ph.D. in rhetoric and composition prepares a faculty member to teach first-year writing *and* many other courses. If we agreed to teach, say, half our annual load in composition—which, as teachers, we were certainly willing to do—would it mean the beginning of a two-tier English faculty: those who teach university service courses and those who teach literature? We responded in two ways. One, we began working on building our professional writing major and developing a minor in writing so that we would have enough upper-level courses to justify new rhetoric/composition hires beyond the need of first-year writing. This, we felt, was consistent with the model for hiring practiced by most other departments—hiring faculty to teach a balance of courses, both general-education and majors courses, both lower-and upper-division. We were clear that we would hire composition faculty only as we had need within the major—and we worked to create that need. And two, we took a public position on the importance of working among faculty where everyone taught first-year writing. We wanted to create a new kind of department identity, with a new kind of culture. This resolve was our first step toward independent departmental status in writing.

EXEGETES AND SERVANTS

How an academic community values composition is one of the pressing issues that departments of English must respond to. Scholes blames much in the kind of situation described above on the historical developments that established departments of literature in the first place and then collared literature professors in their "role as exegetes of quasi-religious texts." He continues, further explaining the problems with the development of English: "The glamour that has attended the notion of 'literature' itself for the past two centuries is just one of the things we must renounce. The glamour of 'theory' another. Which doesn't mean we should forget what we have learned—but we must put our learning to use, for instance, by beginning to deconstruct the opposition between the 'English' courses and the 'services' courses taught by English departments" (85). Whereas literature—which at the end of the nineteenth century was not considered a serious enough subject to have a place within departments—eventually established disciplinary status for itself by supplanting Latin and Greek, it made this move by shifting "the balance of emphasis from the production of texts to their reception" (75).

The result, as we are now well aware, instilled the notion of the "service course" with pejorative feeling and the activity of textual production (unless it be the production of more sacred texts or commentary on these texts) with mercantile status—even "pre-academic." Sadly, this is a received value not often challenged by the field of composition studies. Instead, we resist the notion of service as beneath our dignity as well—hire adjuncts and second-tier faculty to teach these courses for us—and look for ways to elevate our own growing theoretical field to front-door status. As James Sledd (1991) warns, we become boss compositionists.

The rejection of this value allowed us to obtain a different vision of writing as liberal learning. In our own situation at GVSU, the vicious loop, wherein literature teachers find that the only real value is in teaching those who would, like themselves, become literature teachers, would not be changed by *making* people teach freshman composition. One of the staunch opponents of the suggestion that we form an independent writing department tried to make a case that first-year composition was "pre-academic." Throughout these discussions, the high rhetoric that entrenches the study of art and literature was invoked over and against the practical value of service courses—even against our professional writing courses that are akin to the course work of a century earlier when oratory and rhetoric prepared preachers, legislators, and lawyers for the practical demands of a life steeped in the powers and pleasures of language.

Finally, our chair addressed the unresolved matters of department growth and composition staffing by appointing a task force to develop models for restructuring the department in a way that satisfied the conflicting demands of specialists and first-year writing needs. The models that emerged included positions we had already rejected in practice (everyone teaches composition), but also the more radical proposal to create a separate department of academic, creative, and professional writing. Out of the five models presented to the department, the main issue that divided faculty was whether a separate department of writing was the answer or not. Clearly, most of the non-composition faculty preferred not to teach composition, but neither were they eager to see writing faculty take the program and build a new department, especially with the creative writing majors in tow.

CREATIVE WRITING: IS IT ABOUT LITERATURE OR WRITING?

Since initiatives are open in a system of faculty governance, nothing prevented the writing faculty from proposing a separate department of writing that included creative writing, which we felt we could persuade the department and faculty governance to adopt. The discussion now heated up. Nobody in the department seemed to care if professional writing was in or out of the department. And many would be glad to have another unit take care of all the first-year writing staffing. But creative writing was perceived by many to belong with literature and the reception of texts. Oddly, some found the notion that creative writers were about the *production* of texts too much like, well, like what is done in professional writing. If professors of literature were comfortable in their "role as exegetes of quasi-religious texts," some also seemed to value creative writing more for its devotion to keeping the idea of aesthetic production alive and in its place as foil to the interpretive offices. Perhaps on a more practical level, the literature faculty also coveted the seventy-five or so creative-writing majors that, together with the sixty-five or so traditional literature majors in the English department, would help maintain literature's prominence in relation to yet another curricular threat—English education and its over seven hundred majors—which over the years had, like composition, moved further away from its traditional focus on literature as such and more toward a concern with methodology, literacy in general, and the realities of the larger community.

As support in the English department for a separate writing department extended to more of the literature faculty, the issue of creative writing became the most contentious issue. Those literature faculty who supported a separate writing unit did so on grounds that they liked our proposed curriculum and felt it would give the literature faculty clearer focus and purpose. With first-year writing out of the way, literature faculty could pursue their mission unimpeded—and without the perennial annoyance surrounding the issue of who should be teaching composition. In addition, they knew that most of the hires over the past half-decade had gone to English education and rhetoric/composition; perhaps without composition in the department, the literature folks would themselves gain some visibility in the eyes of administration.

But those who opposed moving creative writing out of English did so with claims that a principal goal of creative writing was to introduce students to great literature. Furthermore, creative writing had the look and feel of the liberal arts, while professional writing (to some) did not, and first-year composition was even described, as we said above, with terms like "pre-art" and "pre-academic."

The need to defend academic writing and professional writing as "liberal arts" surprised us, for those of us in rhetoric and composition, from our earliest training in the field, have understood the continuity academic, public, and workplace discourse has with the oldest of the ancient liberal arts. For twenty-five hundred years, nobody would have thought to consider rhetoric and writing as anything but rooted in the liberal arts tradition. This contrary position among several literature faculty (who, in self-contradiction, apparently had no reservations about the place of communications studies in the liberal arts or a theater program separate from English) revealed their deep biases against any education with practical dimensions and worldly affections. Our proposal, they feared, would soil the purity of creative writing and cause these students to stray too far from the ethereal calling of literature.

Since the program we proposed for an undergraduate major in writing would offer creative writing students twice as many writing courses without reducing the number of literature courses, some shifted their argument to the actual sequence of literature courses and the way those courses would be taught out of the context of the whole English curriculum. Without a historical pattern in the literature training, without the pattern of coverage currently offered by the English major's course of study, creative writing students would still suffer a loss, they argued. But this niggling response gives up the high doctrine that only the study of literature can transcend to liberal arts (claiming now that these courses have to be taught in a particular sequence), and thus it lost nearly all of its rhetorical power outside the purist flock in the English department itself.

Although the place of academic writing in the liberal arts and the view that creative writing *needs* to be taught within the context of an English department of literature has remained an issue for some with traditional viewpoints, these issues were not difficult to address, and we responded to the task force charge of producing an outline of courses to demonstrate just what a course of study in writing would look like. As a practical matter, our planned course of study for the creative-writing track within our writing major satisfied most people.

The creative-writing track will require eighteen credits of literature (the same as was required in English). The theoretical justification for these credits has more to do with studying literature as *genre* than with studying literature as history, so while we do require one American literature course, students will choose how to focus the other fifteen credits. Students are also asked to take twenty-four credits of writing (compared to just twelve credits taken as an English major). That is, this curriculum, while not reducing the number of literature courses, doubles the number of writing courses. This sort of curriculum model resembles that of art and design, where studio courses outnumber content courses—but where "content" naturally informs each and every studio course.

By allowing for the possibility for creative-writing students to take nine credits toward the English minor as part of their major curriculum, we want to encourage them to minor in English. Indeed, we anticipate that many students will complete what amounts to a fifty-four-credit program in writing and English. For creative-writing students, this could mean a total of twenty-four credits in writing, twenty-four credits in literature, and six credits in linguistics—compared to the old program as English majors of eighteen to twenty-one credits in literature, twelve credits in writing, and three to six credits in linguistics. This, we argued, would be a very strong curriculum.

PROFESSIONAL WRITING: "BUT HIS FATHER, YOU KNOW, WAS IN TRADE"

Finally, the professional writing component became the last curricular matter to develop in the public forum that had grown up around the proposal. Our primary goal had to do with defining the purposes of such a program against the existing curriculum in communication studies. Regardless of the fact that we had a growing group of professional-writing majors within English already, communication studies wanted to know how our proposed major would distinguish our students from their own majors, who studied rhetoric and forms of writing for such purposes as news, journalism, and public relations.

A writing major, we explained, would not aim to prepare students for any *particular* occupation such as journalism or public relations. Because our program emphasized writing and rhetorical facility, our students would identify more closely with the historical, rhetorical, and liberal tradition of writerly craft and would minor in areas like public relations, journalism, art and design, or English in order to sharpen their practical focus or prepare them for further academic study.

In fact, our forty-two-credit writing major is designed to accommodate a number of different minors based on a concept we presented as "triplets." Nine credits of the professional writing track ask students to commit to a writing-related academic or professional area in either the School of Communications or the English department. These sets of three courses not only channel students' writing into particular areas, but also encourage students to pursue a minor in communications or English—and perhaps someday philosophy, business, computer science, or any number of other academic areas. That is, with nine credits in one of these academic units already counting toward the writing major, students will be only twelve credits short of a full minor, and we would encourage students to take advantage of that opportunity.

Communication studies was supportive. Our university was founded in the 1960s when curricular integration and innovation ruled the day, especially among what were now the older faculty in communication studies. As a practical matter, the professional writing major would transcend the limitations of the English curriculum, but it would not adopt any radically new purposes as a course of study. As a philosophic matter, however, it had another battle to engage. Part of what was not sitting well with a few in English was the taint of worldly purposes associated with the professional writing program. Recurring to the discussion above, one faculty member argued that one could not possibly speak about a business memo and a short story in the same breath without wincing. *Quid ergo Athenis et Hierosolymis*—"What has Athens to do with Jerusalem?" asked Tertullian.

The analysis of this concern could run deep, but at the least what we might see going on here is a view of writing that radically separates kinds of writing as so essentially different that they have nothing to do with each other. When viewed from an essentialist perspective, the content of writing subsumes the writing itself. Writing as an activity, writing as a verb rather than a noun, is hard for the essentialist to imagine. On the other hand, an interest in the *production* of texts has been the lynchpin of writing studies for many years. The phenomenology of writing experience has been the elusive aim of a whole generation of scholars in writing studies. And such concerns are predicated on the idea that the question "what happens when we write" is worth investigating. Furthermore, writing as an activity with social (rhetorical) consequences brings under one pedagogical banner everything from the sonnet to the sales report. Failing to understand the rhetorical tradition, failing to understand the pragmatic character of a liberal education, failing to see that teaching both the sonnet and sales report draws on a pedagogy and a tradition in liberal education is to shroud reality in a metaphysical dualism that marks off the modern world, much more so the twenty-first century.

But perhaps there is a simpler explanation. After some of these arguments that objected to mixing Athens and Jerusalem were offered through department email, one literary bystander rejoined:

> I found the latest round of arguments niggling, . . . and appealing to the kind of snobbery I thought had died along with the last person who said, "But his father, you know, was in trade" and meant it to sting.

BUT WHAT CONTENT WILL YOU TEACH?

This question still lingers outside of English. Our colleagues in philosophy, biology, music, and theater may still imagine that freshman composition is an introduction to literature (as it was when they were undergraduates, the last time they had direct contact with the course). Most within English know better, even if they don't agree. Many outside of our own program do not realize that business and technical writing, genre studies, and rhetorical theory and history are a central part of what defines the content of the discipline of writing studies. And though they readily accept theater, art, and music (to name but a few examples) as practical arts, disciplines that focus primarily on how to do something with the historical, theoretical, literary, and cultural knowledge we obtain, writing is often thought of as relying inextricably on the content areas of English literature. Postmodern understanding of what counts as "text" broadens the outlook of many within English departments, but outsiders are often shocked to learn what is being taught in literature classes also.

Scholes's solution is not to set up separate departments of writing. He wants us to reimagine English studies, weave the disparate threads back into one strong cord. This may well be a possibility in Grand Valley's future. We can imagine, for example, the department of literature one day being reintegrated into the department of rhetoric and writing, not as the queen of "content," but as a branch of rhetorical study and as a research area of written artifacts of the literary tradition.

For now, however, we have imagined a department of writing in ways that gather in a great array of what concerns us all. Academic writing is everybody's business in the university, and it's the principal business of a department of writing. We have, as a group, committed to teaching half our annual load in composition—or, as we are now calling it, academic writing. One of our many short-term goals is to better publicize what our first-year courses do, so as to clear up some of the misunderstandings that lead colleagues in other disciplines to continue to associate composition so closely with literature. Creative and professional writing, as major and minor courses of study, provide students the opportunity to develop knowledge and skill in rhetorical and artistic production of texts. We intend to continue emphasizing the study of literature as a part of a writer's education, but now we can open up for further study the current and historical written artifacts related to business, technical, and professional writing.

WRITING AS PART OF THE LIBERAL ARTS

One of the first reactions of many of our colleagues, both inside and outside the English department, has to do with the seeming inseparability of writing and reading, of composition and literature. But we have pointed out that writing and reading exist in every discipline, not just in English studies, and that academic fields that once seemed inseparably tied to others have often moved on to become viable independent units within the academy. English itself is one such field, having arisen from departments of philology and rhetoric in the nineteenth century. But there are many others: statistics, computer science, anthropology, linguistics, biochemistry, and on and on. The effect of these "divisions" is, as much as anything, to enlarge our sense of what constitutes liberal learning. And perhaps most importantly for the new fields themselves, independence allows for new and equally profitable connections with other fields: separate from English, for example, linguistics can build new connections with the social sciences; and, as an independent academic unit, writing can build new connections with communications, history, philosophy, business, computer science, and more. Indeed, separate from English, writing can finally begin to see itself once again within the context of the liberal arts most generally—rather than as a "basic skill" relegated to preliberal education. It can now exist *alongside* other parts of the liberal-arts whole, rather than beneath them, servicing them, holding them up.

In that sense, "English Studies" remains alive at our institution—not only in English and writing, but also in communications, philosophy, history, and other departments. We look forward to maintaining close ties with our English colleagues, some of whom will no doubt continue teaching "Writing" in our new department along with the "writing" they always have and always will teach in their own classes. We look forward to jointly sponsoring poetry readings and literary festivals and other writing and reading related activities. But we also look forward to sponsoring new events and activities with other departments—departments we'd previously communicated with only *through* the English department. New, more direct lines of communication have opened up.

Our experience confirms that the independent department was best for us, in our situation at Grand Valley State University. Other English departments might have rallied around the first-year course, choosing to recommit to it as a regular part of the job. With a genuine commitment, such an arrangement would likely succeed. But we invited our colleagues to choose their own commitments, and they chose to remain committed to teaching literature, linguistics, and English education—which they are trained to do and which they do very well. Their renewed focus on these three areas mirror our own renewed focus on our three areas—academic, creative, and professional writing. We are confident that in both departments better teaching, and better learning, will result.

2

INTERNAL FRICTION IN A NEW INDEPENDENT DEPARTMENT OF WRITING
And What the External Conflict Resolution Consultants Recommended

Eleanor Agnew
Phyllis Surrency Dallas

In fall 1997, the Department of Writing and Linguistics at Georgia Southern University was formed when the Department of English and Philosophy was reorganized into two separate units. We, as tenured faculty who witnessed this reorganization, saw our new department of sixty full-time faculty embark upon a honeymoon period. With high morale, most of the faculty were energized to work on new projects and to create a distinctive identity for the department. The new acting chair, Dr. Larry Burton, envisaged a strong writing program with a major and a renovated first-year writing sequence. His vision also included the expectation of more research and scholarship in writing studies from faculty who had focused on teaching for most of their careers. The sense of harmony within the department seemed palpable as we got along well. At the annual Christmas party, we sang Christmas carols together around the piano. At the spring picnic, we played baseball and volleyball, drank beer, and laughed. Because of our respect for the acting chair, we faculty petitioned the administration, requesting that Larry be made chair. When this appointment became official in the spring of 1999, most of us came to his celebration party and congratulated him. The new Department of Writing and Linguistics was now launched with a permanent leader.

However, by the fall of 1999, the honeymoon ended abruptly, as buried feelings exploded. No longer could we maintain the appearance of departmental harmony, which often disguises an ugly undercurrent, according to William Massy, Andrea Wilger, and Carol Colbeck, researchers at the Stanford Institute for Higher Education, who studied three hundred faculty across twenty universities. This veneer "pervades faculty institutions. Faculty often appear unwilling to pursue issues that may be divisive or provoke debate. Unpleasantness is avoided at all costs"

(12). As the number of composition/rhetoric specialists grew in our department and discussions about our new mission evolved, this veneer quickly evaporated, as shock waves of discord rippled through the department. One cause for resentment stemmed from the fact that the creation of the new department was driven by senior administration rather than by faculty. Furthermore, faculty with training in literary studies harbored mixed feelings about having been assigned to the new department of writing. To complicate the situation further, the new department existed without a major. In the end, external conflict resolution consultants were hired to analyze the problems within the department and to offer recommendations about how the chair and the department should proceed.

THE PROBLEMS

In fact, the state of our department during this 1999–2000 academic year was described as a "crisis" in February 2000 by the conflict resolution consultants who were called in by the chair and dean (Consortium 12). They noted that faculty had a right to feel anxiety. Besides the usual factor of a heavy workload, the consultants pointed out that an administration with a number of acting rather than permanent positions can increase faculty insecurity and tension. We had this factor—an acting president, acting provost, and acting dean—and others. As their report put it in polite terms, "Manifested behaviors resulting from this crisis include multi-layered conflict, problematic communication styles and methods, significant divisiveness, [and] escalated tensions. . . . Behaviors such as stereotyping, scapegoating, suspicion and attribution of negative intentions to others are exhibited by some faculty" (11). Let us describe it more bluntly.

Morale in the department plummeted. The department had broken into factions. The groups, who, as the consultants delicately put it, had "differences regarding the vision of the department," also had differences about how writing should be taught and about whether faculty members' "contribution" and "importance" should be based on degree and background (12). In other words, should Ph.D.'s in composition and rhetoric be called upon to make a larger contribution to the chair's goals merely because of their degrees and backgrounds?

BACKGROUND OF THE SPLIT

The top-down origin of the split may have contributed to the dissension. The first inklings of the split came in October 1996, when the vice president for Academic Affairs (VPAA), Dr. Harry Carter, and the dean of the College of Liberal Arts and Social Sciences (CLASS), Dr. Roosevelt Newson, addressed the faculty of what was then the Department of English and Philosophy. They believed that an opportunity existed for the department to examine its structure. The current chair had announced his plans to step down from his administrative position. In addition, the Georgia governor and legislature had ordered a 5 percent redirection of state money to fund new programs; and CLASS, alone among Georgia Southern's colleges, had so far not redirected any of its appropriations. The money was there. Besides, according to Drs. Carter and Newson, the department had become "unwieldy" because of its size (seventy-seven faculty members—a number that made Georgia Southern's English department the largest on campus and larger than the one at the flagship institution of the state). As a solution, the VPAA and the dean tentatively proposed three possibilities for the department's future: (1) retaining the same management structure (one chair with responsibility for budgetary matters and personnel decisions regarding hiring, tenure, promotion, and annual evaluations with merit raises); (2) keeping the same management structure but creating two additional administrative positions (associate or assistant chairs responsible for programs); or (3) dividing English and philosophy into two separate departments. The administrators wanted faculty to examine the possibilities and a new committee to "discuss these (and perhaps other) options" (Department of English and Philosophy Minutes, 4 Oct 1996).

Although the VPAA and the dean saw the issue in terms of management and budgets, the faculty began discussing the proposal in terms of philosophical differences, professional issues, course assignments, and privileges. Promotion, tenure, and hiring decisions had been complicated in the past. The department housed disparate segments: a graduate and major literature program with a traditional emphasis on Anglo-American historical periods, as well as creative writing, a few upper-level and graduate composition and linguistics courses, first-year composition, English as a second language, and a philosophy minor. The faculty were diverse in background, degree, and rank. It was composed of tenured and tenure-track Ph.D.'s in literature, composition and rhetoric, philosophy, and linguistics. To complicate matters further, a large number of tenure-track and non-tenure-track M.A.'s in literature taught both in the English department and the learning support department as joint appointees. We also had some temporary faculty, both full- and part-time, with M.A.'s and Ph.D.'s in literature and composition/rhetoric. During that initial meeting, some faculty expressed anxiety about what a restructuring would mean for literature faculty: Would they face lay-offs if in the future they taught only literature?—a legitimate question in light of declining numbers of English majors. Would their release times, which had been mainly supported by first-year comp, be reduced or eliminated? Would individuals lose tenure—a question obviously related to shrinking enrollments in specialty courses. Philosophy faculty wondered how their program would fit into two separate departments. A straw ballot was held. Even though this vote would eventually reveal that an overwhelming majority of the faculty wanted to remain as one department, the redirection committee was appointed the following week, charged with envisioning possible scenarios. By November the redirection committee had devised three models for consideration, two of which followed the senior administration's tentative proposal. These models are described below.

Model I: Chair and Three Program Directors

In Model I, the English department would remain united. The chair would be aided by an assistant or assistants and by three program directors, one for writing, one for literature, and one for graduate studies. Under this model, all three directors would participate in personnel decisions, which would have been one of the advantages. The programs would now be closely connected, giving graduate students the opportunity to train in composition. However, the major disadvantages, according to the committee, were that the chair's responsibility wasn't significantly reduced, the roles of the directors weren't clearly delineated, and the size of the department wasn't affected.

Model II: Two Separate Departments

In Model II, the English department would be split into two departments—one, literature and philosophy and the other, writing, rhetoric, and linguistics—with an assistant for each chair and a division of the existing committees as appropriate. The advantages of this model were perceived as the chance for both departments to grow and govern their own programs. But the redirection committee foresaw the loss of unity between the two departments and "potential problems . . . through the coordination of interdepartmental programs"(Department Minutes, 5 Nov 1996). The committee also acknowledged that the chairs of the separated departments would retain entire responsibility for personnel matters.

Model III: A School

In Model III, the English department would be split into two departments within a new school. Again, the chairs would remain responsible for all personnel decisions, while the assistants would handle nonpersonnel matters. The committee saw this model as ensuring the opportunity for both departments to grow and have "added clout" because they would be part of a school. In addition, this plan would help to preserve "unity of programs" (Department Minutes, 5 Nov 1996). But it would add a position—administrator of the new school—for which the duties and responsibilities were not yet defined. The committee listed several provisos for Model III: (1) The philosophy program would eventually join with religious studies to form a new department; (2) regardless of the final outcome of the restructuring efforts, composition and literature would work closely together; (3) The division of the faculty would be based on "current classification and teaching specialties"; and (4) "the division must not exploit or attempt to marginalize any of our faculty or programs and [f]unding . . . for any new department or division should be commensurate with that of literature, and neither group should suffer any loss as a result of a division" (Department Minutes, 12 Nov 1996).

Despite assurances of budgetary and programmatic support from the administration, faculty felt uncertain. While the VPAA and the dean may have seen the question of restructuring as fairly simple, that first faculty meeting and subsequent ones raised fundamental questions. Both composition professors and literature specialists (as reported in the minutes of department's meeting, 12 Nov 1996) believed that the new Department of Writing and Linguistics would be marginalized as "a service department" because the literature and philosophy department would house the English major. Some faculty members believed the language of the committee's document reinforced this distinction and suggested "demotion" (Department Minutes 12 Nov 1996) for some. Demotion was associated with the document's provision involving cross-teaching. "[B]ased on need, experience, and expertise," faculty from the two departments could teach upper-level courses in the other unit. Although the document outlined this cross-teaching, the reality was that only a few upper-level courses in writing and linguistics existed, most of which the literature specialists would not be teaching. The literature faculty were guaranteed that they would "regularly teach in the freshman writing programs," to be housed in the Department of Writing and Linguistics, while no such guarantee about sophomore or upper-level literature courses from the new Department of Literature and Philosophy was offered to faculty who would go into the new writing unit, even if they had degrees in literature and even if they had already taught these upper-division courses, according to the Redirection Committee's recommendation document. This guarantee of security for literature faculty is nothing new to people in composition studies; after all, the hierarchical, class structures of English departments and the positioning of composition and writing faculty as "other" has been amply discussed by people like Donald McQuade and Robert Scholes. The question also arose whether the literature department would be marginalized by future writing programs. As one literature professor stated, writing programs would be "'sexier'"(Department Minutes, 12 Nov 1996). The groundwork for friction between the literature and composition specialists within the new Department of Writing and Linguistics was laid even before the split took place because of "issues . . . [of] insecurity, multiple identities, authority, and self-determination, as well as . . . similar Nietzschean acts of self-assertion and ongoing struggles for intellectual and cultural substantiation" (McQuade 483).

The departmental deliberations never considered severing literature and composition entirely, even though Model II called for two separate departments. All of the proposed models kept the link between literature and composition, which would come back to haunt us later. Many prominent historians and scholars like John Trimbur and Maxine Hairston have questioned the assumptions linking these fields. Trimbur sees the link as "accidental and overdetermined," a result of "a particular historical conjuncture when written composition replaced rhetoric just as English departments were taking shape in the modern university" (27), while Hairston more than fifteen years ago called for the realignment of composition studies with communications and journalism (1985).

Although in the original straw ballot, the majority of the faculty supported remaining united in one department, by the time they voted on the models, their will had changed. Most of the faculty recognized that writing and its pedagogy and research needed more attention; the department had heard from area high school teachers clamoring for more help with teaching students how to write and from area businesses seeking employees with finer writing skills. The rational for a separate writing program was there because, as Daniel Mahala and Jody Swilky have phrased it, "a need [exists] that originates beyond the boundaries of the specialist community" (626). As the year wore on, then, faculty

who initially could not imagine existence except in an English department began to see Model III as the most viable proposal to meet the
administration's concerns, to address faculty issues, and to satisfy the
academic and professional needs of students. During the vote on the
models, Model I (with program directors) garnered twenty votes; Model
II (two different departments) received fifteen; and Model III (one
school overseeing two related departments) got twenty-one. When faculty were asked their preference about their second choice, Model I had
thirty votes; Model II, twenty-seven; and Model III, forty. Model III won
because most of the faculty had selected it as their first or second
choice; the clear loser involved the creation of two independent units
that weren't linked under one school.

Model III, then, was the choice. However, something happened to the
proposal on the way to the board of regents, the governing body for the
university system of Georgia. The deans' council voted against the school
model. After this vote, the academic vice president created the new position of associate dean, whose job would be to supervise both departments and coordinate interaction between them. The position, however,
was not clearly defined, even, apparently, to the associate dean himself.

The Department of English and Philosophy was officially disbanded.
As our new independent department of writing was about to learn, academic units, like companies that reorganize, may "forfeit the advantages"
of the reorganization if employees "are shaken [and] demoralized"
(Tudor and Sleeth 87).

NEW FACULTY DISTRIBUTION

Assignments for the majority of the faculty were clear cut: Ph.D.'s in
composition and linguistics and M.A.'s in English went into writing and
linguistics; most Ph.D.'s in literature went to literature and philosophy.
However, the senior administration had to consider some faculty members whose degrees and primary teaching responsibilities did not meet
the reassignment guidelines exactly and to decide what to do with faculty
on leave getting their Ph.D.'s. The administration assigned all of these
individuals to writing and linguistics. When the dust settled, the new
Department of Writing and Linguistics inherited a faculty whose backgrounds were almost entirely in literature, the six Ph.D. faculty with
degrees in composition or linguistics being among the exceptions. Of
the rest, there were seven Ph.D.'s in literature, thirty-eight M.A.'s in literature, three ABDs in literature, and three M.A.'s in literature who were

seeking the Ed.D. Between 1997 and 1999, we hired seven new Ph.D.'s in composition and rhetoric, unlike the independent writing department at Metropolitan State University (described in this book), which had "little luck in obtaining new tenure-track positions" (Aronson and Hansen, this volume, 52). After the postsplit honeymoon period, the resentment boiled over. Although many faculty tried to adjust to their new situation, some who had ended up in the Department of Writing felt displaced, "betrayed" by the administration, as some put it. Many had not wanted the split in the first place, but it had been inflicted upon them from above. Second, the agreed-upon model, Model III, was modified without any input from faculty. Finally, if a split had to take place, they would have at least rather been assigned to the Department of Literature. Clearly, the top-down nature of the split fostered negative feelings. In fact, David Russell indicates in "American Origins of the Writing Across the Curriculum Movement" that a bottom-up model is preferable (34).

As the consultants described our internal problems, there was "a substantial degree of miscommunication[,] . . . malicious and false gossip, bitter and defensive arguments, and destructive criticism[,] . . . yelling, accusing, gossiping, personal attacks and finger-pointing"(Consortium 8). There were some attempts to sabotage the chair's leadership in moving the department ahead—the consultants referred to it as "a crisis in confidence at this time"(12). Passionate postings appeared on the department listserv, as colleagues confronted one other about the proper way to teach composition.

TWO POINTS OF VIEW

The faculty with master's degrees in literature, who had been teaching writing for many years in what was once a literature-privileged department, were understandably nervous. Where would they fit in? Would they now have to alter the teaching methods that they had been employing for many years? Would they be expected to publish in composition and rhetoric? They were in the majority in our department but felt demoted by the changes that had taken place and by the new departmental vision. They feared landing at the bottom of a different type of two-tier arrangement. Massy, Wilger, and Colbek's study of twenty institutions revealed how universal these feelings are. The "senior faculty" (as they defined those who had been working at institutions for the longest time) "believe that administrators eager to reward publication treat [new hires] with greater 'privilege'. [They] feel that their stature has been diminished and that they often are viewed as teaching fodder. . . . in addition [they] claim [the new hires] lack historical perspective and push too vigorously for immediate change" (12).

Consider the other point of view. The new hires with Ph.D.'s in composition and rhetoric were culture shocked to come into a freestanding department of writing and linguistics and discover that their more traditional colleagues were not familiar with theory and would question pedagogical practices that have been supported in the field for thirty years. They never expected to have to explain or justify their theoretically based practices to the majority of their colleagues.

Massy, Wilger, and Colbek found this, too, was commonplace in the institutions they studied:

> Another complaint frequently mentioned by [new hires] is that their senior colleagues refuse to recognize disciplinary changes. They cling to traditional theories, sabotage attempts to update curricula, and resist recruiting new scholars in "cutting edge" areas. One junior English professor explained that the split in her department was not over workload but theory. Senior members "don't recognize as valuable" much of what younger members do. The result is a "remarkable abyss" between senior and junior faculty in terms of how they relate to the discipline (12).

While Massy, Wilger and Colbek defined "senior" faculty as those who had been working at institutions for the longest time, in most university systems, the label "senior" also implies tenure, a terminal degree, and an associate or full professorial rank. In our department, however, only six "senior" faculty fit this traditional profile. The rest included faculty who had attained tenure but did not have terminal degrees or associate or full ranks. Therefore, at our institution, the "senior" and "junior" designations cut across the usual degree and rank boundaries, perhaps adding to the discomposure.

ANALYSIS

Of course, problems among university colleagues occur everywhere. In an August 1, 1997, article in the *Chronicle of Higher Education,* Gary S. Krabenbuhl, dean of the liberal arts college at Arizona State University, is quoted as saying that every university has "dysfunctional departments where emotional energy is lost in nonproductive ways, factions don't trust one another, and they have a hard time doing their work. Instead, they are places of gossip and distrust." In Arizona's case, the division was between "those who earned their degrees from elite private institutions and those who did not" (quoted in Wilson A10). In the end, the friction became so intense that the dean sent department members to a psychologist for counseling.

Unlike Arizona, the faculty in our department were polarized based largely on degree and background—Ph.D.'s versus master's, composition-rhetoric background versus literature background, new hires versus veterans. But we wonder if it is possible that the fighting and one-upping were exacerbated because of the low status, low salaries, and perception as a service department, which *both* groups have in the whole academic system. As Turner and Kearns point out, "We are often seen as marginal members of the academy, neophytes who must justify our place and demonstrate our expertise" (this volume, 95). Aronson and Hansen (this volume) agree with Sharon Crowley's point that "even if composition were to achieve a disciplinary status that is recognized beyond its own borders, its image might not alter appreciably within the academy" (Crowley 254).

In 1996, James Stewart and Rhonda Spence reported in the *Educational Research Quarterly* that "Salary differentials have widened considerably in the past decade between faculty in the arts and sciences and those faculty in business and engineering." They propose that higher levels of dissatisfaction are found in faculty whose salaries are at the lower end of the academic scale (31). Joyce Scott and Nancy Bereman also confirm what we all know. In their 1992 article in the *Journal of Higher Education,* they state, "There is a notable relative decline in the salaries for faculty in the arts and sciences as compared to professional and technical fields, confirming differential treatment of disciplines in the salary allocation process. Whereas average salaries in business, computer science, and engineering more than doubled, those in education, fine arts, foreign languages and letters did not" (688).

Where, within the College of Arts and Sciences, which appears to be at the bottom of the hierarchy itself, does writing fall, at least in the eyes of the rest of the academic community? Clearly, not at the top.

In his 1991 article "Depoliticizing and Politicizing Composition Studies," James Slevin decries the exploitation of composition teachers and notes that "such views ultimately constitute *all* composition faculty, even those with full-time, tenure-track appointments, as something of an underclass. And so they get *treated* as an underclass, through an elaborately detailed set of norms that gives insufficient credit to, indeed discredits and therefore marginalizes, what they do. . . . [T]his . . . is a political, social and economic fact of our professional life" (7).

Similarly, Susan Miller suggests that the nature of the work writing teachers do symbolically renders them as "maid-figures" to the rest of the academic community. As Turner and Kearns state, "It did not take us long after separation from the English department to discover just how vulnerable a new academic unit can be, especially when it lacks the prestige of a strong and *known* disciplinary tradition" (this volume, 93).

This may be one of the significant triggers of contention in our department. Senior or junior, Ph.D. or master's, faculty in a department of writing—and in the profession as a whole—do not get the recognition they deserve from their intradepartmental university colleagues, their administration, or the public at large—many of whom perceive them as Miller's "maid-figures," responsible for the quality of writing produced for the rest of their writing lives by all students who enter the system. What do writing faculty hear frequently from other members of the university community? "What are you people doing over there? The students who come to our courses, our graduate schools, our workplaces . . . can't write!" The larger academic perception of what it means "to be able to write" may be as wrongheaded as the writing context that they provide for students. However, educating the world about the fluidity of anyone's writing ability may be too great a task to take on, especially for "maid-figures" who are already swamped with papers. Perhaps tackling the real adversaries of our profession, the persistent stereotypes, is too daunting a task. Instead, we have fought among ourselves.

The conflict resolution consultants who were called in to our department interviewed all faculty and administrators and held small focus group sessions for several days. They came back with their report, describing our department as "in its infant stage of development" but "broaching adolescence." They recommended, among other things, that the chair should restructure the department to include two associate chairs, should "implement a conflict management system for the department," such as a mediation panel, should "intervene early in conflict," should "work more towards building consensus around directions for the department," and should fight to convince upper administration to lower class sizes and no longer guarantee all incoming students a seat in freshman composition (11–15).

Right now, despite this history of conflict, the possibilities for our program seem great. The creation of the new department with the chair's vision to promote writing has given the impetus to new initiatives, which the upper administration has supported. A proposal for a B.A. in writing and linguistics has started its way through the academic channels. The first-year composition sequence has been revamped. For the last four years, the department has sponsored the Student Success in First-Year Composition Conference, which has attracted participants from public and private high schools, colleges, universities, and technical schools from Georgia and South Carolina. The Georgia Southern Writing Project, a site of the National Writing Project, has hosted three summer programs and in the summer of 2000 held its first Youth Writing Project. The department has also succeeded in transforming a departmental tutorial center into the University Writing Center, which has, in order to infuse life into the university's languishing writing-across-the-curriculum commitment, offered presentations to more than twenty-five hundred students in seventy-five classes across campus. To expand teaching repertoires and to enhance professional development, thirteen faculty members participated in the Portfolio Pilot Project in 1999. And the opportunities for change are not confined to the department. With a new president, provost, and CLASS dean, as well as a new strategic plan, Georgia Southern is embarking on an era of self-examination and redirection. In one of his first acts, the president eliminated Learning Support, thereby doing away with credit-bearing remedial courses in English, reading, and math. As a consequence, an ad hoc committee in the department is considering how to address the needs of basic writers. We can only hope that our efforts to build a strong department and academic programs will not be sapped by further infighting. Indeed, have we stopped fighting?

Despite the internal tensions, no longer do we in writing and linguistics accept labels that, to use McQuade's words, designate "composition [as] commonplace and déclassé" (491). No longer do we want to expend energy thinking about the dynamics of the relationship with literary studies, in which the teachers of literature are, to quote Scholes, "the priests and theologians of English," who have power, prestige, privilege, while, again quoting Scholes, "teachers of composition [are] the nuns, barred from the priesthood, doing the shitwork of the field" (36). Instead, we want to direct, as Gottschalk writes, our "mind, energy, and resources on . . . the teaching of writing" (1995, 2).

3

WRITING IDENTITY
The Independent Writing Department as a Disciplinary Center

Anne Aronson
Craig Hansen

*People who know how to teach students to write well in the English Dept.
are valued by my colleagues, but I sometimes wonder whether this collegial
respect comes from a genuine admission that teaching writing is a valid
discipline or from their relief that somebody else does the dirty work.*
Comment from an informal survey on the WPA-L listserv

Is an independent writing program—actually, an independent department—in our case—any different from any other writing program? In fact, we share the familiar struggle for academic identity and meaningful recognition. The perception of writing as a service course is so pervasive in academic culture that any attempt to expand that perception creates dissonance. Yet, in our attempt, we have experienced some progress, some frustration, and have learned much along the way. In this chapter, we describe our attempt to create a different identity—where writing is more than the service course, where writing is a major, and where writing is a recognized academic discipline.

HISTORY

Our development as a writing department reflects in many ways a comment by John Trimbur: "[T]he relations of the study and teaching of writing to English departments is both accidental and overdetermined—the result not of a necessary belongingness between the two but of a particular historical conjuncture when written composition replaced rhetoric just as English departments were taking shape in the modern university" (27). Whether the English/composition relationship is historical accident or sensible partnership, circumstances at our institution allowed us to separate writing from English department "belongingness." These circumstances need some explanation.

Although part of a large state system, Metropolitan State University is atypical in a number of ways. Metro State has a tradition of alternative approaches to education: until the late 1980s, there were no traditional academic departments, majors, or grading systems. Writing, as a discipline and an area of instruction, was part of a "communication cluster." Consequently, when, as new faculty members, we developed the department of writing in 1993, our closest connections were with the areas of communications and media studies—not with the English department. This, along with certain other characteristics of Metro State, has given us unusual freedom in envisioning and developing a department devoted to writing.

Though Metro State is now more like other institutions in many respects, most of Metro State's nine thousand students remain nontraditional—a diverse, urban group of working adults (the average age is thirty-three). The faculty also maintains some nontraditional characteristics. Full-time, tenured, or tenure-track faculty—half women and half men—meet within colleges as a whole (as opposed to departments) to make curricular and policy decisions. Although the administration has made efforts to establish more formal procedures, Metro State is what Stephen Ball refers to as an interpersonally administered educational institution. It is a site characterized by lots of face-to-face contact, sometimes elusive decision-making processes, and personal relationships between subordinates and management. Further, Metro State has a distinctly entrepreneurial feel; it's an institution where change is fundamental and ever present.

Given this overall institutional context, we experienced little resistance to the initial concept of a writing department. This concept from the beginning was for a broad-based program, one that included academic writing instruction, a writing center, and programs in creative, professional, and technical writing.

MARKETING

We have done very little to market our department as a department—nor have we actively marketed our two undergraduate majors (described in more detail later in this chapter)—as we have experienced steady growth. Similarly, we have not felt a need to justify the department within the university: we have generally had the support of both faculty in other departments (and colleges) and the university administration. In terms of our majors, the professional and technical writing areas have attracted students because Metro's adult student population tends to be vocationally oriented. However, we have been somewhat surprised by the growth in creative writing. Though this does not readily lead to well-compensated employment, adult students have stories to tell; this, coupled with a rich pool of instructors (more about that below) has resulted in a strong program. Overall, we have 220 students as undergraduate majors and over fifty master's students.

Despite this general disclaimer, we have undertaken a few specific direct or indirect marketing efforts. For example, as a department, we have sponsored readings, writing panels, and other events. We have also cosponsored a creative writing journal, which we advise. This effort—we hope—has created a higher profile for creative writing. Another example is the M.S. in Technical Communication program. As a start-up M.S. program, we needed to reach potential students currently in the workplace. To this end, we have held information sessions, invested in professional-quality brochures, created an advisory board of industry representatives, and managed to plant a few stories in student or local newspapers. This has been an expensive and very time-consuming effort. Finally we, like programs across the country, have invested department time and resources into creating a reasonably thorough website (http://www.metrostate.edu/cas/WRIT/TCindex.htm). The site, primarily designed and programmed by department faculty (in their spare time), with some student help, generates inquiries from within and without the university.

STRUCTURAL SUPPORT

Metro State, like many state-sponsored colleges or universities, has not been awash in resources. Nonetheless, the College of Arts and Sciences has made some investment in the development of the writing department—however limited. There is overhead in creating and maintaining a department, which the university has provided without question. But, despite seven years of solid growth, we have had little luck in obtaining new tenure-track positions. In the past two years, we gained one full-time position (because it was grant funded for two years) and one half-time position. Our full-time faculty still remain hard-pressed, especially in terms of advising. Just this year, we have succeeded in gaining a clerical support position shared between the writing center and the writing department. Previous to this, we shared a pool of support with many other departments, which was often frustrating for all concerned.

In another important area of structural support, release time, our situation has largely been determined by our faculty union contract and is quite similar to release time arrangements with other departments. Our department chair position receives a standard release with some additional release for managing specific programs (e.g., the M.S. in Technical Communication). Our department also received a one-time, four-credit course release to design, develop, and implement the M.S. in Technical Communication.

Structurally, our department is quite different from every other department in the university—though this may not persist. First, we have had department cochairs since the department's inception—the only cochairs in the university. This is not a formal part of our structure, but rather something that arose from convenience when the department started and that has continued to work well (with the same two cochairs). Secondly, the writing center is associated with our department, but the director reports to the dean. This reporting structure is mandated by union rules (and, in fact, our new support position will not report to the department either: faculty are prohibited from supervising clerical and professional employees).

Finally, our diversity of responsibilities and programs is very unusual—from involvement in writing assessment of new students, to composition classes, to tutoring, to several undergraduate and graduate programs. The writing department has become larger and more complex than most other departments and requires a high level of commitment by the department cochairs and the faculty. Indeed, a possible drawback of independent writing departments is the heavy load of administration; in ours, the chairs have the double burden of writing program administrator (WPA) and department chair.

In one area we are structurally similar to most other departments: our university was envisioned from the start to use many practitioners and professionals with advanced degrees to teach. It is not unusual for a writing program to use adjunct faculty (which we do), but all other departments at Metro State also use large numbers of adjuncts, called "community faculty." The vast majority of these faculty teach only one or two classes a year, which poses some challenges in ensuring consistency within our program.

Writing-across-the-curriculum (WAC) has been handled through infrequent workshops and internal conferences. However, the university is seriously committed to a writing-intensive curriculum (one of its traditions), and students in professional programs, such as nursing or accounting, do a fair amount of writing as part of their class work. Most recently, the writing center has been at the center of WAC initiatives. The writing center has grown in scope and service in recent years, after a difficult early start, where it was primarily grant funded.

CURRICULUM

When we began the Department of Writing, we had a small number of intermediate-level writing courses, primarily devoted to academic or business writing. Our department now has a rich curriculum including general education composition classes and an array of upper-division classes in creative writing, journalism, and technical communication. At the lower-division level, we offer a first-year sequence ("Writing 1" and "Writing 2"), developmental courses, and courses in business and technical writing. Since the typical student transfers to Metro State with some college credits, we have never had to offer vast numbers of lower-division sections. Building on our "cluster" heritage, our majors are interdisciplinary: that is, they include classes from related departments. For example, the screenwriting major in the media studies department requires creative writing, and our technical communication major requires a media studies class. This arrangement is not only efficient, but helps maintain collegial relationships across related departments.

By union contract, the faculty controls the curriculum. Consequently, we have developed the department's curriculum without any administrative interference (although they have voiced opinions). We do, of course, have to gain approval for all new or changed curriculum through a college faculty committee. Our curriculum does show some signs of ad hoc development, and we continue to refine and expand it.

As mentioned above, the writing department offers several degree programs:

> *B.A. in Writing.* This major has two tracks: one with a creative writing focus and one with a professional (but not technical) writing focus.
>
> *B.A. in Technical Communication.* This is a highly structured, interdisciplinary program.
>
> *Minor in Creative Writing.* This minor has attracted students from diverse majors—from English to accounting.
>
> *M.S. in Technical Communication.* We have aimed this program at working adults by offering evening and weekend classes and by sometimes customizing the program to student needs.

When we started the department, there was no major (or concentration, as it was then known as) in writing. We have developed all these programs since 1993.

LABOR CONCERNS

In our department, tenured or tenure-track faculty teach most of the upper-division classes, while community faculty teach the majority of the lower-division offerings. At one point, community faculty taught 70–80 percent of all of our classes. More recently, the ratio has changed so that tenured and tenure-track faculty teach about 40 percent of the classes. This is due, in part, to a small increase in these faculty, but it is also due to increased teaching loads for tenured and tenure-track faculty.

Minneapolis/St. Paul is a major urban center with an active arts community and many new technology companies. This creates a large pool of qualified adjunct faculty for professionally-oriented classes (such as "Technical Writing"), all genres of creative writing, and specialized classes (such as "Writing for Publication and Profit"). We train new faculty on an individual basis (essentially by appointing a full-time faculty member as a mentor). We also have an annual meeting with all faculty to discuss issues of concern and interest (use of new technology, grading concerns, etc.). Our university has a teaching and learning center that offers new faculty orientation, as well as workshops and an annual conference for all faculty. Our writing faculty have been involved in designing or participating in these sessions.

TENURE

Tenure and promotion at Metro State are granted by the administration. Faculty for the College of Arts and Sciences vote to recommend tenure, and this vote is important in a successful tenure application. While our faculty have been granted tenure without undue difficulty, tenure could become problematic, given a different mix of faculty or a different dean. The reason is one common to all involved with writing instruction: these programs involve high levels of unrecognized administrative effort, relatively few opportunities for high-profile research, and a general misunderstanding of writing as an academic discipline.

We believe being a separate department offers distinct advantages for the tenure process. First, departmental status tends to support the viability of writing as an academic discipline. Second, we can recommend tenure as a department before the case is submitted to the college faculty for a vote. A departmental recommendation, supported by testimonials with explanations of the department's work, is very persuasive (and is good public relations for the department). Third, as a separate department, we have been able to develop degree programs that help anchor the teaching and research activities of our faculty: this also strengthens the tenure case.

PRACTICE, ART, PROFESSION AND DISCIPLINE

In an effort to learn more about how our Metro State colleagues perceived our department, we recently sent out an informal survey to faculty and professional staff asking them, among other things, about what they saw as the primary function of our department. Some responses were terse and uninformative (e.g., "to teach writing"); others were comprehensive and better captured the complexity of what we do. One response—clearly from a friend of our department—stands out. The purpose of our department, according to this writer, is "to provide leadership at the university in all activities related to writing as discipline and profession, practice and art." We wish we had formulated this eloquent mission statement for the department ourselves. We'd like to unpack the terms of this definition (in a slightly different order) as a way to comment on our experience as an independent program that has worked toward establishing disciplinary identity.

Practice. Practice is, of course, key in our work as an independent writing department. Practice pervades the curriculum, as students negotiate tasks as diverse as writing a public service announcement and writing a sonnet. More significant, perhaps, is our emphasis on having a staff of practitioners. These writers—poets, novelists, technical writers, editors, freelancers, journalists—are essential to the success of our program. The union contract that governs our hiring practices has reduced the number of credits adjunct faculty can teach to ten—two or three classes each academic year. A few of our faculty—those who see writing instruction as their vocation—are justifiably unhappy with this situation. For most, however, the teaching load fits well with their other writing and work activities. Take, for example, Suzanne, a recent hire who is carving out a reputable career as a fiction writer and poet; she teaches a couple of composition classes for us a year and works as a caterer. She would not want a full-time adjunct position, given her commitment to developing her writing. Another example is Donna, who has a full-time job as an editor of an international engineering journal. She teaches two classes a year in editing and document design. Both of these women are gifted teachers; their effectiveness in the classroom stems both from their abilities to inspire, motivate, and guide students, and from their practical experience as writers.

The situation is different for those of us who are principally academics—the tenured and tenure-track faculty. We all have professional writing experience, but most of us in recent years have made academic work a priority over professional writing. As our department has gained majors and now a graduate program, however, we have been drawn to developing our work as writers. This is not to say that scholarship is not writing practice; obviously it is, but in the context of our curriculum, it is only one limited piece of what we offer. Anne's recent sabbatical consisted of taking courses in writing creative nonfiction and working part-time for a communications company writing and editing grants and other documents for nonprofit organizations. On his recent sabbatical, Craig wrote a novel, as well as a variety of academic writing projects. We think that these sabbatical proposals were warmly received by everyone from the dean to the president of the university at least in part because writing is perceived as a discipline in which practice is necessary for teaching.

Art. This term has at least two possible meanings relevant to our department mission. On the one hand, "art" is *techne* in rhetoric: the methods, techniques, and strategies that are used in practicing effective writing. In imagining rhetoric as an undergraduate major or course of study, David Fleming considers "art" an essential element in the curriculum. Rhetorical art, he says, is "a theoretical vocabulary providing the language user (speaker, writer, listener, or reader) with a way to isolate, analyze, and manage communication situations, goals, resources, acts, and norms." This art, says Fleming, becomes internalized through "practice" (183).

But "art" also alludes to the status of writing as a fine art, a practice of the imagination, an act of creativity. One of the most difficult "marriages" in our department is that between the most vocational and application-oriented of writing activities—technical communication—and the most creative and impractical of writing activities—poetry, fiction, and other creative genres. It is easy to think of these seemingly incompatible uses of written communication as discrete subdivisions within our program, and in many ways they are. But because they live in the same structurally autonomous department, because technical communication specialists work side by side with novelists, we have had an interesting opportunity to see the possibilities for cross-fertilization. One example of a connection between creative and professional writing is demonstrated by the course,

"Written and Visual Communication," a general education composition course that exposes students to the relationship of the verbal and visual. The course has been taught individually or in teams by technical communication specialists, poets, artists, composition specialists, and media scholars. While one class session may be devoted to words and images on an e-business web page, another class session may look at synesthesia in the poetry of Ezra Pound. Bridging the divide has also influenced our own research; Craig recently presented a paper on the aesthetics of technical writing. While these connections are possible in any curriculum, the structure of our department forces us constantly to revisit links among the various kinds of writing we teach.

Profession. Information on professional opportunities is made available to our students through the curriculum, internships, classroom contact with instructors who are also professionals, guest speakers, and advising. We are continually in the process of learning what the range of career opportunities is for our students. We try to foster connections with public and private employers and to stay informed about social and economic trends that affect career tracks for writers. While the job market is fairly open for graduates specializing in technical communication, it is less so for those focusing on professional writing. Recently we have discovered the value to students of gaining expertise in an area outside of writing. One recent graduate, for example, who had a background in botany and biology in addition to a major in writing, is now employed as a public information specialist at the USDA. Another student, who has pursued New Age philosophies as a hobby, is now an editor for Llewellyn Publications, a growing company specializing in New Age materials.

Discipline. This is the most complex and problematic term. Since the department's beginnings, we have seen the work of our department as disciplinary in that we are communicating knowledge and a way of knowing that writers across the many divides of genre and profession share. We realize that the disciplinarity of composition is much debated, particularly in discussions of first-year composition. Sharon Crowley, for example, has forcibly argued that the low status of this service-based course makes the "goals of disciplinarity—the pursuit of knowledge and the professional advancement of practitioners"—virtually unattainable (253). Others disagree, arguing that there is a disciplinary identity in composition: its grounding in rhetoric (Goggin), its unique focus on student writing (Miller 1994), or its concern with critical literacy (Sullivan et al.).

As a department that offers majors and advanced study in writing in addition to composition, we believe we are better positioned to meet disciplinary goals than programs that focus on first-year composition only. We have identified a disciplinary core to our department, driven by questions that are familiar to most writing professionals: What role does written language play in construction of self and other? How is writing related to the use of other symbol systems, particularly the visual? What is creativity, and what are the possibilities for creative use of written language? What constitutes a genre? How does writing affect audiences, and how is writing affected by audiences, situations, technologies, and social/historical contexts? How does writing relate to reading, thinking, and learning? What is the relationship between the professional and the personal in writing? Who has power and agency in a specific writing situation? We believe that these questions are as relevant in a first-year composition course as they are in a technical communication capstone or a fiction-writing course.

That said, we do acknowledge real tensions between what we consider our disciplinary efforts in the department and our service function. We see Crowley's point when she says that "the imagined construction of composition as 'low' work exerts so much ideological force within the academy that even if composition were to achieve a disciplinary status that is recognized beyond its own borders, its image might not alter appreciably within the academy" (254). After all, the questions listed above aren't precisely the questions that some administrators, employers, and colleagues in other departments expect us to address, particularly in composition courses that fulfill general education requirements. In their minds, the questions that drive curriculum might be something like these: What is the appropriate way to write an annotated bibliography or a feasibility study? How can ESL students learn to write better in English? What's the proper use of the comma? The tension between discipline and service recently came to light when we were informed by our dean that the administration was unhappy with the quality of student writing and could possibly earmark money to hire a faculty member in writing-across-the-curriculum. Although we would welcome a WAC hire in the department, our strategic plan was to build on creative writing first. Clearly the pressure to meet the service needs of the university community were derailing our desire to build up a significant curricular component in our department.

This tension between service and discipline emerged in our survey of perceptions about the department. We asked respondents to rank in order of importance what they felt were the "functions or activities" of our department. We gave them the following choices: "providing help with career development"; "supporting or developing writing as an academic discipline"; "improving student writing"; "sponsoring student publications"; and "providing opportunities for tutoring or mentoring in writing." The clear winner was as expected; sixteen of the twenty-one respondents said our top-ranked function was "improving student writing." Similarly, the item that received the most "2" rankings was "providing opportunities for tutoring or mentoring in writing." We consider these two functions as representative of our "service" orientation. However, eleven of the twenty-one respondents placed the item "supporting or developing writing as an academic discipline" among the top two of the department; nineteen placed it within the top three. The written responses to the question about our primary function were also revealing. Although many reiterated the importance of service ("help students develop skills in writing for academic work and daily life"), many respondents perceived that we were doing more: "I see two: to help all students improve their writing and to offer serious study in writing for those who want to focus/major on a 'small' specialty." This response still dichotomizes the apparent service function of first-year courses and the disciplinary function of advanced courses, but it is a step in the right direction.

CONCLUSION

Both of us have taught in departments where writing was part of an English department and was identified almost exclusively as a service-oriented program and not as a discipline. Our experience at Metro State has led us to strongly favor independent writing programs—particularly independent writing *departments*—for several reasons.

First, independent writing departments have institutional power that is usually unavailable to writing programs embedded within other departments. A writing department's budget requests, staffing needs, and curricular plans must, at least structurally, be treated the same as those of other departments. Furthermore, the WPA can become a department chair, on equal footing with the chairs of English, accounting, and psychology.

Second, the structure of independent writing departments works toward resolving some of the professional development and tenure issues that have plagued composition specialists. In a separate department, faculty have a much greater opportunity to help establish criteria for tenure and promotion that differ from those of English departments. In a practice-oriented field of study, faculty are more likely to be recognized for practice, particularly for writing practice outside of the academy and for teaching practice.

Finally, with an independent department structure, writing programs are likely to be regarded more as disciplines and less as the purveyors of skills instruction. We believe that majors and minors play an important role in persuading other academic departments that writing is a discipline. We agree with John Trimbur that composition has been overinvested in the first-year course, isolating it "without a larger curriculum in writing to keep it company, to extend the work it initiates of examining and producing forms of writing" (11). It is much easier to reimagine "composition" as a discipline when we place it within the larger—and in some respects simpler—context of "writing." Trimbur is also concerned that in becoming an authorized department with institutional power, composition will lose its edginess, its ability to critique the center from its position at the margin. "The objection has been raised that instituting programs of study in writing amounts to a status-conscious bid to exchange our identification as low-class service providers for academic legitimacy, disciplinary standing, and professional advancement" (23). Charles Schuster puts this a different way, arguing that faculty in a discipline like English hold private office, while composition faculty hold public office. The English scholar works away from the public; the composition scholar's responsibilities always bring him or her in contact with university and local constituencies. But in many institutions, including Metro State University, the educational environment calls on *all* programs to have a public function. The idea of "service," perhaps better articulated as responsibility to the community within and outside the academy, is something that pervades the educational missions of most colleges and universities. In placing themselves firmly in the context of this public calling, independent writing programs and departments need not give away their community focus for privileged disciplinary status. Writing can be a discipline with a focused curriculum and still be committed to the democratic, community-oriented values that have always marked composition studies.

4

SMALL BUT GOOD
How a Specialized Writing Program Goes It Alone

Louise Rehling

My story is of a technical and professional writing program at a state university that grew out of a special major in the mid-1980s, then, unwanted by the English department, formed itself as an independent, interdisciplinary home for a career-oriented minor. The program now also offers a bachelor's degree and a certificate, yet it remains disconnected in terms of administration, faculty, and budget from English, even though that is where both composition and linguistics are housed.

Thanks to its independent status, our program has no responsibility for service courses or general education requirements; nor are its students required to take English courses (beyond graduation minimums). This allows us to focus on developing a specialized, quality curriculum—which is often a challenge for technical and professional writing programs that are housed in English departments. Of course, our focus and our independence also keep us small, yet we have managed to turn that quality into a virtue, with benefits ranging from staffing flexibility to creating a supportive, networked community for our students.

Ah, but, of course, our story also includes its share of mistakes (for example, a university requirement for the initial tenure-track appointment to be joint with English) and travails (we are often misunderstood, undervalued, and subject to benign neglect). Nevertheless our ability to thrive by flying below the radar may have implications for other writing programs that hope to develop specialized degrees and/or those that fear there is no life beyond English.

HISTORY

Technical and professional writing only in recent decades has emerged as a distinct academic field of study. A course of study focused on writing in the workplace prepares students for careers in a well-compensated profession, one that is becoming larger, more prominent, and increasingly more sophisticated in its expectations.

The present Technical and Professional Writing Program at San Francisco State University grew out of the Career and Technical Writing Program, which offered first a minor in 1983 and then an undergraduate certificate in 1984.

THE CAREER AND TECHNICAL WRITING MINOR AND CERTIFICATE

The initial program was designed by an interdisciplinary team that included tenured/tenure-track faculty from three university departments, all located in separate colleges (then called "schools") of the university: the English department (College of Humanities), which includes a composition program and offers writing courses required for all undergraduates; the design and industry department (College of Creative Arts), which teaches graphic design and industrial product design and which requires an "industrial communication" writing course; and business administration (College of Business), which requires a "business communication" writing course. This team also received crucial assistance from a part-time instructor who also was a professional technical writer and editor. He taught the first actual courses in Career and Technical Writing (CTW).

From its inception, the CTW program was interdisciplinary. It included coursework not only under a CTW prefix, but also from English, design and industry, educational technology, the Center for Interdisciplinary Science, journalism, computer sciences, business, broadcast communication arts, and other departments. It was agreed that the program would be housed in Humanities but would function as a freestanding minor, independent of any department. The minor and certificate were identical twenty-four-unit programs: the minor was taken by students matriculating for a bachelor's degree; the certificate, by students who were either post-bachelor's or who (with a minimum of fifty-six undergraduate units already completed) had decided not to apply for a degree.

The CTW program provided two core courses, in writing and editing, and an internship/final project course. The program borrowed an applied graphic design course from design and industry for a fourth core requirement. It also assembled an interdisciplinary list of electives from across the campus in writing, editing, graphics, and publication, as applied to a number of fields or professions. CTW allowed computer programming and applications courses to be taken for elective credit. The program also designed one elective of its own in grantwriting and another in museum and gallery writing (the latter cross-listed with anthropology, art, and classics).

All CTW courses (about three were offered each semester) were taught by part-time faculty. The final projects were carried out under the aegis of willing individual faculty members. The associate dean of the college, one of the faculty members from English who had helped to found the program, was also its first supervisor, acting as coordinator, advisor, and internship director.

The CTW minor program was aimed at students who were interested in studying the humanities, but who also wanted some career-oriented education to increase their employability upon graduation. The program also welcomed students who were already majoring in science, business, or some technical field, and who wanted to improve their writing skills in that field or who wanted primarily to be writers rather than researchers or practitioners in that field.

During CTW's years of operation, its student body was a mix of those two populations, with humanities majors outnumbering the science/technical majors by about five to one. This ratio fairly closely matched the academic preparation of professional technical writers at the time, with the majority being drawn from the ranks of English, creative writing, liberal studies, and similar majors.

THE TPW PROGRAM AND BACHELOR'S DEGREE PROPOSAL

The CTW program proved to be quite popular, considering its small size, negligible budget, and low profile: at any given moment, it accommodated about fifty students who were actively pursuing a minor or certificate, plus numbers of others taking individual courses out of interest. In addition, students began inquiring from the outset about a major. In fact, individual majors were designed for about a half-dozen students each year between 1984 and 1990.

It was because of the continuing demand for a major that the faculty active in the program prepared a bachelor of arts degree proposal, which was approved, and the degree was implemented in fall of 1990.

This new bachelor's degree retained the core component and interdisciplinary skills electives already in place for the minor and certificate. The core, however, was strengthened for majors by requiring an internship (rather than the culminating project that was still allowed as an option for the minor and certificate) and a completion-level course. In addition to the skills electives, the forty-five-unit major also required a subject matter focus in a professionally related department or interdisciplinary theme. Additional electives now offered by the program were included as well.

The faculty group proposing the new bachelor's degree thought that they might encounter questions or resistance from California State University (CSU), which needed to approve new degrees offered by any of the universities within its system, including San Francisco State. Our degree was unprecedented for the CSU system: in fact, it continues to be the only freestanding technical and professional writing major in either the CSU or University of California system and, to our knowledge, at any four-year institution in California.

The proposal made its case, however, that the degree was an appropriate offering in the humanities (requiring much understanding of writing and communication theory and process, along with considerable research skills and practice), while also providing students with concrete professional skills and employment options. The location of the program in the San Francisco Bay Area, with its many high-technology employers, also strengthened the case.

Leadership

The bachelor's degree proposal specified that the program could be offered with two faculty positions, one of which needed to be tenure-track for the director (then called "coordinator"), who would also do all advising and who also would develop and supervise the internship requirement. The program would offer a bachelor's degree, a minor, and a certificate. The name for all three would now be Technical and Professional Writing (TPW).

The proposal also specified that the program, because it was quite interdisciplinary, must be freestanding (as the earlier program had been), that is, not a part of the English department or any other department. This stipulation resulted from recognizing that other technical and professional writing offerings and concentrations within the CSU system were usually offshoots of English, and so those programs were limited in their coursework and in their independence. However, the new TPW program aimed to provide a broad range of training for a number of different professional paths, most of them not even remotely connected to English. The discipline also had developed as a distinct scholarly field, with its own journals and areas of specialization, most not familiar to scholars in other areas of English. Moreover, as the computer industry had been growing exponentially in size, sophistication, and ubiquity, employers of TPW graduates were demanding increasingly specialized training in types of writing, editing, and presentation that were beyond the interest and expertise of the English faculty.

The English department, for its part, had never had (and still does not have) any desire to own or even coordinate TPW. English at San Francisco State University is a department dominated by faculty devoted to literary studies. Creative writing is an entirely separate department. And, while the composition program (along with linguistics and ESL) is included within the English department, composition's undergraduate offerings are primarily designed for students to meet university reading and writing requirements and also for prospective K–12 teachers. Composition has never offered university service courses in technical writing or business writing, nor does it offer graduate degrees in rhetoric, professional communication, or related fields.

Therefore, the English department agreed that the programs should remain separate and that TPW would flourish best independently. Despite their joint stance, the university's provost insisted that the first TPW tenure-track hire should be through the English department. Because there was no other way to move forward, TPW and English agreed, although very reluctantly.

This first tenure-track faculty member intended to supervise TPW was hired in fall of 1990. As an English-TPW consensus hire, he needed to demonstrate dual qualifications. And, indeed, he had a publications record in literary studies (as well as creative writing) and also had workplace experience as a technical writer and editor. However, his lack of focus created difficulties right from the start, so he never was able to develop the TPW curriculum nor even to teach its existing courses effectively. Before the first year was out, it became clear that he was not fulfilling the program's needs or expectations. Unwilling to leave his position voluntarily when initially asked to do so, he was denied retention after his second year. His formal connection with the English department had not aided him in any way to become retainable, for he was not recognized there as a desirable colleague to teach literature courses. Nor did he have credentials or experience for teaching undergraduate composition requirements or teacher preparation courses.

The consequence of this initial consensus hire was negative fallout for the fledging TPW degree program, which lost credibility both among university administrators and among disappointed students. TPW applied to refill a tenure-track position for 1992–93; however, budget exigencies forced a hiring freeze across campus. As a result, the associate dean again filled in, serving as interim coordinator for one year. Meanwhile, the college dean's request for return of the TPW tenure-track position was refused for yet another year, so one of the part-time TPW core-course instructors was hired to serve as interim coordinator for 1993–1994.

Finally, the program was given its position back, and I was hired to serve as TPW's director, beginning in 1994–1995. In this position, and for serving as program advisor, I earned one credit of course release time from the expected four-course load of my academic year appointment. (I also coordinated the internship program and taught two classroom-based courses.) Technically, although I was appointed to TPW, because the program was too small to have department status, I was classified as an assistant professor within the College of Humanities, but was not formally part of any department. All parties had learned the unfortunate lesson of the previous appointment, so the university approved this unusual arrangement. And, indeed, my background fit me particularly for a position in TPW. Although I had earned my doctorate in English with a focus in literary studies, I had since developed a specialization in technical and professional writing through several positions in industry and through college appointments in which I taught composition, business and professional communication, and technical writing service courses. I also had published scholarly research in technical writing journals.

It was someone with this type of background that the program needed to develop its interdisciplinary offerings independently of English or any other department. Nevertheless, I found that my background put me somewhat at a disadvantage when I applied for tenure. Although I received early promotion to associate professor, my initial tenure bid (which at San Francisco State occurs when the faculty chooses to apply) was denied by the university provost, despite strong recommendations by my interdisciplinary Hiring, Retention, Tenure, and Promotion Committee and my college dean, based on my documented teaching, scholarship, and service record. The critical grounds for denial, apparently, were my number of years of tenure-track teaching experience, because my years as a college lecturer and, more importantly, my relevant workplace experience were discounted. The unique requirements of the program made my qualifications too unconventional to fit the expected mold for a humanities professor. Although I did receive tenure when I reapplied the following year, the initial negative decision suggests a concern for future tenure-track hires in the TPW Program.

CURRENT PROGRAM: DESCRIPTION AND ISSUES

The technical and professional writing program that I direct has maintained its overall design and position within the university structure since it began, but it has matured in other ways that I believe are consistent with the original vision of its founders and that also reflect changes in the discipline and in circumstances outside the program itself.

Curriculum

In my first year in TPW, I researched ways to strengthen the program, not only by reviewing scholarship in the discipline, but also through conversations with students, with TPW faculty, with faculty and chairs of departments in which TPW listed skills electives, with San Francisco Bay Area technical and professional writing practitioners and/or supervisors of TPW student interns, and with professors and administrators of technical or professional writing programs at other institutions nationwide. I then proposed revised course descriptions, a new scheduling plan, and revisions to degree and certificate requirements. The university approved these changes in 1995, and the new program has continued (with minor modifications) since that time.

The approved revisions retained the overall structure of the major, minor, and certificate programs. The most significant changes were

- updating and deepening TPW course content, refining its professional emphasis, while also minimizing both gaps and overlaps in coverage;
- offering required TPW core courses every semester and offering TPW electives alternate semesters on a predictable schedule;
- redesigning the core course segment to include only TPW courses and adding an additional TPW elective to that core;
- modifying the list of interdisciplinary skills electives to include more courses oriented to technology and professional applications, to add electives covering oral communication, and to eliminate lower-division and survey courses;
- clarifying the subject matter focus selections and requiring skills electives in disciplines outside the focus.

These revisions were designed to make the program both more coherent and more relevant to current professional expectations for career writers. The revisions also reflected national trends for academic programs in technical and professional writing by focusing the curriculum, making it both more rigorous and more responsive to workplace trends.

Staffing

In addition to revising the TPW curriculum, I also reviewed its policies for recruiting, hiring, training, and reviewing adjunct faculty. Each year four to six lecturers teach the several TPW course offerings not assigned to me, its sole tenure-track faculty member. The preference always had been for these faculty to have combined experience with both workplace writing experience and teaching (or corporate) training, as well as to hold a master's degree. I tightened these criteria somewhat (requiring, for example, a minimum of five years of relevant workplace experience) and also made them requirements, rather than preferences.

This change—while popular with students even as it also added to the rigor of the program—complicated hiring, especially because the San Francisco Bay Area market for technical and professional writers has become more competitive with each passing year. Local expert practitioners of technical and professional writing now are extremely well paid; jobs in the field often are demanding, requiring long hours of work; and for those practitioners who want to moonlight, contract writing and production jobs are readily available. Meanwhile, the college standard pay rate for part-time and short-term lecturer faculty is shockingly low. And I have had no success in convincing college or university administrators to adjust that rate based on market factors. Therefore, I have had to sell our part-time teaching positions as a form of pro bono service and professional development. This has required me to maintain particularly active contacts with professional associations of practitioners (while still keeping up scholarly affiliations in the field of college composition and in business, professional, and technical communication).

Having individuals whose primary job is not teaching also can lead to problems in the classroom. While most TPW instructors have done an exemplary job, bringing their skills as communicators to bear and drawing on their prior teaching and training experience, as well as their educations, others have led me to rework the old "those who can, do . . ." adage to conclude "but those who do sometimes can't teach." I have maintained an early TPW requirement that all new instructors in the program get both midsemester teaching evaluations and a peer teaching evaluation, then discuss those with me. I also have learned that an up-front commitment to helping new lecturers to choose textbooks and to plan their syllabi, class activities, homework assignments, grading schemas, and so on pays off down the road in the form of more confident, appropriate methods and better organized classes. However, this, too, demands significant time beyond that required for the administrative and advising roles of the director.

This type of work, along with a heavy advising role, professional association involvement, and other program development duties, make my assigned release time inadequate for the job. In addition, not having another tenure-track faculty member to call upon has made it difficult for me to have backup for my roles as director, advisor, and internship coordinator. Currently, after six years in the position, I am attempting a leave of absence with a part-time acting director taking over some of those responsibilities, but that has been difficult to arrange and the outcome is still uncertain.

Students

Because TPW is such a small program and because technical and professional writing is relatively new, both as an academic discipline and as a well-recognized profession, TPW does not have high visibility on campus. Students in advising sessions frequently comment that they learned of our program by happenstance (and often too late to change their majors). When we surveyed our alumni a few years back, less than half of them said that they heard about TPW from faculty or advisors. So TPW cannot rely on those traditional channels for recruiting students. The program has, however, promoted itself through its bulletin board, website, and biannual career events. The growth of career opportunities in the field has also attracted students, although many of these are graduate students who enter our certificate program. Undergraduate students, who are less likely to have professional workplace experience, often remain unaware of career opportunities in this field until they begin researching employment options during their last year of college. Nevertheless, given that TPW offers only a limited number of entry-level courses and sections, enrollments have generally been sufficient to meet course limits, and sometimes the program experiences excess demand.

Structural and financial support

While departments throughout the university have budget allocations (based on faculty teaching units) that they manage, program budgets must be separately funded. For other university programs, such funding comes from special university support, foundation grants, corporate donations, or other external sources. However, TPW has had to rely exclusively on allocations determined and administered by the dean of the College of Humanities.

TPW does not have any budget of its own (except for a few hundred dollars annually designated for purchase of instructional support and typically used for guest speaker honoraria, office assistance, books, and supplies). TPW also relies on the college to fulfill its requests for relevant software and equipment, computer classroom assignments, lab aides, and other materials and services essential for its somewhat technology-driven curriculum.

Even when class enrollments and excess demand have warranted it, requests for additional sections and for new courses have routinely been denied; we are stuck in a no-growth holding pattern. In fact, I have sometimes had to fight to retain our schedule of current offerings, which are arguably the minimum required to offer our bachelor's degree, minor, and certificate.

TPW's small size and lack of financial resources also has limited us in terms of administrative resources. For example, while department chairs throughout the university are awarded part-time pay to oversee their departments' administration and advising during the summer break, as the director of a small program, I have not been deemed eligible for such pay. As a result, my only choices have been to volunteer my services in the summer or to discontinue the advising and internship support so critical for program students. Also, only this year, after many years of requests, has the program been approved for a half-time office staff position. Previously, TPW has had only a few hours a week of student work-study clerical support, further burdening the director with duties typically handled by support staff. This also exacerbated the problem of maintaining a summer presence, because work-study funding typically has not extended outside the academic year.

I do feel that TPW has been fortunate in having a college dean who has generally been supportive of at least maintaining the TPW Program. However, a change in the leadership of the college could change that circumstance as well. Being small and independent puts TPW in a precarious position in an institution largely organized around larger departments.

Evaluation

For its first program review, completed in 1998, the Technical and Professional Writing Program at San Francisco State University conducted a self-study (with contributions by all of its faculty and the dean of the College of Humanities), surveyed its alumni, and invited external reviewers to make an independent assessment. The results of this process were uniformly and highly positive. TPW continues to experience strong enrollments, despite its low profile on campus; and its graduates report both their own exceptional successes in the job market and the growing reputation of the program among businesses and nonprofit organizations in the San Francisco Bay Area. The TPW alumni group is active, and TPW receives many employers' internship postings and job leads. As an independent program, TPW has flourished.

Of course, TPW's independence is not the norm for programs of its type. Despite their interdisciplinary concerns and increasingly separate identities, most technical and professional writing programs are located within established departments of English (or, less frequently, within rhetoric, writing, composition, communication, or journalism). Although this positioning can be successful, it often has led to limitations and misunderstandings affecting curriculum, students, resources, recognition, and, especially, the recruitment, retention, and promotion of qualified faculty.

In response to the documentation and discussion of such problems in recent years, the issue of program home currently is much debated in the field. Meanwhile, the discipline of technical and professional writing continues to develop and to establish itself separately, creating a rationale for the independent program alternative.

Individual contexts matter enormously, of course, in justifying the decision to establish an independent program. For example, TPW can be a dedicated career-oriented program because, at San Francisco State, the English department is not responsible for teaching service courses in technical or business writing and does not have doctoral students for whom it must find teaching positions. And the university's mission includes a respect for professional preparation programs and interdisciplinary courses, in addition to more traditional liberal arts majors.

Even with that context, TPW obviously experiences some drawbacks from its independence. As noted above, small size is associated with limited budgets and resources. Also, an independent program can be isolated and its faculty marginalized or its work poorly understood. Bearing those problems and TPW's unique context in mind, I can nevertheless identify important benefits that TPW has experienced from having an independent program home.

Curricular Benefits

Independence allows the TPW Program to focus on career writing exclusively, establishing a coherent and rigorous sequence of core course work. The program does not need to prioritize offerings from a larger home department.

This control allows TPW to define a program with more interdisciplinary breadth and carefully selected elective options. TPW also can balance theory and practice in the manner most appropriate to its specialization. Finally, being independent, TPW can be more nimble about adjusting course syllabi and can more readily value teaching technologies in light of workplace practice.

Faculty benefits

Being an independent program means that TPW makes its own staffing decisions and can prioritize workplace experience or specialized competencies over more traditional academic preparation. This leads to more internal harmony among faculty, because all choose to teach what they teach and feel qualified to do so. Faculty independence also allows TPW to encourage fieldwork, collaboration, service learning, and other nontraditional teaching methods that seem especially appropriate for technical and professional writing instruction.

Identity benefits

Independence gives me, as TPW's director, a chair's seat on some committee tables. Small size also allows for centralized advising and close networking among students. TPW also is more clearly recognized by writing practitioners and their employers outside the academy. Finally, TPW's independence contributes to the profession by affirming the status of career writers.

CONCLUSION

A specialized program for a specialized field, the independent Technical and Professional Writing Program at San Francisco State University may be small, but it is a good program in terms of achieving its core objectives. For others considering an independent writing program, it may provide a model of at least some hoped-for virtues.

ACKNOWLEDGMENTS

Dr. Jane Gurko, former associate dean of the College of Humanities at San Francisco State University, provided a first draft of much of the initial program history summarized here. I revised her draft for inclusion in the

Technical and Professional Writing Program's first required self-study report for academic program review, then further revised that material for this chapter. In addition, for my analysis of program benefits and drawbacks here, I drew on a paper of mine, "The Virtues of Program Independence," previously published in *Proceedings of the Society for Technical Communication*, in 1998.

5

INDEPENDENCE FOSTERING COMMUNITY
The Benefits of an Independent Writing Program at a Small Liberal Arts College

Elizabeth J. Deis
Lowell T. Frye
Katherine J. Weese

In his preface to *Developing Successful College Writing Programs,* Edward White laments that "college and university writing programs usually develop organically as needs appear; they are not so much planned or organized as inherited and casually coordinated" (1989, xvii). Insufficient planning and inadequate organization may bedevil a writing program that emerges in response to local problems or needs, but such difficulties are not inevitable. On the contrary, effective writing programs can and do grow out of a clear perception of specific educational needs within a particular college or university. Such a contingent origin is perhaps the best guarantor that a writing program will develop from the bottom up rather than from the top down, a model of curricular change praised by David Russell in "American Origins of the Writing Across the Curriculum Movement," and that there be an appropriate "fit" between a writing program and the educational community in which it emerges (Hartzog; White 1989). At least that has been the case at Hampden-Sydney College, where, in response to specific local concerns about student writing, faculty and administrators devised and implemented the Rhetoric Program, a multi-faceted writing program that is administratively independent of all academic departments, even as it draws on the expertise, interest, and energy of faculty from across the curriculum. A strong commitment to flexibility, communication, and cross-curricular faculty involvement—combined with a willingness to evolve in response to periodic internal and external program reviews—has enabled the rhetoric program to face and surmount many difficulties in the past twenty years, achieving in the process significant intellectual status on campus. It has been called by faculty and administrators alike the heart of Hampden-Sydney's academic program.

HISTORY AND DESIGN OF THE RHETORIC PROGRAM

Hampden-Sydney College is a small, private, liberal arts college for men in rural southside Virginia. Its interest in good writing is as old as the college itself: its first president, Samuel Stanhope Smith, announced in 1775 that at Hampden-Sydney "a more particular attention shall be paid to the Cultivation of the *English* Language than is usually done in Places of Public Education" (Tucker 22). Two hundred years later, a perceived decline in the quality of Hampden-Sydney student writing led the faculty to demonstrate this "particular attention" by constructing an independent writing program. It is important to stress that impetus for the program came from the faculty who worked every day with student writing; it did not originate in a top-down, administrative decision with lukewarm faculty support. Earlier in the 1970s, the experience of freshmen at Hampden-Sydney was similar to that of freshmen at most American colleges and universities: those with high verbal scores on college entrance exams were exempted from instruction in writing, while the majority of entering freshmen were enrolled in English 105, a one-semester traditional writing course grounded in the study of literary texts. By the mid-1970s, concerned faculty in the college—and particularly members of the English department, who were specifically charged with the teaching of writing—became convinced both that completion of English 105 could not ensure proficiency in writing and that writing instruction should not be the responsibility solely of the English department. Motivated primarily by this local experience but also by growing national attention to writing and writing pedagogy, faculty both in and outside the English department set to work inventing a program that would strengthen student writing.[1]

The resolution passed by the faculty in the spring of 1978 stated simply but boldly that "all graduates of Hampden-Sydney shall have demonstrated the ability to write and speak clearly, cogently, and grammatically" (Minutes of a Meeting of the Faculty, Hampden-Sydney College, Spring 1978). But the faculty approved at the same time a detailed proposal of what the rhetoric program would look like and how it would be administered. Since its founding, the rhetoric program has comprised four principal elements: (1) a required course sequence; (2) a program of testing; (3) a writing center for tutorial support; and (4) cross-curricular faculty participation.[2] Over the years the program has evolved in many ways, but these features still define it. First, the instructional core of the program is Rhetoric 101 and 102, a two-semester course sequence required of all students. Enrollment in sections of these courses is limited to fourteen, ensuring significant attention to each student's writing. A set of course guidelines, constructed and regularly revised by the rhetoric staff, governs but does not prescribe the content and structure of all sections. Instead, instructors have considerable freedom in designing syllabi to achieve common goals. Final grades are determined primarily by the portfolio of writing the students produce, but in addition all students write common essay and editing exams at the end of each course.

These final exams are features of the rhetoric courses, but they also contribute to the second major element of the rhetoric program: a serious program of testing and evaluation. Every August, entering freshmen and transfer students write an in-house diagnostic editing exercise and an essay so that they can be placed in an appropriate rhetoric course. The final course exams ensure a common experience across rhetoric sections and establish a programwide standard of achievement. Finally, all students must pass a challenging rhetoric proficiency exam before they can be graduated from the college. This three-hour timed essay exam on a topic "not foreign to the students' experience" is, perhaps surprisingly, an aspect of the program fiercely defended by faculty and students alike, who see in it tangible evidence of the college's commitment to excellence in writing.

The third major component of the rhetoric program is the Writing Center, where students have come for tutorial services since the late 1970s. The availability of trained faculty and peer tutors has allowed the rhetoric program to establish and maintain high standards for student writing—in rhetoric courses, in courses across the curriculum, and on the proficiency exam—secure in the knowledge that students can receive the help they need to meet those standards.

In the next two sections of this essay, we describe in some detail the fourth principal element of the rhetoric program: the legislated involvement of faculty from across the curriculum in the enterprise of strengthening student writing. Through the years, close attention to writing quality within and beyond the rhetoric program proper has encouraged faculty to assign a good bit of writing in a wide range of courses. As a result, even without a formal program of writing-intensive courses, both faculty and students are aware that writing plays a key role in learning and that students improve their writing if they are asked to examine and discuss their work at different stages in the writing process.

COMMUNICATION WITH AND INVOLVEMENT OF COLLEAGUES

In *Developing Successful College Writing Programs*, Edward White notes the importance of improving the "campus climate for writing," concluding that a key to establishing a good climate is for "all members of the campus community, particularly the administration and the faculty outside the English department, [to] begin accepting their share of responsibility" for writing instruction (1, 15). At Hampden-Sydney, writing is part of the academic culture in precisely the ways that White advocates, primarily because faculty and administrators have accepted the pedagogical arguments that underlie writing-across-the-curriculum (WAC) programs. Because we are a small liberal arts college, we interact frequently with colleagues in all departments and have come to understand not only the importance of managing a cultural shift among the faculty in attitudes about writing, but also how best to accomplish that shift through an informal approach to WAC.[3] We have done so by creating constant and diverse (major and minor) ways of interacting with our colleagues and communicating with them about writing. One might say, then, that we have a strategy instead of a program, a strategy centered on persuasion—friendly but persistent, varied, often low-keyed.[4]

That persuasion takes concrete form in several ways. First, our colleagues across the curriculum participate in the rhetoric program itself: some teach theme-based 102 courses that allow them to adapt their own intellectual interests to the rhythm and demands of a writing course. Close to two-thirds of those who have taught a rhetoric course indicated in a survey administered by the writing center that teaching writing has influenced their teaching within their own discipline, evidence that the emphasis on pedagogy that characterizes a writing course heightens teachers' awareness of their teaching practices in the disciplines. Second, the great majority of faculty help score the rhetoric proficiency exam. All proficiency exam readers are well trained in the art of scoring exams holistically: we conduct workshops for new faculty each spring and only then invite newly trained readers to score exams; refresher workshops are offered each fall semester for veteran graders. The training workshops ensure reliable scoring of the proficiency exam and, according to the survey administered by the writing center staff, also influence the ways in which faculty grade papers written in their classes.

In addition to involving colleagues directly in the rhetoric program, its directors and staff often serve as consultants about students' written work; the writing center, through "outreach" strategies, is a focal point in this regard. Results from a broad-based student survey, the College Satisfaction Experience Questionnaire (CSEQ), administered collegewide in 1998, show clearly that students believe that they are receiving significant, valuable instruction in writing at Hampden-Sydney.[5] More than 50 percent of the faculty have consulted with writing center staff about constructing and grading assignments, and faculty tutors have been invited to visit classes as varied as math, economics, and physics to discuss writing assignments. Finally, the rhetoric staff adopts and maintains toward colleagues outside the rhetoric program an attitude that communicates the assumption that they not only are interested in developing students' writing but also have valuable expertise in the writing conventions in their own fields.

MAKING ADJUSTMENTS TO THE PROGRAM

The original plan for the rhetoric program mandated periodic review of the program by internal and external reviewers. With the understanding that regular assessment keeps academic programs alive, growing, and changing, program directors and staff members have paid careful attention to suggestions and criticisms made by all reviewers and have made adjustments to the program when such changes are appropriate and possible.

Furthermore, because the rhetoric program's independent status means that "ownership" of the program and thus responsibility for it rests with the community at large, faculty across the curriculum regularly offer criticisms and advice on nearly every aspect of the program. Such interaction provides valuable information about how features of the program are working and equally importantly about how the program is perceived; so we take seriously all critiques, knowing that, at the very least, we who are most closely involved in maintaining the program demonstrate thereby a determination to keep lines of communication open to the entire community. And for the most part, such advice— along with reviewers' assessments and rhetoric staff attention to developments in composition theory—has spurred valuable staff discussion or has led to beneficial changes. We sketch below several case studies illustrating such changes.

Case #1: Additional Courses

As noted above, the faculty resolution that created the rhetoric program established Rhetoric 101 and 102 as the course sequence required of students; however, over the years, other courses have been created.

Perhaps the most noteworthy of these is Rhetoric 100, the addition of which serves as an example of the need for flexibility and creativity in adapting features of a program in order to solve problems while maintaining the goals most essential to that program.

The original plan for the 101–102 course sequence included both a provision to exempt students from 101 if they performed particularly well on a diagnostic examination and a provision that "students whose performance on the diagnostic examination show[ed] serious deficiencies" should be "placed in special sections of Rhetoric 101, where more intensive and extensive work will be expected." The difference between "special" or intensive 101 sections and "normal" 101 sections was ill-defined, except that enrollment in "special" 101 sections was limited to fewer than ten students.

The various provisions regarding Rhetoric 101 provoked the program's first major lesson in the need to heed constructive criticism and to change the program when it becomes clear that change is needed. During the first five-year review of the program in 1983, the instructor who taught most of the intensive 101 sections reported serious problems in those sections: first, "an average of nearly 1/4 [of students in the "special" sections] fail Rhetoric 101"; second, "of those intensive students who do go on to Rhetoric 102, an average of 42% make a D or an F in Rhetoric 102"; and third, "at the end of their freshman year, over half of all intensive students are gone—52% do not return for their sophomore year." This instructor concluded, "I feel this survey indicates a failure to deal successfully with students in the intensive sections of Rhetoric."

While an internal review committee did not recommend any specific remedy, increasing problems with student achievement in the mid-1980s, along with recommendations from external reviewers, forced the issue. Institutional concern with retention bolstered the cause of instructors in the intensive courses, who were frustrated by the requirement to bring less-prepared students to the same end point in one semester that better-prepared students in the "regular" 101 classes had to reach. Finally, students, faculty, and administrators came to the same conclusion at roughly the same time: there was a need for a basic writing course that was congruent with the goals of Rhetoric 101 and 102 but that allowed students to focus on a narrower range of concepts and practices than was required for those courses. Approved by the rhetoric staff and then by the faculty as a whole, with little debate, in 1986,[6] Rhetoric 100 has proved a remarkable academic success; students starting out at that level have shown themselves to be able students who simply need extra time and guidance as they improve their writing. In this case, fortunately, the need for action in response to the combined advice of students and faculty was clear, if somewhat slow in coming, and the changes were justified by the improvements to the rhetoric program and to the college's overall educational program.

Case # 2: Changing the Procedures for Proficiency Exam Scoring

Nothing came so close to jeopardizing the rhetoric program's survival in its first decade as did emerging controversies about the validity, reliability, and fairness of the rhetoric proficiency exam. Most of the problems grew out of the scoring procedure. As established by the founding resolution, the proficiency essays were "to be evaluated by three-person faculty panels drawn from all the faculty," with each panel to include at least one member of the rhetoric staff. But the resolution did not specify how the exams were to be graded or what would constitute a passing score, and at the time the college had little experience with large-scale testing and none with holistic scoring. Problems appeared almost immediately. Faculty outside the rhetoric staff wanted detailed scoring rubrics with instructions for ranking or weighting rhetorical elements; rhetoric staff members worried about reductive, mechanical grading scales. As a compromise, the director of the program constructed a fairly general set of evaluative criteria. It was further decided that the three readers would assign scores of Satisfactory or Unsatisfactory to each essay, with three S's needed for an essay to pass.

Not surprisingly, given this cumbersome scoring system from which little useful information could be gained about either the students' or the readers' performance, rumblings about unfairness and inconsistent standards began to erode confidence in the proficiency exam and to threaten the program as a whole. Still, the program review committee of 1983, relying in part on the recommendations of an external reviewer from the Council of Writing Program Administrators (WPA), urged that measures be taken to improve the scoring of the exams rather than to jettison the test. In response to this tangle of problems, serious attention was paid to research in the field of testing. Conversations with the Educational Testing Service (ETS) complemented readings in Edward White's *Teaching and Assessing Writing*. A new method of scoring the proficiency exam, a version of holistic scoring models by now familiar to most writing programs, was adapted for use at Hampden-Sydney and is still in place. The rhetoric staff, oscillating between rhetorical principles and actual student writing, constructed a six-point scoring guide based on a model devised by Edward White. The guide then was subjected to further revision by the faculty as a whole. As noted earlier, frequent grading workshops have generated a community standard for the proficiency exam and a population of skilled readers who regularly "recalibrate" their scoring; and the use of a numerical scale provides necessary information about the reliability of scorers. As a result of these changes, serious discontent about the exam has virtually disappeared.

Perhaps we could have implemented a good testing system from the start if we had "downloaded" a model developed elsewhere. But the struggle to understand testing issues and the attempt to solve problems that developed in the early years of the rhetoric program helped the faculty as a whole to devise appropriate, in-house ways of addressing the issue and in the process to develop a strong sense of community ownership of the rhetoric program.

Case #3: Reconsidering the Teaching and Testing of Grammar

To outside reviewers, the most controversial aspect of Hampden-Sydney's Rhetoric Program is the emphasis on teaching grammar and editing and the use of frequent editing tests. Since its inception, the program has included editing tests, which, together with a three-hour essay test, serve as exit exams for all rhetoric courses. It should be stressed that no rhetoric course at Hampden-Sydney focuses primarily on grammar or editing: Rhetoric 100, 101, and 102 all teach expository and argumentative writing, and rhetoric staff members emphasize a process-based approach to writing that guides students through drafts. More than in many other writing programs, though, instruction in grammar and editing is seen as part of that process. Until very recently, students in each rhetoric course had to pass a test asking them to edit fifty sentences, each containing a single error in grammar or usage. Such a test can easily be construed as—and for some instructors indeed does become—product- rather than process-oriented. Thus in recent years, as more instructors with graduate training in composition have joined the staff, there has been some internal pressure to reassess not the fact that we teach and test grammar and editing, but the ways in which we do so.

As with other debates about features of the program, this one has proceeded slowly and was resolved in a cooperative, experimental manner rather than by dictate. Our discussion began in the spring of 1997 when Martha Kolln, author of *Rhetorical Grammar: Grammatical Choices, Rhetorical Effects,* conducted a workshop for the rhetoric staff on ways to use her book in the classroom. Some of her observations about our methods of teaching editing—namely, that we stress rules and what not to do rather than positive ways in which students can manipulate the language rhetorically to better communicate their meanings—led the staff to reexamine some of our practices to see if we might institute a more positive approach to grammar and editing.

Intrigued by Kolln's approach, a special committee on teaching and testing editing conducted a staff workshop on the issue, during which a consensus was reached that Rhetoric 102, which focuses on research and style, would be an ideal course in which to experiment with different pedagogical approaches to grammar and editing. Many at the workshop expressed dissatisfaction with our standard editing test as a tool to measure students' grasp of stylistic concepts and choices; as a result, we established several experimental 102 sections, taught by interested staff members, who used Kolln's book rather than the standard handbook for grammar instruction and who did not administer the traditional fifty-sentence editing exam. Instead we devised an alternate exam to assess students' learning of the materials in the Kolln book and other rhetorical matters introduced by their instructors.[7] While these experimental sections were under way, instructors of these sections met regularly with other members of the teaching and testing editing committee to discuss the progress and problems of the classes. At a workshop following the first semester of experimentation, instructors of the new sections discussed not only the final editing exams, but also their experiences using *Rhetorical Grammar* in the classroom. They generally agreed that the experiment had been a successful one and expressed their belief in the usefulness of Kolln's approach.

Because attitudes about the importance of teaching grammar and editing are deeply embedded in the rhetoric program, many staff members are firmly attached to our traditional editing exams, which constitute for them a significant pedagogical tool. In addition, members of the Hampden-Sydney community at large, including other faculty, students, and alumni, consider the rhetoric program's emphasis on grammar and editing to be an essential part of writing instruction. For students who have gone through the program, the editing exams become a common experience, a rite of passage. Because the program is independent of all academic departments, there exists a strong sense of communal ownership and the feeling that one simply cannot change the program at will. Throughout the process of addressing the issue of teaching and testing editing, then, we have proceeded slowly and democratically. Before any binding, programwide decision was made regarding what would be perceived here at Hampden-Sydney as a fairly radical change in program policy, there was careful consideration, in a series of workshops, of instructors' accounts of their teaching experiences with new approaches, as well as of student work itself, both experimental editing exercises and tests and the student essays produced in the experimental sections. As this evidence was considered over time, interest in the changes grew among the staff. Finally, at a staff meeting in the spring of 2001, the staff approved by an overwhelming margin the proposal to retain the traditional editing tests in Rhetoric 100 and 101 but to adopt for the program as a whole the approaches to editing and grammar developed in the experimental sections of 102.

At our small, close-knit institution, changes mandated by a program director without the lengthy process of consideration that has taken place in this case would likely be met mostly with resistance and resentment. But our process of ongoing assessment and communication about proposed changes and our policy of establishing experimental sections to test hypotheses about the value of programmatic changes smoothed the way for this dramatic change. Our experiments with ways of teaching and testing grammar and editing constitute a recent, significant example of how the rhetoric program remains flexible but cautiously so, responding to criticism from sources both outside and inside the college in order to benefit our students.

CONCLUSION

Our experience has shown that, in order for an independent writing program to survive—more importantly, in order for such a program to accomplish its educational goals successfully over a period of time—program directors and staff members must be receptive to the constructive suggestions and criticisms of colleagues, of students, of administrators, and of outside reviewers. Establishing lines of communication and keeping those lines open are crucial to maintaining others' trust and support. If there is a sense of campuswide ownership of and responsibility for a writing program, especially at a liberal arts college, then independence does not turn into isolation or marginalization but instead becomes a source of strength, allowing true integration of writing instruction into the whole of the institution's academic program. Furthermore, program directors and staff members need to be open to the idea that various features of a writing program—even features they are particularly attached to—may need to be adjusted, either because there is significant and reasonable demand for change or because, over time, shifts in focus are needed to ensure that the program corresponds to the needs of the student body, the teaching staff, the institution's overall academic program, or the world beyond the university gates, where the students must compete for jobs or for places in graduate and professional programs. Program directors need to be flexible and creative in finding ways to adjust features of the program so that the program's central goals are not sacrificed but enhanced. Inevitably, too, the director will have to find appropriate ways to smooth the ruffled feathers of those on the teaching staff and beyond who opposed the changes.

How is all of this possible, and what are the drawbacks of having an independent program that operates this way? It must be said that probably the most significant difficulty with Hampden-Sydney's Rhetoric Program and its particular version of "independence" is that being deeply rooted in the requirements and standards of our own institution's liberal arts curriculum and being deeply committed to interacting with members of the local community can mean that the program tends to be out of sync with developments in the broader world of composition studies. More often than not, assessments of our program by outside reviewers have been highly critical on these grounds, and many reviewers have left campus saying something to the effect that "according to composition theory, and given results of research in the field, this program should not work at all; it simply cannot be as effective as everyone on campus believes that it is." Although being slower to adjust to external than to internal demands leaves us open to the charge of provincialism,[8] we have decided that local demands and standards, along with the experience and evidence accumulated during the program's twenty-year lifespan, outweigh the mandates of current theoretical developments in composition studies.

To date, program directors have worked on this problem by ensuring that issues from internal and external sources are seriously discussed in staff meetings and workshops and with the campus community at large. And, though slow to change, the rhetoric program has not been averse to change: if staff meetings are at times cantankerous events, they are also lively ones, as instructors seek ways to adapt the program they have inherited to new generations of students and to the constantly changing world of work and study. What can certainly be said in our favor is that the time and effort we devote to discussion and debate means that on our campus there is an unusually acute awareness not only of the importance of students' writing but also of various issues associated with the teaching of writing. That the Rhetoric Program at Hampden-Sydney is quite healthy at age twenty-two can be credited to the wisdom of those who devised it, to the college administrators who have supported and even lauded it, and to the hard-working staff members and program directors who have guided and formed it, but also to the faculty members and students campuswide who—along with the professionals in the field who have reviewed it—have contributed their ideas about how a good program could be made even better. This is our way of fulfilling Samuel Stanhope Smith's 1775 goal for Hampden-Sydney College, ensuring that, in fact and not just in theory, all graduates of the college will be able to write clearly and cogently; it is our way of creating the "open communication and rational engagement" (Russell 1992, 41) that is a most natural and appropriate foundation for liberal arts education and a hallmark of effective, enduring academic programs.

ACKNOWLEDGMENTS

The authors wish to thank Professors George Bagby, Larry Martin, Mary Saunders, and Wayne Tucker of Hampden-Sydney College for providing information about the founding of the college's Rhetoric Program. We would also like to thank former director of assessment Onie MacKenzie for providing the results of the CSEQ.

NOTES

1.   Mary Saunders, now a senior professor of English who was hired in 1977 specifically to help develop a comprehensive writing program, recalls that members of the English department agreed that "a two-semester course, probably with exit proficiency exams, would be crucial to giving students the help they needed to improve their critical thinking as well as their writing skills. It was also understood that the job was too big for the English department alone: careful attention from more than a few teachers in one department would be needed to produce improvement." As a result, though plans for the rhetoric program were initiated within the English department, faculty and

administrators quickly decided that "the program would be the business of the whole college."

2.   Wayne Tucker, professor of classics and the first director of the Rhetoric Program, published in the college's alumni journal a useful article on the new writing program, from which some of the information in this section is taken. See "Rhetoric Reborn: A Theme with Commentary". Additional information was provided to us by George Bagby, professor of English, and Larry Martin, professor of English and dean of the faculty, both of whom helped construct the rhetoric program.

3.   In the last chapter of *Programs That Work*, Toby Fulwiler and Art Young identify "entrenched [faculty] attitudes as the chief enemy of writing across the curriculum" (292–94). We maintain that at least at our institution and likely at others, the most effective weapon against that enemy is what David Russell claims is one of the strengths of WAC initiatives—their ability to help the American education system "realize the vision of Dewey: that curricula should be arrived at by means of open communication and rational engagement, not by fiat" (1992, 41). Hampden-Sydney has had the opportunity to implement a more formal writing-across-the-curriculum requirement, but it has consciously decided not to, opting instead for the kind of approach we have described. Other schools have benefited from such "grassroots" methods—administrators at George Mason University, for example, write that "[we] decided to create a grass-roots program through workshops that would involve interested faculty. We felt that a 'seed' program would eventually provide a strong base for more ambitious plans. Rather than beginning the program from the top, as has occurred recently at many institutions where 'writing intensive' courses have been mandated before faculty training has begun, we felt that massive curriculum change would occur naturally though pressure from experienced faculty" (Thaiss et al. 225–26).

4.   This strategy of persuasion is especially effective at small liberal arts colleges, according to a recent article by Thomas Amorose. Citing David Bell, Amorose unpacks the complex concept of "power" at academic institutions; what we call "persuasion" is termed "authority" and "influence" in this article. On the whole, Amorose's discussion of authority and influence in the operation of successful writing programs at small colleges is an apt analysis of how the rhetoric program works at Hampden-Sydney.

5.   In particular, seventy-one percent of students reported that in the course of the year they had written and revised a rough draft, and a

significant number reported that they had spent five hours or more writing a paper and/or had revised a paper two or more times. Almost half of the students surveyed (forty-five percent) reported that they had written more than ten papers during the year (which was not yet complete when the survey was administered), and, most importantly, 85 percent reported that, as a result of their work at college, they had gained "quite a bit" or "very much" in their ability to write clearly and effectively. In comparison, 65.9 percent of students responding to this questionnaire at all selective liberal arts colleges included in the survey between 1990 and 1996 felt that they had gained "quite a bit" or "very much." The Hampden-Sydney numbers in the "very much" category especially stand out: 49.5 percent, compared to 24.2 percent among other respondents. Though this is self-reported, anecdotal evidence, the fact that more than twice as many students at Hampden-Sydney than at other liberal arts colleges reported gaining very much from their study of writing in college speaks to the influence not only of the rhetoric program but also of the culture of writing that has become an established part of Hampden-Sydney.

6.   At Hampden-Sydney, all new courses must be presented to the faculty as a whole for consideration and vote. The independent status of the rhetoric program (and its status as a program and not a department) was a considerable disadvantage in this instance, since there were no tenured department members to argue for the course. This fact makes the faculty's acceptance of Rhetoric 100 all the more significant. We were lucky in this case because the Math department already had in place a Math 100 course, one that students took for credit but which did not satisfy the college's core requirement in math. We modeled Rhetoric 100 on this course and used the parallel when presenting the case for Rhetoric 100 to the faculty.

7.   In the first semester of experimentation, students were asked to revise two substantial paragraphs that contained a variety of problems in organization and focus as well as problems with rhetorical effectiveness at the sentence level. They were then presented with two passages about a similar subject matter and asked to decide which was the most rhetorically effective and to explain why. Because there was some dissatisfaction with this test among instructors, the following fall a new task was designed, this one asking students to revise a paragraph from their final essay exam according to the principles of rhetorical grammar and then to explain in a brief essay why they had made the changes they did to improve their paragraphs. A recent staff review of

this revised test, as well as writing portfolios produced by students who wrote the revised test, suggested that this testing model was effective for Rhetoric 102. The instructors who administered and graded the tests were pleased with the type of test and also with their students' performance.

8. Hampden-Sydney's rhetoric program is certainly a "traditional" writing program and is also "homegrown," as we have explained; however, it is not insular or closed to outside influence. Directors and staff members regularly attend and present papers at regional and national conferences devoted to writing instruction, and several national figures in the field of rhetoric and composition have visited campus to conduct workshops here. Such interaction, we believe and hope, keeps our pedagogical peculiarities from developing into ineffective oddities. On the problem of writing program insularity, see Bruce Horner's discussion of the English 1–2 program at Amherst College in his recent *Terms of Work for Composition* (179–87).

6

NO LONGER DISCOURSE TECHNICIANS
Redefining Place and Purpose in an Independent Canadian Writing Program

Brian Turner
Judith Kearns

In a recent, often brilliant, reading of the *Rhetoric*, Eugene Garver revisits a central distinction in Aristotle's thinking: the difference between professional and civic rhetorics. Like other noble arts, says Garver, rhetoric has both a given (external) end and guiding (internal) ends. Its given end, persuasion, can be achieved by any professional rhetor with the appropriate technical skills or "know-how"; it doesn't require honesty or breadth of vision. Yet the rhetor whose sole aim is suasive victory will eventually raise doubts about his character, and he may bring disrepute to his entire profession, occupation, or discipline. Indeed, his unethical approach can do even greater damage: it can make suasion itself, and by association the whole art of rhetoric, seem less than noble. Still, it would be a mistake to treat the given end of rhetoric scornfully simply because some practitioners abuse the art. The failing of the fast-buck lawyer—his ignobility, if you like—is not that he concerns himself with persuasion, but that he concentrates on it exclusively. By contrast, Aristotle's civic rhetorician never makes persuasion an end in itself. Guided as much by rhetoric's "internal standards of completion and perfection" (Garver 28) as by its given ends, he practices his art responsibly, aware that his rhetorical choices will have consequences not only for himself but also for his auditors and for the community they both inhabit.

The relevance of Aristotle's ancient distinction may seem obscure in an anthology such as this, focused as it is on narratives about contemporary writing programs. Yet in the process of articulating our story of the University of Winnipeg's Centre for Academic Writing (CAW), the authors have come to see the distinction as something of a touchstone and guide, useful in our dual roles as narrators of a program's past and as actors in its ongoing present. Like the histories of many writing programs, the history of CAW has largely been played out from the margins. It has been a story about trying, simultaneously, to accommodate colleagues and administrators who misunderstood our work, to convince them that we deserve a place in the academy and in our institution, and to become a better program according to the "internal standards" of our discipline. During the course of these efforts, CAW faculty have certainly engaged in acts of professional rhetoric, as academics fighting territorial battles must. But what has been more important than any particular act of persuasion, we see in retrospect, is the sense of purpose that directed our efforts to create a stronger program. We were determined not to become what others seemed to think we should, mere discourse technicians or, worse, tenured remediators. That sort of profile and program—the stereotype held by those who see writing as a basic skill, unworthy of academic research—is one that every writing teacher resists, whether she considers herself a compositionist or a rhetorician. What we were not so clear about was how to define ourselves otherwise and how to make the alternative a reality. This is how Aristotle helps us. His distinction between civic and professional rhetoric reminds us not only of what we want to avoid becoming but of what we want to be.[1]

The following narrative is in two parts, punctuated by occasional returns to Aristotle. In the first, we recount the process by which our program, originally situated in the English department, became an independent center, and we explain how CAW faculty dealt with and continue to deal with some of the difficulties resulting from separation.[2] The second part then describes our recent successes, focusing particularly on our role in the development of a new joint communications program but also outlining our plans for still further development.

At times, we realize, the narrative may suggest that CAW faculty knew precisely what we wanted and how to get there or that we were always aware of the distinction between professional and civic rhetoric and conducted ourselves accordingly. Such implications are quite unintended. The fact is that we often fumbled along, trying to win small battles, sometimes with anything but rhetoric's internal standards of completion and perfection foremost in our minds. Even now, as far as we know, the authors of this article are the only CAW faculty to speak of the program's goals and practices in terms of "civic" and "professional." Yet something like a sense of civic rhetoric—we thought of it as a vision of what "the best" writing program should be, for our students, for our institution, for ourselves, and for our discipline—has, we believe, motivated many of our faculty's efforts and been responsible for the continual improvement in our public profile.

WHERE WE ARE AND HOW WE GOT HERE

The University of Winnipeg is an undergraduate liberal arts institution (seventy-five hundred students) located in Winnipeg, Manitoba, a city of about 650,000 that also includes a larger research university. Its Writing Program, as the current Centre for Academic Writing was first called, was established in 1987 as a subdivision of the English department, mandated to meet the needs of the university's heterogeneous population of first-year students, many of them considered academically at risk. At first, a faculty of eight full-time instructors taught only two courses (both of them collaboratively designed and based on predominantly expressivist assumptions); but by 1992, several upper-level rhetoric courses had been designed and three tenure-track assistant professors had been hired. (We would remain a faculty of eleven, but our proportions would gradually shift to our present balance of four instructors, three assistant professors, and four associate professors.) To our delight, the program was even beginning to garner national attention. According to Canada's most popular news magazine, *Maclean's,* "Winnipeg's *writing-skills* program for entering students ha[d] become a model for universities across the country" (78, emphasis added).[3]

In the same year, however, a review of the program exposed increasingly serious theoretical differences about writing pedagogy.[4] The very possibility of such differences, much less the expression and resolution of them, had been suppressed by our administrative structure; as our external reviewers would note, "[A] system of governance designed for flexibility [had] become rigid" (Paré and Segal 7). Both the internal and external sets of reviewers therefore agreed on the need for administrative change. Both recommended autonomy. But it was indicative of attitudes within the university that our internal reviewers recommended we become a center rather than a department. The recommendation seemed to be based on concerns about empire building, fear that upper-level courses would proliferate at the expense of our first-year mandate. Further and quite different "status" concerns were strongly implied by the language of their report. Program faculty should, it said, "focus on the expressive, stylistic and technical aspects of the writing" and "disciplinary faculty [should] concentrate on the disciplinary content" (De Long et al. 35). With such language, the internal report formalized what program

faculty had long suspected: that our colleagues saw us as discourse technicians rather than full-fledged academics with subject matter of their own.
The external committee, on the other hand, seemed to assume that
departmental status was appropriate, perhaps because they understood
that an emerging discipline such as ours could ill afford to be treated differently from other disciplines.

This disagreement over whether we should become a center or a
department marked a pivotal point in our history. At stake was not only
our institutional status but also, we now realize, our pedagogical function
in the university—in other words, whether we were to remain discourse
technicians or have the opportunity to become something more. No one
understood this fully at the time, of course, at least not in these terms.
Relieved by the Internal Review Committee's well-meant efforts to
remove some of the conditions that had made us second-class academics,
pleased that both committees recommended independence, we failed to
see what now seems obvious: without departmental status, we would be
less free to pursue rhetoric's own guiding ends, that is, the standards of
our discipline, but would instead be compelled by institutional restraints
to concentrate on utility, to focus on what nonrhetoricians think writing
is and how it should be taught, and to adjust our courses to the ends of
other disciplines. We were in danger of becoming professional rhetors,
always persuading, compromising, and accommodating, rather than
rhetoricians who could follow their discipline's internal standards.

In 1995, more immediate dangers occupied our attention. It did not
take us long after separation from the English department to discover
just how vulnerable a new academic unit can be, especially when it lacks
the prestige of a strong and *known* disciplinary tradition, as is the case
with composition and rhetoric (especially in Canadian universities).
Within months of becoming independent, CAW submitted its first
tenure applications to the university's Faculty Personnel Committee, a little uncertain of the politics involved but confident that our own personnel committee had done all it could in giving both candidates strong,
unanimous recommendations. We had not, however, anticipated the
consequences of having no senior faculty, no one with enough institutional clout to counteract the Faculty Personnel Committee's emphasis
on traditional research. We were quickly, and painfully, taught a political
lesson (as many compositionists before us have been).[5] The candidates
did ultimately receive tenure, but only after a great deal of lobbying from
our director and from such senior, respected faculty as the dean, the

chair of the English department, and the university's grievance officer. Not long after, we faced another obstacle—though admittedly one far less traumatic in its impact and not at all political in its origins—when a sabbatical application encountered difficulties with the university's Research Leave Committee. The reason for the difficulties was clear: not one member of CAW's personnel committee, which had given its stamp of approval, had had experience with the standards and procedures of the university's committee for judging such applications.

The lack of senior faculty also retarded our progress with committee work. We had been right to see the elimination of our committee service to the English department as an advantage of separation (we now carried a single committee load), but it was one that would not be realized for at least a year or two, because the administrative learning curve was so steep. Where once we had been members of committees guided by experienced faculty, we were now forced to do everything on our own as we got our committees up and running. Moreover, since half of CAW faculty were at this time still instructors, neither required to do research nor allowed to sit on major university-level committees, the bulk of the work fell on the shoulders of the very people who needed more time to do research. Yet another complication was that few CAW faculty had graduate training in rhetoric and composition, so our committees wasted time struggling to find common terms and concepts as we discussed internal issues. Even fewer faculty could speak from experience about the unspoken institutional requirements for achieving tenure and promotion or about the labyrinthine processes of guiding a curriculum proposal through the university's various planning committees.

That we were a new academic unit staffed with junior faculty was not something that we could alter immediately or by sheer effort. But what we could and must do, several of us realized, was to expand our first-hand experience of the institution's protocols and politics as quickly as possible. Not only would such insider knowledge make us less vulnerable to the tacit norms of important committees, it might also give CAW a higher profile within the university and confer at least some of the advantages associated with seniority. We began to nominate one another for service on those standing committees that might have the greatest impact on our operations and/or that might give us the broadest perspective on the workings of the university: Personnel, Curriculum, Research Leave, Academic Standards. When the opportunity arose for our director to serve on other ad hoc or senate committees that might "teach us" something—a committee on Prior Learning Assessment, a committee to select a new university president, and, subsequently, the new president's committee on enrollment strategies—she did so. (Indeed, the election of our director to the Presidential Search Committee was in itself a clear indication that our status was improving.) One of our faculty became the university's grievance officer.

Many readers will see little that is unusual in all of this. Administrative service is, after all, a given in the life of an academic; and few directors of any program would turn down the opportunity to help choose a new university president. But what made our voluntarism special was the context in which it occurred. In addition to managing the heavy teaching and marking loads normally faced by compositionists, CAW faculty had just come through an extraordinarily time-consuming review and were still climbing a steep learning curve; the time available to research and publish was therefore still very limited. Yet time for research and publication had been one goal of separation, and we had learned by experience that publication was what the university's traditionalist personnel committee demanded. Committee voluntarism therefore involved risk: gaining procedural knowledge that would, for example, obviate difficulties in promotion might mean sacrificing the time needed to strengthen curricula vitae.

All the same, we made the commitment. Indeed, we did more. When the opportunity arose to write reports or to serve on editing subcomittees, we did so, because such work showed our colleagues from other departments what we could do. Academics generally assume, unless given strong evidence to the contrary, that the historian can "do history," the mathematician "do math," and the philosopher reason well; and they assume, moreover, that these things are worth doing. On the other hand, writing teachers know from personal experience and disciplinary lore that other academics don't always make these assumptions about what we do. We are often seen as marginal members of the academy, neophytes who must justify our place and demonstrate our expertise. One can rue or rebel against this fact, or one can work with it. We chose (or perhaps, guided by political instincts, eased towards) the latter path, and we have not regretted it. Indeed, working with the stubborn facts of our status over the last five years has altered them more than we could have imagined was possible. Demonstrating our ability to define a rhetorical problem or to revise a report or to distinguish among degrees of mechanical error has given us a certain cachet among our colleagues. Much remains a mystery to them—how we improve our students' writing without concentrating on "grammar" and what we mean by and do with "rhetoric"—but they have at least acknowledged that we "do" some things well and have accordingly given us *some* degree of academic respect.

Admittedly, we were casting ourselves as discourse technicians, but in this case the role has been well worth playing. Performing as technicians on committees will in no way bind us more tightly to a technical curriculum. Indeed, in pursuing the given end of rhetoric by appealing to what is valued by our colleagues, we have persuaded them of our worth; we have improved our ethos and elicited an attitude of assent, smoothing the path for the kind of program *we* value—a broader, more rhetorically based curriculum. We could therefore argue that, in our committee efforts, we have not only acted professionally but also been guided by our civic sense of what is right by the standards of our discipline and of what is good for the community.

Improvement in our institutional status probably owed as much to the very fact of independence as it did to our committee voluntarism. Placement within the English department had created some damaging misperceptions about the writing program's philosophy and pedagogy. Our courses were never belletristic, as colleagues from other departments seemed to assume, but many sections were firmly rooted in the expressive paradigm. From the point of view of physicists and geographers and sociologists who were dismayed by their students' writing, it all amounted to the same thing: we were encouraging "voice," concentrating on invention, doing what English professors have long done— teaching a disciplinary way of writing as though it were "the" correct way to write. Granting the program independence strengthened the university's claim that writing was central in *every* discipline; naming it the Centre for *Academic* Writing and concurrently endorsing our new curriculum, grounded in writing-in-the-disciplines (WID) principles, made the claim a reality.[6] Colleagues from the natural and social sciences, we soon found, welcomed our questions about their specialized discourses and were not at all xenophobic about the idea of compositionists' entering their domains.[7]

To the extent that it allowed us to do teaching that calls for and feeds on challenging research, the new curriculum made CAW faculty feel for a time just a little less like discourse technicians. But only a little: although a WID approach opens up exciting opportunities to investigate disciplinary rhetorics, it also places severe constraints on "outsiders." It is, at best, a chance to work on what Robert Schwegler calls "marginally contestable" discourse (Shamoon et al. 13). Nevertheless, it was all we had at this stage, since the decision to make us a center rather than a department had left us without the freedom to develop a major. Without this freedom, we would have few conventional opportunities to move beyond the study of academic discourse into the province of civic rhetoric.

MOVING INTO THE FUTURE

Eager for new challenges and lacking conventional avenues, CAW was ready to entertain unusual options. We were primed to think laterally. When an opportunity arose to help construct a combined degree/diploma in communications, to be offered jointly between our university and a local community college, we seized it. Our efforts in this venture, as it turns out, have been doubly rewarding: they have further enhanced our professional status by showing that we can take initiatives and secure advantages for our institution; and they have established a stronger toehold for us as academics—as teachers and scholars whose discipline involves much more than technical expertise in composition.

The idea of joint programs was not a new one for our university. In a province with a small population base, cooperative ventures between local postsecondary institutions made good economic sense. The provincial government certainly favored such partnerships. The University of Winnipeg was particularly well suited to a partnership of this kind; as the smaller of the city's universities, it can adapt more easily to experimentation, and in fact, our colleagues in biology, chemistry, and environmental studies had already developed successful joint programs with Red River College. CAW certainly recognized the political wisdom of linking with an award-winning program highly regarded by local employers, as is the case with Red River's diploma program in creative communications. But acting on such indications was not mere opportunism. We also believed that we could strengthen the program by adding courses with a theoretical and rhetorical perspective, courses that would encourage students to think deliberately, analytically, and critically about the practical skills they were learning to apply in the college's journalism, advertising, and public relations streams. One might say, in short, that we saw collaboration with Red River as a rare opportunity to make apprentice professionals in communications think more like civic rhetoricians.

But there were risks involved. The first, admittedly minor, was to perceptions of our professional competence: what if, having initiated such a project, we failed to design a program that would meet the standards of the university's senate and of the appropriate government bodies? The models available were, after all, applied scientific programs, which could help us avoid certain logistical problems but were of less use in curriculum and program design. Given that we were stepping up to the plate for the first time, would we be considered minor-leaguers if we struck out, unable to deal with problems solved by our colleagues in the sciences? More important, partnership with an applied program posed a risk to CAW's evolving academic ethos. The science departments that had set up joint programs faced no risk of this sort, possibly because they were well established within the institution and possibly (though of this we, as outsiders, can't be sure) because applied studies have always been an accepted part of scientific disciplines. Those teaching in the humanities, though, view applied programs with some suspicion; the assumption seems to be that a college's narrow vocational orientation undermines the rigor required of an academic program. As a new, unproven academic unit, already vulnerable to misperceptions about the remedial and mechanical dimensions of the instruction it offers, CAW was especially susceptible to these assumptions. Partnership with an applied program might confirm the perception that we are not a real discipline but a service.

We overcame both of these risks in part because we collaborated with our university's English department. Just as membership in the department had once made the Writing Program, if not quite academically respectable, more acceptable to other faculty, CAW's partnership with English now seemed to buffer us and the new Joint Communications Program from traditionalist, ivory tower criticism. Since English, an established humanity, was equally involved, no one could argue that CAW's involvement with an applied program demonstrated that we weren't "real academics." Indeed, during negotiations, CAW proved its worth to the university in unexpected ways, confirming the wisdom of having made us an independent academic unit. With two of its academic stakeholders involved—two stakeholders, moreover, whose members had worked together closely in the past—the university enjoyed much stronger representation. The result was the birth of a cost-efficient program that had immediate public relations value for the university and soon proved popular with students.

Our work on the joint program has helped make the center more than a halfway house for discourse technicians. Our senior courses are flourishing. Two of them, designated as requirements in the program, now have a steady supplemental enrollment; the others, designated as electives, have a reliable pool of students from which to draw.[8] These increases come on top of consistently high enrollment in upper-level courses, so high, in fact, that our requests to deliver existing rhetoric courses and our proposals for new courses have been routinely granted. Perhaps the most important benefits from developing the joint program have been those we couldn't have anticipated. For one thing, the appetite for communications courses seems to have grown with the feeding; rather than satisfying demand, as we had expected, the new program has stimulated further interest. Applications have increased each year, as have inquiries, not just from high school students interested in the joint program but from Red River graduates who want to supplement their diplomas and from white-collar workers eager to develop their communicative abilities and upgrade their credentials. This last group is far more likely to come to us than they once were—evidence of the second unexpected benefit of our involvement in the joint program: we now have a strong identity. CAW may offer only a small portion of a degree, but from the students' point of view, we now seem much like other departments. The expanding interest in communications has something to fasten itself to.

As the focus of such enthusiasm, we are now taking the next logical step: an appeal for both departmental status and a major in rhetoric and communications. The most recent draft of our proposed curriculum includes a range of general and specialized writing courses, designed mainly to strengthen students' abilities to generate, revise, and edit text for various audiences. Balanced with these are courses grounded in broader perspectives—in rhetorical criticism, theory, and history, for example, and in literary nonfiction, visual rhetorics, and orality and literacy. The blend, we believe, will meet the given end of rhetoric; we know we have to construct a major that will persuade colleagues and students of its value; and a curriculum that addresses the endemic shortage of strong technical skills will do so (far from abandoning our mandate to first-year students, as colleagues feared, we have extended it). At the same time, this balanced design heeds rhetoric's guiding ends; it keeps faculty from becoming discourse technicians, and it reduces the likelihood that graduates will become fast-buck professionals of the sort described in our introduction. The argument we will make this fall is that such a major would not only draw students but enhance the university's liberal arts focus.

We don't want to paint too rosy a picture of our future—there's no guarantee that we'll attain departmental status or that a rhetoric and communications degree will materialize—but we are now secure enough within the institution to explore such possibilities with little anxiety about repercussions and even with considerable optimism. We are, in short, doing very well and are gradually becoming the kind of program we would like to be.

CONCLUDING REFLECTIONS

It has become common practice to conclude narratives such as this with a few words of advice, offered in the hope that a young, marginalized discipline might strengthen itself by sharing its stories. Such advice is, however, often generalized and carefully qualified, largely because the lessons one learns from the history of one's own writing program are not easily transferable. As Timothy Donovan observes, "no single writing program, no matter how artfully conceived in theory, could survive in practice without being adapted to the given institution" (176). Inevitably, writing programs are a product of local exigencies and conditions.

As Canadians writing for a largely American audience, the authors of this narrative feel a particular need to be cautious about giving advice. Our program has emerged not only from unique local conditions, but also from national traditions quite different from those shared by Americans. First-year composition, for instance, has never been the norm in Canadian universities, a fact that reverberates throughout our history. When the University of Winnipeg set a writing requirement, it provoked some hostility (much of it directed at Writing Program faculty), not because the requirement was a bad idea, but because it was a new idea. Even now, we suspect, the students who resist our mandatory course do so mainly because first-year composition is not embedded in Canadian university culture. At the same time, the absence of program models may have offered CAW more freedom to develop our curricula, as well as more flexibility when the opportunity arrived to redefine ourselves in response to changing circumstances.

With these qualifications in mind, we believe that writing administrators and teachers may benefit from some of the strategies we've use— first instinctively, then more deliberately—to strengthen the Centre for Academic Writing. We would argue, for instance, that administrative voluntarism not only teaches faculty how their institutions operate, but also raises a program's profile and creates good will. Clearly, though, faculty need to be judicious about this service, and not only in terms of how much they take on. Those best suited by temperament and ability for such service should be encouraged to work on committees with the greatest impact on a program's success; as ambassadors for a program with no clear disciplinary identity, their performance matters as representation of an established department rarely does. Moreover, our experience suggests that writing teachers should, when the opportunity arises to compose or edit a committee report, university calendar copy, or policy statement, voluntarily extend their commitment. Such work does cut into valuable research time and may play into narrow stereotypes about the grammar skills of writing teachers, but our experience suggests that it benefits one's program in the long run. By demonstrating abilities that colleagues appreciate, a persuasive, well-crafted report may win their professional respect. Also important is the fostering of alliances, not just with the English department but with those who may misunderstand the writing program's goals and methods. In addition to widening the constituency of potential supporters for new initiatives, such alliances create opportunities for program faculty to educate colleagues about what we do, how we do it, and why.

To some of our readers, this advice may sound painfully naive. After all, members of our own profession have referred to us, with some justification, as the workhorse of the academy, toiling "tirelessly, selflessly," until "his strength gives out" and he "collapses" (Schuster 1991, 86). To recommend more committee service for people already overloaded with grading and student conferences might well seem perverse. Yet if we are to become, and to be perceived as, more than discourse technicians, we may simply have to make such extra efforts. To return to Garver and the distinction between civic and professional rhetoric: at one point in *Aristotle's Rhetoric: An Art of Character,* Garver recounts a discussion in Plato's *Laws* of the various demands made on one's character by civil and foreign wars and analogizes rhetoric with war:

> [F]or professional rhetoric a professional skill analogous to the courage of a professional warrior is all that is needed, and so one can hire someone else to do the fighting, or pleading. . . . Are there rhetorical situations where hiring a professional to do the job just won't work? A civic rhetoric is one in which more than the external goal is at stake. The audience is not an enemy, and the civic rhetorician must construct a civic relation between himself and his audience. (46)

As writing teachers in the academy, we are not only in the professional business of developing technical skills but also, whether or not we wish it, in the political business of representing values. We all want opportunities to do more than teach technical skills. Conducting ourselves as civic rhetors—willing to make some compromises for the good of the institution and doing what we can to persuade doubters rather than treating them as the enemy—seems to these authors one satisfying way to create such opportunities.

NOTES

1. In identifying ourselves with civic rhetoric in this way, we were mindful of Charles Schuster's words of caution to those in composition studies: not only should they avoid "the temptation" to conceive of themselves "within narrow, rigid, or oppositional terms," they should also favor "a contested disciplinary definition, one that cannot be satisfactorily located, specified, articulated." On the other hand, Schuster concedes just how "dangerous" such a position is: "the undefinable is often marginalized and misunderstood" (1991, 47).

    Though we do believe that identification with civic rhetoric will ensure that our self-definition is both broad and flexible, we do not wish to argue that this identification is some sort of universal panacea for the fields of rhetoric and composition. Indeed, it clearly won't solve all the problems in our own Centre for Academic Writing. Nevertheless, we believe that defining ourselves and our purposes is better than avoiding definition. Schuster's concession about the dangers of the undefinable is what rings truest for us: if we do not define ourselves, we will inevitably be defined by others.

2. A fuller account of this process can be found in the authors' 1997 article, "Negotiated Independence: How a Canadian Writing Program Became a Centre," in *WPA: Writing Program Administration* 21: 31–43.

3. All writing teachers reading this, we expect, can readily imagine both our pleasure at being singled out for such recognition and our chagrin at the language in which it was couched, which reinforces the narrowest stereotypes about writing instruction. The problem was one that we have often encountered, within as well as outside the university. Even those who praise us most highly have caricatured us as discourse technicians.

4. Of the range of positions identified by Slevin, the main lines of debate among our faculty were drawn between those who argued "for a freshman curriculum that focuses on expressive writing and the development of students' individual voices" and those who maintained "that

freshman English should afford students a critical perception of the constraints and genuine intellectual possibilities of academic discourse, providing them with the opportunity to use for their own purposes, and not just simulate for the purposes of the institution, the genres of the academy" (1991, Politics of the Profession). As Bizzell has noted, such a debate is politically charged, especially when it comes to the needs of students perceived to be "at risk" in an unfamiliar academic environment: "Teaching academic discourse to basic writers has become a particularly sensitive issue because their difficulties with academic writing tend to be a function of the social distance between the academy and their home communities" (64). One of our goals, then, was to move from a "common curriculum" to a program that accommodated divergent, yet deeply held, convictions about writing instruction.

5.   See, for instance, Charles Altieri, Edward Corbett, Stephen North, and Charles Schuster.

6.   Our offerings now allow students to choose a course that teaches writing in their discipline area ("Academic Writing in the Humanities, Social Sciences, or Natural Sciences"); a writing course linked with introductory courses in departments like biology, environmental studies, or administrative studies; or a more broadly based introduction to the norms of academic discourse ("Academic Writing: Multidisciplinary").

7.   Our statement about the advantages of separation from the English department might be taken to imply that they held us back. In fact, it would be unfair of us not to acknowledge the positive role that the University of Winnipeg's English department has played in our history. Studies of writing programs are, we know, full of stories of their marginalization within departments of English. ("Literature and Composition: Not Separate but Certainly Unequal," the title of a chapter in Crowley's 1998 *Composition in the University,* says it all.) By contrast, it was our good fortune to be members of an English department in which we were treated as near equal.

8.   English department courses have almost exactly the same weight as CAW courses in the degree structure, and we have shared responsibilities for administering the program and for advising students. Especially for communications students, but also more generally, these facts in and of themselves mark CAW's status as a separate unit academically as important as English.

II

Beyond the Local

CONNECTIONS AMONG COMMUNITIES

7

LEARNING AS WE G(R)O(W)
Strategizing the Lessons of a Fledgling Rhetoric and Writing Studies Department

Jane E. Hindman

Even before the Wyoming Resolution and certainly ever since, compositionists have debated how we might improve the material conditions of teaching writing. Like the promise of the New World shone for many an immigrant, our vision of a legitimate discipline and—even better—a stand-alone department of rhetoric and writing seemed to guarantee the changes we'd longed for and knew we'd earned. In actuality, however, this dream of independence has been less than liberating for many. Some argue that the status of the profession has improved at the expense of the material working conditions of many professionals. While the discipline of composition studies has apparently survived its legitimation crises, the expertise and authority of a majority of its practitioners are persistently and willfully ignored on a massive, institutional scale.

Understanding the causes of and solutions to this seemingly incontrovertible split between the material labor interests and the more "academic" (that is, abstract as well as disciplinary) objectives is the goal of much recent scholarship. In the September 2000 issue of *College Composition and Communication* (*CCC*), for instance, Joseph Harris considers the conflicting interests between "tenure-stream" faculty and adjunct, part-time, and graduate writing instructors or "comp droids," a term Harris borrows from Cary Nelson. These lecturers, adjuncts, and graduate teaching assistants (GTAs) are the qualified teachers of writing whose status the Wyoming Resolution strove to improve. In reality, however, their labor has made possible the relative leisure of an upper-class type of scholar, one whom Harris calls—following James Sledd—the "boss compositionist" who's sold out his former peers. This "new" boss, Harris argues, is no different from the old boss: like the privileged literature professors before them, tenured writing instructors enjoy the luxuries of light teaching loads comprised of small graduate seminars while the "droids" bear the weight of undergraduate education.

In order to trace the cooption of writing instructors' objectives, Harris refers to Jeanne Gunner's analysis of the Conference on College Composition and Communication's (CCCC) response to the Wyoming Resolution—from its original initiative and on through the 1989 "Statement of Principles and Standards for the Postsecondary Teaching of Writing." Gunner demonstrates how CCCC rhetorically shifted the focus and values of the Wyoming Resolution and thus appropriated the resolve to improve instructors' labor conditions, transforming it into a means for authorizing composition's growth as a disciplinary community, creating more tenure-track positions in composition, and—by implication perhaps—more independent departments of writing studies. Harris uses Gunner's warning about seduction that lures our attention away from present working conditions to note the folly in our destructive illusion that stabilizing the disciplinary status of composition studies will ultimately enfranchise all writing instructors.

Harris's warning is clearly well intended and relevant. So too are James Sledd's criticisms of boss compositionists who side with the interests of management and Jeanne Gunner's cautionary words to those "blinded by the allures of what might be called 'MLA-like' power and status" (108). Our continued professional and disciplinary evolution depends on our identifying the ways our professional commitment to improving working conditions can be and indeed have been co-opted. However, successful integration of the concerns of labor *and* legitimacy within composition requires us to avoid shortsighted, naive, or decontextualized analyses of how our efforts to improve working conditions and disciplinary authority are appropriated. I do not mean to imply that the critiques I've cited are categorically simplistic or restricted; yet, they do seem similar in their tacit assumption about the nature of the problematic shift from material to abstract concerns.

A careful examination of Harris's perspective on the origins of the inequitable caste system in composition reveals that assumption. Here are the alternative methods for improving working conditions that he presents: requiring tenure-stream faculty to teach first-year composition regularly; revising the first-year course so that it becomes less labor-intensive; "mak[ing] the training, supervision and review of adjunct instructors part of our own [i.e.tenure-stream personnel's] regular work as faculty" (61); and creating departmental autonomy or at least "pressing for more direct control over staffing and curricula" (64). As we can see, a change in values and perceptions is as crucial to these alternatives as the changed behaviors they describe, for the problem—as Harris understands it—emanates from

> the attitude of English towards composition in all its unconscious self-right-eousness. For English *does* want full-credit for teaching composition, does want the full-time equivalents and graduate teaching assistantships and ethos of collegial responsibility that comes from such work. But English doesn't want to pay for it. This situation has led to a multi-tiered workforce. (60)

What particularly interests me in this analysis is its implication that getting out of English will provide compositionists and composition what they long for. Carried to its logical conclusion, Harris's diagnosis implies that creating stand-alone departments of composition will not only eliminate the multitiered instructional workforce and equalize ratios between full-time equivalents (FTEs) and salaries, but also enhance the collegial ethos of those who arc responsible for the literacy of university students.

SEEING THE LARGER PICTURE: RECOGNIZING OUR UNTENABLE UNDERLYING ASSUMPTIONS

Because I am now—but have not always been—a tenure-stream associate professor in a stand-alone department—a department that seceded from English over seven years ago, I consider myself particularly well situated to assess these assumptions. Accordingly, one of my goals here is to interrogate this perspective on the sources of the continued inequitable material conditions in which we academic professionals labor. As I see it, Harris inadvertently creates another diversionary seduction, namely the temptation to blame English and its attitudes for problems in composition and/or to believe that we will or can be immune to the professional and institutional realities. Beguiled by this seduction, we imagine that creating a department of our own will be the answer. I can assure you it's not: neither English departments nor "MLA-like" power structures nor our own individual ambition for job security and position is solely or even collectively responsible for academia's persistent caste system and co-optive processes. The multitiered work force, as indeed the process of co-option itself, is a predictable outcome of the academy's institutionally sanctioned hierarchy. Gunner's explanation of how CCCC appropriated the concrete concerns of the creators of the Wyoming Resolution is, to my view, 100 percent accurate, but that shift from the material world (instructors' concerns) to an abstract, self-authorized, professional (e.g., "MLA-like") authority is not a shortcoming of composition or compositionists. As I've argued elsewhere, it is a definitive and inevitable feature of professionalization. The shift that works to authorize our field as a discipline establishes an authority that is part and parcel of our *eventually* being able to improve labor conditions for our professionals. In other words, it is a necessary (though often not very useful or even "right") requirement of building a discipline. Building disciplinary authority is crucial to changing any material conditions within an institutionally sanctioned hierarchy structured on binary oppositions like these: theory/practice; research/teaching; knowledge/experience; discipline/subject; abstract/material.

I agree that achieving Harris's goal "to forge a more collective view of our work" (43), as well as the goals of the Wyoming Resolution and the CCCC's "Statement of Principles and Standards," does depend, as he says, on our "turn[ing] more attention now to the institutional structures in which we work" (58). But we need to understand those structures within a larger context; we must further attend to the nature of the academy itself and of professional authority. It's clear to all of us that disciplinary status does not necessarily change material conditions, that only changed practices alter material conditions. But I fear that the changes in practice that Harris suggests will have no noteworthy or long-term effect on the inequities in a multitiered work force, for they do not address the institutional sanctioning of the hierarchy that creates them.

Thus, my second goal here is to identify the professional practices that perpetuate institutional hierarchies and undermine our local, material goals. I also hope to suggest innovative ways to construct new practices that address the hierarchical structures and values of the institution. To provide a local example and a common frame of reference, I offer the case of the stand-alone department where I've worked since August 1996.

A BRIEF STAND-ALONE HISTORY: SAN DIEGO STATE UNIVERSITY'S DEPARTMENT OF RHETORIC AND WRITING STUDIES

The origins of SDSU's Department of Rhetoric and Writing Studies (DRWS) are typical—and not. As is usually the case, most of DRWS's initial tenure-track faculty, as well as lecturers and graduate teaching assistants, were formerly housed in English (the Department of English and Comparative Literature, DECL). Atypical, however, was the union of that group with other faculty formerly housed in an entirely independent and separate unit, namely the Academic Skills Center (ASC). ASC provided developmental writing, ESL, *and math* instruction to approximately one-third to one-half of the SDSU (incoming as well as transfer) student population; all other lower-and upper-division writing courses had been offered through English. The academic vice president, in response to a faculty team's review of the Academic Skills Center program, first suggested establishing a department devoted solely to composition and rhetoric. Many English faculty opposed this merger of ASC and English composition faculty, at times vigorously and resentfully; however, the proposal was supported by upper administration, particularly the dean of the College of Arts and Letters. In addition to detailing the benefits of a coherent composition program that would encompass nearly all student writing instruction from students' entrance through their fulfillment of the upper-division writing requirement, the proposal specified that an independent graduate program and upcoming minor in rhetoric and writing would add to the academic status of the newly formed department. Originally presented to the vice president for academic affairs in December 1991 and revised in March 1993, the proposal was approved by SDSU's senate in spring 1993.

In fall 1993, DRWS officially opened it doors, elected its first chair, and began to establish priorities. The faculty consisted of the chair, four additional FTEs of tenure-track faculty and approximately thirty lecturers and sixty GTAs offering writing instruction. Tenure-track faculty collaborated with lecturers, whenever university policy allowed, in creating policy regarding evaluation and rehiring of the lecturers, but worked alone to develop departmental structure, as well as retention, tenure, and promotion guidelines for tenure-track faculty. During 1993 one of DRWS's tenure-track faculty members spearheaded the Freshman Success Program, an all-campus initiative to integrate writing instruction with content material from introductory courses in various majors typically taken by first-year students. Faculty teaching both the developmental and 100-level composition courses took an active part in curriculum design, scheduling, and program promotion of Freshman Success.

In fall 1994, DRWS hired a distinguished visiting professor to examine and revise the Lower Division Writing Program and develop the Teaching Associate Program. In fall 1995, that position, the director of the Lower Division Writing Program, became permanent when one of the original proponents of the stand-alone department accepted a position elsewhere. In academic year (AY) 1995–96, DRWS initiated its proposal for a graduate program, a proposal that—in light of English's strenuous objections—DRWS was forced to revise substantially; the department also conducted another formal search when it was awarded an additional tenure-track position. That search actually resulted in two new assistant professor hires since another of the original tenured proponents of the department, the former director of the Professional and Technical Writing Certificate Program, returned to English.

At the beginning of AY 1996–97—the third year of its existence—DRWS supported six tenure-track FTEs. During that year DRWS's graduate committee rewrote the proposal for a freestanding M.A. program.[1] When that effort was approved, the same body constructed the subsequent M.A. program implementation plan.[2] During AY 1997–98, both of the new DRWS tenure-track hires and one additional tenured professor were recruited to work with faculty from other departments to create an interdisciplinary class cluster, the Integrated Experimental Core Curriculum (IECC). One of the DRWS assistant professors was asked to coordinate upper-division IECC efforts in spring 1998; the other taught in the first nine-unit IECC program during spring 1999 and was asked to serve as program codirector in fall 1999. The tenured DRWS professor was recruited to teach a nine-unit IECC course in spring 2000.

AY 1998–99 posed many challenges to DRWS. In fall 1998, the chair accepted a position as associate dean of the College of Arts and Letters, and thus the department's scheduled search for a new director of Technical and Professional Writing was quickly matched by a search for a new chair. The interim chair, the only full professor remaining in DRWS—who also served half-time in linguistics—took over in November 1998. DRWS's faculty was to be reduced even further when one tenured member accepted a postponed-once-already Fulbright sabbatical. And finally, Executive Order (EO) 665 additionally complicated the department's labor. EO 665's mandate that students complete developmental requirements within their first academic year resulted in more than five thousand students enrolling in DRWS. At that point, when DRWS became the largest university department in terms of student load, an additional tenured faculty member—hired in 1993 as a joint appointment in English and DRWS, but stationed at a satellite campus—joined DRWS to assist the interim chair and two lecturers with the overwhelming scheduling and lecturer hiring issues that accompanied EO 665. These same faculty began (and continue even now) to work with local schools to educate secondary teachers about the English Placement Test and the Entry Level Mathematics Examination; to meet with staff from other campus units (e.g., the advising center, test office, undergraduate studies) to coordinate on-campus responses; and to administer DRWS's agreement with San Diego Community College District to offer thirty composition classes and seventy-two mathematics classes on the SDSU campus during each academic year. These already heavily burdened faculty members joined the others conducting two search committees and promoting the graduate program in efforts to complete the self-study required for the department's first external review.

In fall 1999, two new hires—the chair and the director of professional and technical writing—joined DRWS, and the department underwent its first external review. Reviewers recommended additional tenure-track positions, an especially fortunate decision since the former interim chair was appointed faculty coordinator of the Teaching Resource Center, another tenured person took a semester's leave, and two tenure-track faculty resumed their agreement to teach at least one class annually in English. The department conducted yet another tenure-track search, this time for a coordinator of technology and pedagogy. During AY 1999–2000, the department's ongoing revisions of its upper-division curriculum resulted in a major revision of the primary upper-division writing requirement and two new technical and professional writing courses.

As of fall 2000, ongoing projects in DRWS included continuing to respond to EO 665, administering IECC, conducting another departmental search for a coordinator of upper-division writing, continuing to expand the Technical and Professional Writing Certificate Program, developing an undergraduate minor, lobbying for the still-pending approval of a stand-alone graduate program, and responding to the provost's campuswide initiative to revise and/or develop assessment practices.

MATERIAL WORKING CONDITIONS IN DRWS

As you can see in this whirlwind tour, DRWS's first seven years brought several new tenure-track hires. However, several tenured faculty also departed. In fact, of the original five proponents of the proposal for establishing an independent department, only one remains as an active member of the department, and her appointment fluctuates from zero to .50 FTE, depending on the semester. Only one fully active tenure-track faculty member has been with the department since its inception. It's important to remember that throughout the history I detailed above, as few as four and until fall 2000 never more than six tenure-track faculty members were available to share the work load. Thank goodness, highly qualified lecturers, many of whom had experienced considerable power and administrative responsibility in the Academic Skills Center or in coordinating GTA training in the English department, have contributed significantly to the administration of DRWS. In some cases, however, university policy dictates that only tenure-track faculty (e.g., for evaluation of lecturing faculty, teaching graduate courses) or only tenured or full professors (annual review of probationary tenure-track faculty, review of sabbatical and grant applications) are authorized to serve. In most cases, these faculty efforts are not recognized or rewarded.

Thus, and especially because of EO 665, the formation of DRWS has resulted in more work done by fewer faculty. Keep in mind too that all the efforts I've detailed here have been in *addition to* customary faculty duties. These traditional duties include, of course, teaching: three classes each semester for tenure-track faculty (with some of the faculty who administer programs receiving one or two course releases a semester) and five classes each semester for full-time lecturers. Of the very few lecturers who are granted 100 percent contracts, each receives one course release a semester for such administrative duties as assisting with GTA training (two lecturers); coordinating the assessment projects and a developmental portfolio grading project (two lecturers); hiring, training, and evaluating tutors (one lecturer); administering and coordinating the evaluation of developmental students' proficiency exam (one lecturer); directing the developmental writing program (one lecturer) and general math studies program (one lecturer); coordinating departmental technology labs (one lecturer). In addition to teaching, tenure-track faculty must evaluate all nontenured and non-tenure-track faculty annually; individually apply faculty merit increases (FMIs) and form committees to consider FMI applications; serve on the DRWS Executive Council as well as other department committees assigned; serve on various university or college level committees; direct or act as second or third readers of M.A. theses; and so on. Oh yes, and publish, at the minimal level of one referreed journal article each academic year.

I hope it's copiously clear that—at least here in DRWS—a tenure-track position does not a "boss compositionist" make, not even for the Boss. You may even agree with my hypothesis that neither my own position— nor that of any of the other four, five, or six tenure-track faculty members in DRWS—has not been "advanced" as a result of my gaining tenure-track status in a stand-alone department. In fact, and even though tenured members do enjoy the privilege of job security, it seems more likely that the reverse is true. Perhaps you can also agree that it's hasty to contend that "privileged" tenure-track status comes at the expense of non-tenure-track faculty's labor.

If none of these claims seem evident, then try this: compare my work conditions of the last five years with those of my previous appointment as an assistant professor in an English department at another state institution (quite similar in size and reputation to San Diego State). Not that my former post was a cakewalk: there, I was charged with revising the entire first-year composition program; and because I was the only degreed compositionist on the faculty, perhaps in the entire state, I had to coordinate all theoretical and practical matters relating to the writing curriculum. Nonetheless, the sheer size of the English department (in which, by the way, all literature faculty were assigned to teach first-year composition at least once every three years) translated into a drastically different distribution of departmental duties. I, for instance, chaired the Composition Committee, served on the First-Year Composition Task Force, and attended regular department meetings—five fewer committees than in *any* of my semesters in DRWS. My teaching load at that institution was two courses a semester. The university's expectations of research and publication for tenure were similar to those here at SDSU. Which material working conditions sound better to you?

Let me assure you that I don't make this comparison necessarily to argue against creating or joining an independent department of writing: leaving that earlier position to accept a post here at SDSU has suited my enthusiasm to work in a more independent writing program. But it definitely did not improve my material labor conditions. On the contrary—it has greatly expanded my administrative tasks and my teaching load and greatly reduced my time for writing and reading.

Neither did creating a stand-alone department improve the workaday lives of most of our lecturers. In fact, for those adjuncts who came to DRWS from the Academic Skills Center (ten to fifteen of them), working conditions worsened: they lost office space (ASC lecturers formerly enjoyed private, individual offices, and now many of them share one office, computer, and phone with fifteen or more others), forfeited autonomy (according to the policy of an academic department, they now are evaluated and governed by tenure-track faculty who probably don't know them or their work, rather than by colleagues familiar with and dedicated to developmental writing), and surrendered a certain degree of job security (former ASC lecturers now compete with former English department lecturers for the very few renewable one-year contracts and full-time assignments in DRWS). Previously well respected in ASC for their administrative expertise and their success rates with developmental students, these adjunct faculty now face some tenure-track faculty's disdain for "remedial" programs and have been forced to increase their teaching repertoire (with no subsequent upgrade of salary or benefits) to include first-and second-year as well as upper-division composition.

Lecturers joining DRWS from English, on the other hand—another ten or twelve in total—witnessed some improvement in departmental attitude toward their contributions and expertise. Also for some in this group of adjuncts, the smaller number of tenure-track faculty in DRWS (as compared to English) meant increased administrative responsibility (and release time). However, lecturers joining DRWS from English forfeited their former opportunities to teach upper-division literature and creative writing courses. Until fall 2000, none of these lecturers were awarded more than a 60 percent position, a situation that forced many to find additional employment at other schools or outside of academia.

Job security for all these lecturers became more precarious in the stand-alone department: along with departmental status, the dean gave DRWS the mandate to "meet the need" of all students who wanted to register for all writing courses. This newly instituted requirement was further complicated by English's former practice of turning away potential first-year writing students and the subsequent backlog of upper-division students needing to complete their first-year composition requirements. As a consequence of this mandate to "meet the need"—added to EO 665's scheduling nightmares—DRWS's student enrollment fluctuates widely. Accordingly, not only has the size of writing classes increased, but also part-time lecturing faculty have had to be hired for one semester at a time with little to no opportunity for consistent or future employment. Full-time lecturing and tenure-track faculty both are forced to spend an inordinate amount of time trying to predict and/or respond to the sporadic enrollment numbers, which in turn necessitates hiring, firing, and evaluating part-time lecturing faculty. In one particularly horrendous semester, for instance, the four active DRWS tenure-track faculty members were required by university policy to observe, evaluate, and rank approximately thirty new part-time lecturers by the end of the sixth week of the semester.

DRWS, backed by the policies of the California Faculty Association—the faculty union of the California State University system—has pushed for more permanent contracts for lecturing faculty, but even for the lecturers who have been "temporary" at SDSU for more than twenty years, two-year renewable contracts have marked the limits of formally recognized "permanent" status. Very few of these contracts are offered (perhaps four out of the current forty or so lecturers have them). Likewise, very few lecturers are offered 100 percent employment (approximately eight in writing and six in general math studies). Thus, lecturers not yet awarded but competing for full-time employment are likely to try to earn favor by taking on additional, uncompensated administrative tasks, such as presenting workshops during GTA training orientations and regular seminars, organizing an annual textbook fair and review, or editing a departmental newsletter.

In addition to these institutional conditions affecting job security, university attitudes toward lecturing faculty are less than supportive (to say the least). Note, for instance, upper-administration's response to the department's determinations for faculty merit increases: though the DRWS FMI committee unanimously voted to distribute its merit allocations equally among all meritorious lecturing and meritorious tenure-track faculty, that decision (and its concomitant monetary amounts) has been reversed by the college dean and the provost for the last two years. Also reversed were the department's allocations of "highly meritorious" dollar amounts to the lecturers charged with addressing the administrative nightmare caused by EO 665. As you can see, DRWS has not been the formative site for improving lecturing faculty's labor status.

For GTAs, on the other hand, the formation of DRWS has brought some crucial improvements in working conditions in the shape of greatly enhanced teacher training. The two or three workshops that English used to offer newly appointed graduate writing instructors have expanded into a week of orientation that includes DRWS's annual Conference on Pedagogy. That orientation is followed by a full semester of weekly meetings wherein graduate student instructors and trainers discuss issues of evaluating student writing, directing class discussions, and assigning essays according to a common curriculum.

GTA salary has not improved, however: English GTAs of six years ago were actually paid more than DRWS GTAs are now. In fact, DRWS GTAs are among the lowest paid at SDSU. Furthermore, English can lure trained GTAs out of DRWS by parceling out its coveted introductory

literature and creative writing courses to the most talented young teachers DRWS can produce. Moreover—since the DRWS stand-alone master's program has yet to be approved—English continues to share equal
decision-making power with DRWS in the hiring, education, and socialization of DRWS-trained GTAs.

STAND ALONE DEPARTMENTS AND THE [IM]POSSIBILITY OF RADICAL CHANGE

This experience has opened my eyes wide to some basic realities of
work in an academic institution, realities about which I had been totally
"clueless." Here's one: if it isn't "English [that] *does* want full-credit for
teaching composition . . . [but] doesn't want to pay for it," then it's the
dean. And if it isn't the dean, then it's the provost or the president. And
even if English or the dean or the provosts *did* want to pay for it, they
couldn't afford to. Thus, the CCCC's 1989 "Statement of Principles and
Standards"—especially in its contention that "to provide the highest quality of instruction, departments offering composition and writing courses
should rely on full-time tenured or tenure-track faculty members" (331)
and in its recommendations that writing classes be limited to no more
than twenty students and no faculty member teach more than sixty writing students a term (335)—is in a word, unrealistic. Richard E. Miller,
whose article "Let's Do the Numbers" details some of his experiences as a
writing program administrator at Rutgers University, assures us "a change
of this order of magnitude . . . is never going to happen at my institution"
(1999, 101). As Michael Murphy likewise argues in "New Faculty for a
New University," requiring tenure-track faculty to teach all sections of
composition "would obviously increase total instructional costs prohibi-
tively," double or even triple them (22). And Murphy also points out,

> for better or worse, most university central administrations seem to have
> decided once and for all that in certain disciplines there simply is not
> enough of the work that traditional teacher-researchers do to go around, or
> at least a large enough budget to support that work without reservation. (22)

It is *this* situation—not simply the attitude of English but also the
decisions of central administrators, as well as the traditional, hierarchical structure of the academic institution—that has led to a multitiered
work force in the academy. Clearly then, creating a stand-alone department will not of itself resolve the class problem in composition. Neither
will requiring tenure-stream faculty to teach first-year composition,

revise its curriculum, or participate in the training, supervision, and review of adjunct instructors. Such measures may well improve intradepartment collegiality and enhance senior faculty's respect for the rigors of first-year writing instruction. These are, therefore, worthy practices. But they have little if any impact or effect on the source of the academy's hierarchical hiring practices. This hierarchy dictates the fact that *no* academic department has "direct" (in the sense of complete or pioneering) control over staffing and curricula, particularly not one charged with administering what may be the only course(s) required of every student who attends the university.

Here's another harsh reality: what Harris labels as "unconscious self-righteousness" in the attitude English has toward composition is far more pervasive than his standpoint allows. In DRWS, our atypical origins in a "skills center" (as well as in an academic department, but others across campus tend to forget that half of the history) certainly contribute to the common SDSU perception that ours is a service department, that what we do in DRWS is correct grammar, that our tenure-track faculty's "research" is unlikely to be "rigorous," even less likely to be "theoretical." Unless and until our stand-alone graduate program takes off, that view of our marginal academic status will probably prevail. But this attitude is not uncommon, it isn't maintained by English alone, and it's not based only on the fact that first-year composition is usually taught by graduate students and lecturers.

Rather, and once again, this problem for composition is instituted in the structure of the academic institution itself. Historically, ideologically, and practically, a familiar and often rehearsed set of binary oppositions not only allows the very existence of the academy, but continues to authorize its reality and assign value to the various forms of work conducted therein. A list of the most characteristic binaries includes research v. teaching, theory v. practice, knowledge v. experience, abstract v. material—where, of course, the privileged value is listed first and the "v." indicates an ongoing battle. Seemingly omnipresent in the Western tradition (and dating at least as far back as Socrates's privileging philosophy over rhetoric), these oppositions sustain the "class consciousness" that separates tenure-track research faculty from lecturing teaching faculty *throughout* the university. They likewise separate rhetoricians from compositionists even within our own discipline, theoretical from applied researchers in other disciplines, soft from hard scientists in other colleges.

Thus, it's from within *and without* English departments that the academic expertise and rigor of rhetoric and composition tenure-track faculty are questioned by those who view "real" research and "real" academic work as distinct from practice. These academic edicts do not fade away when writing and rhetoric gets out of English. In fact, it is occasionally the English literary faculty who justify to others in the academy the theoretical complexity of our "service" discipline and thus support compositionists' efforts to earn authority according to institutional practices and ideology. If and when English faculty do not lend such support, creating a stand-alone department of writing studies can help to ensure that at least one's immediate colleagues appreciate the (sometimes) highly theoretical, academically rigorous, and competitive quality of research in rhetoric and composition. It can guarantee that one's colleagues can recognize and attest to the respectability of the journals wherein one is published. But creating a stand-alone department has not yet eliminated the hierarchical levels of review nor the institutional evaluative standards that discipline tenure-track as well as lecturing faculty. It's not likely that it ever will: equitable or not, the process of professionalization is for now the only means we have by which composition can establish professional authority and thereby justify individual compostionists' demonstrations of how they meet the academy's hierarchical standards. And that process is enabled by the transformation of material concerns into a more abstract "MLA-like power and status."

MANAGING THE (BEFORE AND AFTER) MATH OF MINIMAL INSTITUTIONAL CHANGE

If creating a stand-alone department doesn't necessarily change material working conditions for composition instructors, then what will? If achieving legitimacy as an academic discipline in our own right results in disavowing individuals' concerns, then how are we to reinstitute those goals? To my mind—as you've probably guessed—Michael Murphy and Richard E. Miller are traveling in the most promising direction. As Murphy's move "Toward a Full-Time Teaching-Intensive Faculty Track in Composition" demonstrates and my own experience verifies, the argument that it's immoral to offer such low pay and little job security for adjunct faculty has had little effect on administrative practices; in the face of the large pool of willing workers, it's not likely to have positive effect in the foreseeable future. Thus, Murphy focuses his attention on the larger context of work in composition, that is on the practices and perspectives of university administrators; and in doing so, he makes an important rhetorical shift in the ways we might improve material working conditions in composition. Conventional disciplinary think-ing—including the CCCC "Statement of Principles and Standards"—has implied that because a "professional," that is, a tenure-track Ph.D., is most intellectually prepared to teach composition, the quality of educa-tion is compromised when departments employ large numbers of lec-turers on a consistent basis. But as Richard E. Miller reminds us, "the truth is that the question of who's qualified to teach first-year writing was settled a long time ago by the market" (1999, 99). Additionally, the conventional arguments regarding the qualifications for teaching first-year writing are not verified. It's quite possible they aren't even true. I, for one, am not convinced that any tenure-track professor would neces-sarily be a better writing instructor than any lecturing faculty, nor that research in composition necessarily improves one's teaching. In fact, at the three state universities where I've taught—especially at the major research institution—undergraduates *benefitted* from the expertise, focus, energy, and commitment of graduate student and lecturing staff. Thus, the rhetorical shift Murphy makes is a shrewd as well as sincere strategy. He explains that

> as the work of part-time faculty relates to *the sustained intellectual integrity of the discipline*—that is to the discipline's ability to offer students consistently rigor-ous and effective instruction in advanced literacy. . . . [T]his argument stands a much better chance of success with program and university administrators, as well as with the education-consuming general public, who will ultimately have to be convinced in order for significant changes ever to be realized. (18, original emphasis)

Because he served as a long-term lecturer himself, Murphy's argu-ment for formalizing lecturers' professional status and job security—vis-à-vis a form of teaching-tenure contingent on their teaching ability and their commitment to staying current with research in the discipline—is ethically as well as strategically persuasive. Thus, I'll do no more to reconstitute it here and refer interested readers to the original. Let me only underscore my conviction that the strength of Murphy's vision lies in his recognition of the larger institutional and professional context within which composition instructors and programs operate. His pro-posal for how we might initiate institutional change *and* sustain our dis-cipline's scholastic integrity addresses not only the structure of the institution but also conventional administrative practices. It integrates material with professional concerns.

Murphy's proposal also gestures to the increasingly common belief that "except in its most rarefied and privileged corners, . . . [a]cademia is simply no longer in an economic position to maintain even the pretense of aloofness from the daily concerns of the world outside it—beginning with the market forces that shape student demand" (16). Joseph Harris also recognizes this imperative, declaring that "we . . . need to admit that we are indeed workers in a corporate system that we hope to reform"; however, he continues, "almost all the routine forms of marking an academic career . . . militate against such a view of our work" (51). Like Harris, I find sound ways to revise our routine in Richard E. Miller's *As If Learning Mattered,* particularly in Miller's contention that an academic who produces abstract critiques of the systems within which she works is much less likely to effect change than one who embraces her position as "intellectual bureaucrat" and uses her positioned authority to argue for local changes. In other words, we could use this implication that academics must learn to be accountable to consumers of education to uncover further strategies for improving material working conditions in composition.

The same reasoning applies to our methods for proposing and implementing a stand-alone department within the current academic system, a system in which—Miller argues—"the boundary between academic and corporate culture is being steadily eroded" (1999, 98). Though the ideology of corporatization may appall us, we must recognize the fact that abstract, ideological battles do not affect institutional outcomes. However, our tactical maneuvers might. I support Miller's notion that "we'd be better off facing, head-on, what it means to work in the corporatized University of Excellence" (1999, 98). Thus, in an earnest gesture to Miller's call for us academics to imagine ourselves as intellectual-bureaucrats, I turn to a volume he recommended to me, Eliezer Geisler's *Managing the Aftermath of Radical Corporate Change.*

Let me reiterate: my invocation of the expertise of a corporate management consultant is not meant to sanction the corporatization of the university, but rather to make the most of others' wisdom in assessing the success and failure of attempts to institute change in large organizations. In turning to Geisler's analysis of business process reengineering's (BPR's) failure to sustain successful change in corporations, I hope to uncover further explanation for why, against all in-house intentions, creating a stand-alone department here at SDSU continues to serve the interests of the few rather than the many. In suspending my disbelief at

least long enough to conceive of BPR and creating stand-alone departments as similarly conceived solutions (instituting radical organizational
change) to similar problems (ineffective management of resources and
work processes), I hope to find some useful tools or strategies to grow by.

Geisler's crucial argument is that BPR, "the latest in a long series of
proposed solutions and 'revolutions' in business thinking," has been a
dismal failure because it was ill conceived and applied (3). A "systematic, synergetic, and synthetic approach to corporate problems," Geisler
argues, is the key to sustained and comprehensive organizational
change (36). Because it did not "provide adequate answers to pressing
issues and to identifiable problems at *all* levels of the organization," BPR
not only failed to accomplish the improvements it promised, but in
some cases further weakened the corporations banking on its promises
(52, my emphasis). This explanation jibed with my intuitive understanding of why creating a stand-alone department of writing, the latest in a
long series of "revolutions" and proposed solutions to the problems in
composition, not only failed to solve those problems (at least here at
SDSU), but in some cases intensified them.

Time and space do not permit me to detail how Geisler's accessible
analysis of BPR's weaknesses, as well as his ideas for restoring balance
after organizational changes, suggests to me some very practical guidelines for DRWS's future. Many of my department's specific applications
of Geisler's methods to our challenges would probably not apply to
other contexts, for academic problems demand local solutions based on
local contexts. How else can a good manager discover a "systematic, synergetic, and synthetic approach"? Nonetheless, I will present here a
brief overview of how Geisler's analysis of the process of organizational
changes might apply to the history and the future of DRWS, and I'll
hope that my presentation triggers imaginations and inspires interested
readers to turn to Geisler's volume themselves.

In a concise table (See Figure 1), Geisler categorizes the reasons for
the failure of BPR, a list comprised of weaknesses in groundwork, implementation, and organizational structure, as well as in the "untenable
underlying assumptions" of BPR itself (50). Even a cursory glance at
those assumptions reveals conceptual similarities between BPR and the
dreams some of us have had for the changes to be wrought by creating
stand-alone departments. Consider, for instance, the particular untenable assumption Geisler calls "transferability of culture" (50). Is not
composition's desire to reduce or eliminate class consciousness in its
labor force an example of an attempt to create a culture that—so far—

has not been transferable to its larger organizational context? If Geisler is correct that "even in a situation where a new vision is thrust upon the organization, the existing culture remains as an institutionalized frame of mind," then it's no wonder that our efforts have failed (45). Whether corporate or academic, a manager who misrecognizes these tacit labor laws evokes visions of change based on false assumptions.

Figure 1
Categories of Reasons for Failure of BPR

GETTING READY

Lack of adequate preparation
Unrealistic expectations
Lack of measurable targeted goals
Creation of overly optimistic backdrop
Lack of a coherent vision

IMPLEMENTATION

Cynicism and resistance to change on part of employees
Lukewarm support by senior
    management
Delegation of task to consultants without adequate direction
Lack of employee involvement
Focus on cost-cutting and narrow technological objectives
Inadequate investments in cross-functional teams and in information
    technology
Choice of wrong champion
Too little time to implement and evaluate the changes
Focus on tasks, not processes
Overhaul of parts, not entire systems
Generally, taking the easy way

WEAKNESSES OF THE ORGANIZATION

Lack of coherent organizational strategy
Absence of slack resources needed for adequate implementation
Entrenched hierarchy and its rigidity
Resistance from middle managers who feel threatened

WEAKNESSES OF BPR: UNTENABLE UNDERLYING ASSUMPTIONS

Vision precedes obliteration
Full understanding of work processes
Unabridged, unbiased and definite evaluation criteria
Obsolescence of current logic
Improvements are no longer enough
Transferability of culture

(Geisler 50)

An equally false presumption we may rely on is that people outside the culture of composition and English (e.g., "senior managers" within the academy such as the dean, provost, and president, as well as "stakeholders" within the community such as employers or parents) have adequate or accurate information about the work that gets done in composition. Similarly, we may assume that others agree with each other or with us about what an independent unit should be or do. "Another false assumption [among the organizations Geisler reviewed and in academia as well]: that managers possess undisputed and definite criteria to evaluate work processes" (43).

Clearly, unless we recognize such untenable underlying assumptions about how change happens and address their inadequacies, our hopes for substantive change in composition (whether it be housed in English or in an independent department) will be dashed. And Geisler's analysis of the assumptions that are likely to undergird plans for change helps me to understand what were previously befuddling realities: for instance, DRWS pays its faculty to train English GTAs, some of whom never take a course in DRWS and teach only one semester of composition; furthermore, our own department chair has no statistical evidence of DRWS's remarkable success in educating more students at less expense than any other department on campus.

Geisler's summary of the specific weaknesses of organizational architecture also helps me detail what I already understood in the abstract, namely that the academy systemically opposes and co-opts the material goals of individuals and even of departments. For instance, the resistance to change that results from an "entrenched hierarchy and its rigidity" certainly describes the academic institution's persistently multi-tiered work force; likewise, that phrase explains why my department's unanimous decisions to undermine class consciousness (e.g., by awarding equal dollar amounts to meritorious lecturing and tenure-track faculty) prove unsuccessful. Geisler's explanations regarding "resistance from middle managers who feel threatened" account for the source of the campus and state-level lobbies against DRWS's graduate program, which have delayed approval for more than five years. And the "absence of slack resources needed for adequate implementation" describes the DRWS situation wherein four to six tenure-track faculty have been faced with administrative tasks previously divided among thirty or forty or more; it could also explain why only one of the original five tenure-track faculty in DRWS remains.

As you can see, even though they are based on his experience as a corporate management consultant, Geisler's explanations of the structural actualities of an organization—as well as his views on the untenable underlying assumptions about how to effect change therein—clarify the reasons why proposed "radical" changes in a university usually fail. They can explain why creating a stand-alone department may well yield minimal improvements in the material working conditions of compositionists. Put to good use, they can also stimulate realistic expectations of what an independent writing department can do. Thus, I'll conclude by suggesting how Geisler's categorizations of the failures of BPR—as they are applied to what I've presented in the brief history of DRWS—suggest a plan for creating a stand-alone department. Again, and as I hope I've made clear, no plan for a stand-alone department will succeed unless proponents take into account the limitations and opportunities of their unique local contexts. Nonetheless, the following may provide useful thinking.

My own analysis of the restrictive hierarchical structure of the university notwithstanding, Geisler's views on the shortcomings of implementation plans show me ways that improved preparation could facilitate success in addressing the limitations of the multitiered work force. At the outset, it's important for proponents of a stand-alone department to account well and liberally for labor and resources. In the proposal for DRWS, however, lecturers' labor status was not mentioned at all. A proposal that includes a specific labor plan for lecturing faculty—addressing such issues as renewable contracts and permanent status, opportunity for merit awards, adequate office space—has a better chance to counteract the rigid and entrenched hierarchy of the academy's work force. If the creation of an independent writing department is suggested and/or strongly supported by upper administration, as was the case with DRWS, then proponents may have an even better opportunity to address labor inequities in their proposal.

The "choice of a wrong champion," Geisler tells us, is another way that proponents fail to implement change successfully. In retrospect, we might see DRWS's lending so much of its severely limited tenure-track faculty's time and energy to, say, the IECC project as an example of choosing the "wrong" champion. Perhaps the department could have better negotiated the dean's requests for DRWS faculty's expertise in curriculum developments, insisting on more space or permanent faculty resources in exchange. Likewise, the department's intense concentration on EO 665 concerns consumed an inordinate amount of its limited resources. Championing developmental efforts may seem particularly self-destructive when here at SDSU—as everywhere in the CSU system—upper administration has vowed to eliminate all "remedial" writing programs within the next three years. Thus, applying departmental resources to efforts to restructure the assessment methods that determine "remedial" status or the curricular mechanisms that integrate developmental writers, for instance, may have been more strategic than additional support for current practices.

Overcoming the lack of resources necessary for adequate implementation of an independent unit is another potential pitfall that strategic planning may prevent; in the case of DRWS, time quickly became the most precious commodity, especially time to reflect. Crisis management and a lack of coherence inevitably result when there is "too little time to implement and evaluate the changes" in a fledgling program (Geisler 50). I cannot emphasize enough how important it is to budget for and liberally allocate release time for all those involved in preparing the documents and decisions required in the formative years of a stand-alone. Planning for these needs is crucial because in most contexts, creating a stand-alone writing department will greatly reduce the ratio of tenure-track to lecturing faculty and at the same time greatly increase the number of administrative tasks typical in any academic department, many of which must be done by tenure-track personnel. Furthermore, the circumstances of a newly formed department exponentially increase the number and importance of the institution's seemingly incessant calls for "official" departmental documents, crucial testimonials that, in turn, delimit the terms and conditions of a department's future. A departmental mission statement (preparing this alone can take months); proposals and implementation plans for graduate, major, or minor programs; promotion and tenure guidelines for tenure-track faculty; procedures and policies for hiring and evaluating lecturing faculty; self-study documents; a five-year strategic hiring plan; assessment plans; new course proposals—each of these crucial documents requires group collaboration, careful planning, forethought. In a perfect world, each of the tenure-track faculty members of a new department contributes to these tasks and nonetheless performs administrative duties comparable to those of her peers in other departments. Barring that luxury, faculty—especially untenured members—of a new department should be awarded release time corresponding to the amount of administrative time they commit. Accordingly, proponents of any new department should take care to include in their proposals sufficient release time (no fewer than one course each semester; even two credits of course release did not compensate for the number of administrative hours some DRWS faculty worked), an adequate number of tenure-track faculty (five is not enough), and sufficient "soft" monies to fund the faculty who take over the teaching responsibilities of those who receive release time.

Other observations and applications of Geisler's advice to DRWS's case history are surely possible. It's quite likely that you readers have insights that my own involvement obscures. Furthermore, it's obviously true that my own perspective is based on the advantage of hindsight and that, as they say, everything looks clear in the rearview mirror. I was not among the group who formed the committee, and thus I have no direct experience of that context. It may well be true that the original proponents did not advocate improved labor conditions for lecturers or insist on greatly reduced teaching loads for tenure-track personnel during the first years because to do so would have compromised the proposal's success. Facing severe opposition from English, as well as the professional and personal trauma of severing ties with former colleagues, the proponents of DRWS faced remarkable challenges and clearly succeeded in numerous ways. In addition, and as we must recognize, institutional contexts necessitate complex negotiations of many factors. To some if not all faculty in DRWS, the commitment to championing developmental students and programs takes precedence over any other concern, regardless of its success. Likewise, while DRWS's tenure-track faculty participation in special projects like the IECC may not have supported the department's most pressing needs, it was politically savvy. So who's to judge its ultimate success?

In Stanley Fish's typically glib, but nonetheless wise, words (this time on the topic of administration),

> it is only in the situation that you will know what you want . . . and once you
> know what you want, what you then decide to do will depend heavily on the
> history of the institution, the resources at your command, the calculation of
> short-term and long-term risks, the structures of reporting and responsibility,
> the degree to which you can afford to ignore these structures of reporting
> and responsibility, and so on. (2000, 109–10)

The point, then, of reviewing DRWS's first years is not to pinpoint culpability or create a blueprint for others' success but to reflect on where we thought we wanted to g[r]o[w], where we've been, and where/how we want to be. I'm convinced that applying Geisler's analysis of the process of organizational change enhances that reflection, for it allows us to locate and learn from others' failures. Furthermore, because it isolates potentially unrealistic expectations for radical change in organization, it helps us avoid disappointment and conceive of revised institutional practices that have a chance to be effective.

One last thing: in the less-than-pretty picture I've painted of the actual working conditions in the early years of DRWS, I do not want to imply that joining a stand-alone department does not have significant benefits, some of which cannot be measured in terms of office space, course loads, or numbers of committee assignments. On the contrary, my five years in DRWS have been exhilarating in many ways: I've worked with a small group of more or less like-minded people to develop an innovative graduate program that is responsive to the needs of the particular students it (will) serve(s); I've participated (but not had a vote) in the hiring of three new tenure-track colleagues and a new chair—even chaired one of those committees; I've collected data concerning the actual and perceived needs of upper-division writing students at SDSU and developed an upper-division writing requirement that addresses those needs; in addition to developmental, intermediate, technical and professional, and advanced composition courses, I've taught at least one different graduate course each year, two of which I originated. As you can see, a stand-alone department does indeed offer opportunities for autonomy and growth not available in other contexts, even if it is not the utopian work place some of us had hoped for.

Neither do I mean to be pessimistic about a stand-alone department's, or even the profession's, capacity to effect change in the academy. I do believe in the possibility of improving the material working conditions for compositionists. But I also believe that—because the nature of the institution insists upon traditional chains of command and an ideological commitment to binaries—the possibilities for change are much more limited than we like to dream. Nonetheless, change can and will eventuate if and when we get a perspective large enough to identify the institutional strictures within which we labor. Let us not be afraid to use whatever means necessary to acquiring that perspective.

NOTES

1. Even prior to the formation of DRWS, graduate students could choose an M.A. in English with an emphasis in rhetoric and writing studies. In proposing a stand-alone master's degree, DRWS added to its original graduate offerings to include a full graduate curriculum.

2. Though sent through all campus committees and approved by the full SDSU senate in spring 1999, at this writing—over a year and a half later—the plan has still not been approved by the California State University system's chancellor.

8

CREATING TWO DEPARTMENTS OF WRITING
One Past and One Future

Barry M. Maid

It's tempting to start this piece by invoking Martin Luther King's famous "Free at last. Free at last." The temptation to celebrate once given the opportunity to be "out on your own" is great. It's not unlike the feeling many of us may have had when we found ourselves at age eighteen at college and "on our own." We were free to live our lives the way we wanted without parental intervention. As some of us learned the hard way, just doing what we wanted or what felt good at the moment was not the most prudent course. Likewise, when given the opportunity to build a new academic unit—a full-fledged independent writing department—the temptation is to celebrate and "create brave new worlds." For good or ill, the reality of putting together a new academic unit is hard work and fraught with pitfalls. What I hope to do here is to give those who may find themselves in the situation of creating a new unit some sense of what happened at the University of Arkansas at Little Rock (UALR) and how that experience is helping me to shape things at Arizona State University East. Recognizing what others have done will help those forming new units better understand the task that lies ahead for them.

I've been fortunate in my career to now be building my second completely independent writing department. Initially, I was thrust into the position of helping to develop a new department in the late spring of 1993 when Joel Anderson, the provost at the University of Arkansas at Little Rock, decided to split the English department, which I chaired, into English and rhetoric and writing. It was an exciting time. I had spent almost an entire year attempting to restructure the English department in order to keep it together—despite an increase in the number of faculty and expanded diversity in the programs we offered. As chair, I saw it as part of my job to keep the unit together. I can't begin to count the number of times I touted the department as a "microcosm of the university—encompassing linguists, who worked like scientists;

compositionists and folklorists, whose work was like social scientists'; literary scholars, who did humanities work; and the creative writers, who were artists." It was wonderful public relations. In fact, on closer study, it reveals lots of people thrown together whose only commonality was that they somehow shared this indefinable mythical umbrella called "English Studies." I created multiple new structures that attempted to give more autonomy to individual programs—especially the writing programs, which were expanding and drawing large numbers of students.

I think the defining moment of the futility of my effort occurred at one faculty meeting where the entire faculty was discussing my proposals. Listening to my colleagues, I had one of those moments of insight. I thought, "This unit has over one hundred people on the payroll. Its budget, including salaries, is more than $2,000,000 a year, we serve over six thousand students a year, and they want to run it like the junior high school English Club." From that moment on, I felt there had to be a better way. So, when the continued discussions led to the flashpoint that ultimately split the unit, I had done significant thinking of how to reshape an academic department—especially one whose strength was its writing programs. As a result when the unit was split, it was relatively easy for me to put together a proposal of how to implement the split and take it to the dean. Suffice it to say, the dean ignored my proposal.

It's tempting to say that if the dean had only listened to me, many of the problems the newly formed Department of Rhetoric and Writing faced in its first few years wouldn't have happened. I know better. However, I do think that some problems could have been avoided and others lessened. Although I certainly won't claim any powers of prophecy, the fact that I had been struggling with these issues for over a year—developing multiple scenarios and attempting to envision their consequences—gave me some advantage in making suggestions. Now, watching the Department of Rhetoric and Writing at UALR and some of the other new departments across the country, I have a fairly good idea of how I want to help create whatever we decide to call the new department here at Arizona State University East, which will house the new program in multimedia writing and technical communication.

FUTURE AND PAST

In order to look to the future, the creation of a still unnamed new writing department at ASU East, I think we first need to look to the past. History, and the context in which history happens, plays a much larger role in the present and the future than we usually surmise. In a recent Writing Program Administration listserv (WPA-L) post, Ed White, who has consistently preached caution when it comes to leaving English departments, had this to say:

> So I don't mean to cut off the discussion of the issue, which is really an interesting one, but rather to suggest that conditions of this "split" tend to be so particular that we should be very cautious about generalizing from what others have done. (2000)

I have to agree with Ed here. We do need to be cautious. We also need to look at each particular case very closely. That's what I propose to do here.

THE SPRING OF 1993

I'm not sure what it was about the spring semester of 1993, but that term saw the creation of three independent writing units. The first one occurred when the University of Texas at Austin created the Division of Rhetoric and Composition. The last one happened at San Diego State. In between those two, the University of Arkansas at Little Rock created the Department of Rhetoric and Writing. What seems interesting to me is that the entire country had been aware of the rancor that was present in the English department at the University of Texas. That split should have been predictable. At San Diego State, Shirley Rose and Sherry Little had been working for several years to institute a split, having to deal with multiple levels of administration and faculty governance before it could happen. Again, it was something that those who watch writing programs would have known was in the works. But, at least outwardly, there was no indication there was something in the works in Little Rock before the spring of 1993. The fact that something may have been brewing at UALR first hit the scene when on March 23, 1993, I posted a message to WPA-L with the subject "Another Program in Crisis." There I said:

> Here at U. of Arkansas at Little Rock we're looking at a potential lit/writing split. The whole situation is complex, but from my perspective we're making it even more difficult by focusing on details (such as the role of full-time non-tenure track instructors) rather than what I see are the larger issues (traditional views of scholarship and the proper role of professors as opposed to new definitions of scholarship a la Ernest Boyer). At UALR the lit folks tend to be traditional while the writing people are looking at new models.

Then less than two months later on Friday, May 7, 1993, I posted to WPA-L and every other mail list that seemed even remotely appropriate, the following message:

Subject: YES !!!

As of the Fall 1993 semester, the Writing Center, the Freshman Composition Program, the M.A. in Technical and Expository Writing, and all appropriate undergraduate curriculum at the University of Arkansas at Little Rock will all be housed in the separate (from the English Department), tenure-granting Department of Writing and Rhetoric (tentative name).

I will supply more details later. It's possible I might take the afternoon off to celebrate.

Please forgive me if you get this message on multiple lists. I'm about ready to call CNN to have them announce it to the world.

Barry Maid
Only till the Fall, Chair of the Department of English
bmmaid@ualr

WHAT HAPPENED IN LITTLE ROCK IN 1993—A PERSONAL PERSPECTIVE

I'm aware that any rendition I give of the creation of the Department of Rhetoric and Writing at UALR is going to be only one side of a multi-faceted story. It has been difficult keeping my own story separate from the story of the department, only because I served as WPA from July 1982 to June 1987 and was then department chair from July 1987 until the split in 1993. There is no question that my job forced me into the middle of what happened. What follows, then, is a narrative that I began writing on Saturday, May 8, 1993. I drafted sixteen pages that Saturday. I've gone back to that draft several times over the past seven and a half years. Finally, now, I feel comfortable incorporating some of that original text with my more recent reflections.

The Story Begins

I'm tempted to begin, "Once upon a time." After all, what I'm really doing is telling a story. Instead, however, I think I'm going to begin with a "warning label." What I have to tell is the story of one university. What happened at UALR is specific to the institution. That doesn't mean it can't happen elsewhere, rather it means it may have to happen somewhat differently elsewhere.

From my perspective, the story of why a department of rhetoric and writing exists at UALR dating from fall 1993 really goes back to fall 1981. I was the first writing person hired by the department, and I got there in August 1981. My first year I was assigned to teach freshman composition, codirect the writing center, and supervise part-time composition faculty. A year later, I became director of Freshman Composition—a position I held till July 1987 when I became department chair.

During the five years I was writing program administrator (WPA), some interesting changes took place in the department—some planned, some, perhaps, serendipitous. First was the fact that the department recognized that for statewide political reasons it would never house a traditional M.A. in English. As a result, in the early 1980s the department put forward an M.A. in what we called Technical and Expository Writing. To the surprise of many, the program received statewide approval. And after a slow start (with regard to students finishing their degree), by 1993 the program was accepting around twenty-five to thirty students a year and was granting between fifteen and twenty M.A.'s a year.

Several other things happened in the early and mid-1980s. First of all, we hired five other writing faculty. Part of this was made possible by the fact that in 1984 we wrote a proposal and received continuing money from the Arkansas Board of Higher Education for a project we termed "Quality Writing." We used some of the money to hire faculty and some to run programs—writing across the curriculum (WAC), training of part-time instructors, work with high school teachers. In addition we managed to hire a full-time writing center director, put our first generation of computers in the writing center, and implement a system of peer tutoring. We had also managed to get some state money to begin a small Writing Project site. At that time we had pieces but no whole.

In February 1987, I was elected department chair—slated to take over July 1. That in and of itself was somewhat significant. In 1987 it was exceptionally rare to see a writing person as a department chair, even though the administrative ability WPAs gain make them natural choices. (In fact, I remember having Liz Neeld pull me aside at a party at the Conference on College Composition and Communication (CCCC) in March 1987 and explain to me that I would, at that time, be the only writing person serving as a department chair and how important that was.) In my case most of my colleagues saw the job of department chair, as they had seen the job of WPA, as a clerical one—a paper-pusher. I think they elected me chair for the same reason they liked the way I ran the composition program. I ran the program so that it was essentially invisible to the tenure-track faculty. They assumed I would run the department in the same way, and they were right.

Being a WPA had taught me much about the university. Unlike most faculty, I understood the importance of support services. I regularly worked with the registrar's office, the dean of students office, the counseling service, and the bookstore, as well as many academic areas across the campus. I was clearly aware that there was a large world beyond the English department.

I learned many things upon becoming department chair, but perhaps one of the experiences that taught me the most, especially in the beginning, was student advising. In 1987 we had a very modest program in English. We had around sixty majors and were graduating fifteen to eighteen students a year. By the time of the split in May 1993, the department had nearly 220 majors and had graduated nearly 80 English majors in the past academic year.

There was really no secret to all of this. I simply gave students permission to want to be English majors. I found many students drifting their way into my office to talk about being English majors but not thinking it was a viable option. Almost all of them asked the classic question, "What can I do with an English major if I don't want to teach?" My answer was simple. I told them that English majors learn only three things—reading, writing, and thinking. I told them if they could use a calculator, they could then do anything. Students' eyes lit up. They almost all became English majors. I recognize that's kind of a reductionist way of looking at things. However, what I emphasized to my students was that we teach them skills and that those skills are marketable. I know this is heresy to many academics, but I completely accept that part of our job is to prepare students for successful lives in the workplace—a workplace that is outside of the academy. Believing this, I was able to connect students to the workplace. We already had several real-world internships in place. I tried to stress those and expand on them. (I am leaving this next sentence intact as it was written in 1993. I realize that my analogy now seems unnecessary. But the world of English departments was different in 1993.) What I told students was that my ideal was to have them graduate with a "portfolio in hand"—just like a graphic artist or a photographer.

Clearly, this concept of real-world connectedness stresses writing. Indeed, when most of our students graduate and look for jobs, they, more often than not, look for jobs where they can utilize their writing skills. I had one more advantage working for me. We had an eighteen-hour writing minor on the books. It had originally been created for students with an interest in creative writing. By creative use of internships, I was able to have students put together an English major where they would primarily, but not exclusively, take literature courses and a writing minor. That meant they were required to take forty-two upper-level hours in the department. It also created a renewed demand in literature courses. All of a sudden, literature faculty, who had been teaching one section of literature (if it made) and then freshman composition or world literature, were having literature courses with twenty to thirty students. Eventually, most of them ended up teaching nothing but upper-level literature and sophomore world literature.

The Unwitting Role of the First-Year Composition Program

When I took over the composition program in fall 1982, almost all the tenure-track faculty taught in the program. Since we didn't have enough faculty to teach all the sections, we supplemented by using a large number of part-time instructors. In 1982 we probably used around twenty to twenty-five part-time instructors a semester. By the time I left the composition director's position, the numbers had changed only slightly—affected more by the fact that fewer full-time faculty were teaching twelve hours. As composition instructors continued to receive more release time for alternative duties, we staffed the courses by hiring growing numbers of part-timers. I honestly don't know what we would have done if enrollment had risen dramatically back them. I do know that even then we weren't offering enough sections of composition. Finally, in fall 1989 our then chancellor realized that he was talking to a group of around four hundred incoming freshman during an orientation session and that none of them would be able to enroll in composition because the sections were all closed.

We were faced with a crisis. Immediate action was called for. My WPA and I did not have sufficient time to consult with the appropriate faculty committees to get authorization to do extraordinary things. We simply acted on our own—with the full blessing of the administration. First of all, since our graduate program was in technical and expository writing, we authorized the use of our first teaching assistants. (Previously our graduate assistants had been assigned to do clerical work for various faculty.) Second, we received approval from the provost to move six of our part-time instructors to full-time for one year—at a full-time salary. The dam had burst. The flood gates were open.

Interestingly enough, once this had happened, most of the full-time tenure-track faculty were fairly reconciled to the notion that we would hire permanent non-tenure-track instructors (an idea that was anathema to them several years before). Things were going fairly well in the department. There appeared to be no reason to rock the boat. At that point we just needed to convince the administration that if we were to hire people in such positions, they would be treated reasonably. The sticking point with the provost was course load. Several years before, the previous dean of science had hired full-time instructors in the math department and had given them a five-course teaching load. In what was perhaps their finest hour, the entire Department of English went on record opposing the five-course load. The load issue had us at an impasse until I finally had the good sense to call Ed White and ask him to send us some WPA consultant-evaluators.

Bruce Appleby of Southern Illinois University and John Brereton of the University of Massachusetts-Boston did a thorough evaluation of our composition program. They said some kind things about the program, and they were adamant in recommending that full-time instructors not be allowed to teach more than twelve hours a semester. Our provost decided to follow their recommendations. It was downhill from there. We managed to get the faculty to agree to hire non-tenure-track, full-time instructors to teach composition. We wrote an amendment to our governance document that supposedly defined their role in the department. In many ways the document that was approved by the English department in June of 1990 was flawed from the beginning. While parts of it were very specific, other parts were hopelessly ambiguous. My response back then was to pass the thing, forward it to the administration for approval, and then redo it after the administration kicked it back. In the meantime we would have already hired our first full-time non-tenure-track instructors.

Strangely, that document never got forwarded to the administration for approval—something we discovered only in February of 1993. (For the record, according to departmental governance neither the chair nor the WPA was responsible for sending that document on for administrative approval.)

We hired nine full-time, non-tenure-track instructors in fall 1990. We added two more in fall 1992. These instructors were expected to teach four sections of composition a semester. They would be evaluated primarily on their teaching. They would also be expected to engage in professional development activities. Through use of the Quality Writing money, we were able to send them to one professional meeting a year. Most became regular attendees at CCCC. A couple chose other rhetoric and composition conferences.

At the end of 1991, my WPA moved to a position in central administration. This left us with no WPA, and none of the remaining writing people had any interest in the job. When I realized my WPA was moving into central administration, I visited with several of my writing faculty to see if anyone was interested in assuming the position. As I expected, no one showed any interest. I recognize that there were also eleven non-tenure-track instructors and a director of the writing center (a staff, not a faculty, position). I made a decision based entirely on politics. My decision was that I felt only a tenure-track faculty member with a Ph.D. should be WPA. I have no question that a number of the other people could do the job well; however, part of the job was to work with the English department faculty and other units across campus. The bottom line was that at this point in UALR's history, a tenure-track Ph.D. would simply have more credibility across campus. As a result of having no internal volunteers, I agreed to serve both as chair and WPA. Finally, in September 1992, the administration authorized a search for a new WPA.

The Beginning of the End—Though No One Knew It at the Time

Ordinarily, faculty are happy when they get permission to search. However, the UALR English department, like many academic units, had a history of wanting to define its own needs. It was clearly upset the year before when the provost had given us a new tenure-track faculty line but dictated that we must hire someone whose main responsibility would be to teach undergraduate technical writing courses. The department also was uncomfortable with the idea of going outside to search for an administrative position.

Having been aware for some time that programs with different interests and values were competing, I had called an open department meeting in September of 1992 in order to begin discussions of departmental reorganization. I had hoped to have the unit recognize the problem and begin working through some kind of innovative structure that would enable curricular units to operate on their own. (I envisioned cluster groups such as composition/rhetoric, technical writing, American studies, British studies, and so forth.) People would be completely enfranchised in those areas in which they taught and would not have input into areas in which they did not teach. Ultimately, I had hoped we would recruit through cluster groups and also evaluate faculty based on criteria appropriate to the group.

As things worked out, I chose this meeting as the appropriate time to announce to the department as a whole that we had been given permission to search for a director of Freshman Composition. (I had already run this past the department's standing recruitment committee. They had assented, though not all were happy with the provost's directedness.) Many of the faculty were unhappy with the decision to go outside for a WPA. Yet, when I explained there was no viable inside candidate, they had problems accepting that fact. Finally one of the faculty asked directly why a certain member of the writing faculty wasn't going to do the job. I replied that he wasn't interested. (Indeed, I had asked him the previous spring.) Nonetheless, this persistent faculty member specifically asked the writing faculty member directly if he would serve as director of Freshman Composition. To everyone's surprise, the member of the writing faculty said he would be happy to serve as composition director. The original faculty member then instantly nominated the writing faculty member to be director of Freshman Composition. The nomination was instantly seconded.

I was aware that nominations for administrative positions from the floor of an open meeting were clearly out of order and in direct violation of our rules of governance. I also had enough experience dealing with faculty to know that once they build up momentum it is wiser to let them do what they will do. Imprudent decisions can always be, and usually are, reversed. At this point someone raised the issue of who had the right to vote for WPA. The reference was directed toward the eleven non-tenure-track instructors. I frankly had not prepared for this question at this time. I did remember that we had passed something before hiring the instructors that gave them voting rights on issues that concerned them; however, I had no recollection of the details. What I did at that point was consult our governance document, only to find that it had never been officially amended to include the reference to the instructors. As a result, I read to the entire faculty the section on voting rights. It had apparently been drafted sometime in the early 1970s and gave full voting rights to all members of the department (not faculty) who had more than half-time appointments. By my interpretation this included even the department secretaries, though they were not present for this meeting (and, by my sense of the historical politics of the department, that would have been the intent).

The question was called, and the vote was unanimous. We had just filled a position we were advertising for. I had visions of losing a faculty line. I asked the writing faculty member who had just been elected why he had changed his mind. He responded, as I suspected he would, that given the choice of serving or hiring an administrator from the outside, he felt he had an obligation to the program and the faculty (especially the non-tenure-track faculty).

My next step was to report the results to the dean. Needless to say he was incredulous. Actually, what he said was something like this: "Two years ago your department, which has one of the fastest growing and strongest master's programs on campus (the M.A. in Technical and Expository Writing), elected a specialist in Irish poetry to run that program. Neither I, nor the graduate dean, nor the provost understood that." Actually I had been questioned multiple times by the three named administrators, especially the provost, about the department's sense of stewardship of its own graduate program. The dean then continued, "Now, you want to take the best teacher in the department (indeed, he had been named the best teacher in the entire university the year before) out of the classroom to put him into an administrative slot that has already been advertised." His questions then moved toward what he saw as the inherently self-destructive tendencies of the English department.

I'd prefer not to discuss the dean's observation that the department was self-destructive. I do think, however, that the department's decisions in choosing these particular faculty members to administer writing programs (and, remember, the graduate program was a pure writing program) reflects a lack of understanding and undervaluing of the administrative function, as well a lack of value for writing programs in general. This is not to say the department necessarily devalues faculty members by placing them in administrative positions; rather, it fails to understand that different faculty members have different skills and that the unit will function most effectively and efficiently when faculty do what they do best. To take the best teacher in the department and begrudgingly place him in an administrative slot, where he would do significantly less teaching, says to him that his teaching isn't that important. More importantly, however, it deprives a group of students of the benefit of having him as an instructor. Likewise, to place the specialist in Irish poetry as the coordinator of a graduate program in writing says that the administrative position is really nothing more than paperwork and that the faculty member's worth is greater doing paperwork than teaching and doing his own scholarship. I thought then and continue to think that these are strange messages we are sending our colleagues. And I don't think the UALR English department was unique in sending these messages.

Finally, the writing faculty member decided it was in the best interest of all concerned if he withdraw his candidacy, which enabled us to continue our search for a WPA. Nothing in an English department is ever easy. Since the department had never gone outside for an administrative position, this raised all kinds of questions and fears. The dominant concern was that the person be above all "a colleague." That translates to a publishing scholar. What the faculty were unaware of was that they were creating the potentiality for the situation that appeared in the *ADE Bulletin* "Case Study" in spring 1993. (This is a situation where people are hired and evaluated on one job but not retained because they didn't successfully do a different job.)

The Search Begins

The UALR English department elected a standing Recruitment Committee each spring, long before we knew whether we would be recruiting and even longer before we knew what specialties we would be recruiting for. People usually decided whether they would choose to serve on that committee based on the location of the Modern Language Association (MLA) Annual Convention and whether they wanted to ruin their Christmas vacation by interviewing candidates at MLA. That year the committee was composed of an eighteenth-century specialist, a Shakespearian, a poet, and a specialist in African American literature— not a composition/rhetoric person among them. In order to get a slightly better sense of what we were looking for, the department allowed (my choice of verb here is deliberate) me to send one tenured composition/rhetoric specialist and two non-tenure-track instructors along to MLA. However, these three extra members of the committee were designated nonvoting members from the beginning.

All of us went off to MLA and interviewed nine candidates. I think we were all clearly impressed by the quality of the people we would be able to choose from. We went home and, though it wasn't easy, decided on one top candidate to bring to campus. At UALR, even though the position has been approved, the process dictates that we get permission from the provost to bring our candidate to campus. To our great surprise, we were denied that permission. What had happened in the interim was that as of January 1 we had changed administrations. Our chancellor had stepped down as of December 31. The new chancellor wouldn't be on campus until March 1; but the provost (who was serving as acting chancellor) visited with the new chancellor, and they both reviewed the budget. They discovered significant shortfalls and froze all positions.

And Finally the Straw that Broke . . .

The faculty were getting testy over this when we entered another point of crisis. Our rules of governance called for an election for department chair every three years in either January or February. Originally, I had no intention of serving as chair more than six years. That's long enough for just about anybody. However, no other candidate was emerging, and I felt I could continue even though I felt no obligation to serve a full three more years.

I was fairly confident at that time there were no other potential candidates. I will be the first to admit that while most of the faculty were comfortable with my administration, some would disagree with anything I did, just because I was the one who did it. Frankly, most of the faculty were fairly content, and no one else wanted the hassle. I set the date for the election meeting and told some friends that I expected some kind of procedural objection from the floor.

I was slightly surprised. Rather than wait for the meeting, two of the faculty came to my office and informed me that there would be a problem if the non-tenure-track faculty were given the right to vote for chair. I explained to them that, as I understood our governance, the non-tenure-track faculty had that right. I checked with the dean who agreed with me and suggested that I run the matter past the attorney for the University of Arkansas system.

I drove to the system office, armed with governance documents, but feeling a little silly. I probably should have known that lawyers deal with minutiae every day. After explaining the details to the attorney, his first response was to break out into laughter. He then responded with "Leave it to faculty to argue over who gets to vote on what is by board policy a dean's decision." He was, of course, right. Both the dean and I knew that, but in my college the faculty has always elected a candidate, whom the dean has then appointed. After reviewing the documents, the attorney informed me that the right to vote was clear. Since the

1990 document that gave the eleven instructors only two votes was never approved by the administration, my original interpretation was correct. Everyone had a vote.

Having received the ruling of system counsel, I went to what was probably one of the ugliest meetings I've ever attended. Most of the tenured faculty were outraged that anyone could suggest that non-tenure-track faculty could possibly have any rights. An outsider observing the meeting might have thought that people were going berserk. They would have been wrong. What happened was, as I later chose to term it, that faculty were subscribing to what I have come to call "Academic Fundamentalism." The tenets of AF are simple: You can be saved only if you have a terminal degree and are tenured. The longer your vita, the higher up you are in the priesthood.

Understanding this, it came as no surprise when tenured faculty affirmed that, despite the ruling of the attorney, non-tenure-track faculty could not vote. When the non-tenure-track faculty objected, they became the objects of personal insults. Some of them had their jobs threatened. When I informed the faculty that they had no authority to hire or fire, the faculty then said they would abolish the positions. It went on and on, getting more ugly and ridiculous. It was clear that many of the faculty failed to understand that the UALR English department was really governed by UALR central administration, the UA system, and the UA board of trustees. In addition, they failed to understand that we were also constrained to abide by the laws of the state of Arkansas, as well as the United States. Faculty governance to them, plain and simple, meant that they had the final say on everything. Sadly, in the past no one had ever told them otherwise.

Not surprisingly, nothing was resolved at that meeting. Ultimately, faculty started visiting the dean and the provost. On February 17, 1993, Lloyd Benjamin, the dean, sent the English faculty a memo called "Current Events," where he outlined procedures that he and the provost had decided would help remedy the situation. Among other things, he asked that the faculty provide the provost and him with information and that all elections be postponed. Perhaps most telling was this item:

> 4. I am aware that comments (verbal and written) have been made that have been perceived as threatening, inappropriate and damaging to the academic environment. Such activity is considered unprofessional and should cease immediately.

Then on March 18, 1993, Joel Anderson, the provost, sent a memo titled "Where We Go From Here" to the English faculty. It begins with "Twenty eight of you sent me 79 pages of letters and memoranda, exclusive of a number of attachments." The provost continued in his memo asking me to call a meeting of the department, which the dean would attend and where he (the provost) would preside. Finally, in that same memo the provost asked the English faculty to consider the following four scenarios: "Status Quo," "Composition Sub-Unit Within Department," "Reassignment of Composition Program and Writing Center," and "Two Departments—One Literature, One Writing."

That meeting was held on the morning of Thursday, April 15, 1993. The day before, at the provost's request, I had turned in to him and the dean a short report on my findings from talking with national leaders in composition/rhetoric (see "The Decision" in Appendix A). The provost listened while faculty spoke on all sides of the issue. This time the discourse was professional. The provost said that he and the dean would come to a decision shortly. We adjourned just before noon. I remember getting in my car shortly after the meeting and driving to Stillwater, Oklahoma, to attend the South Central Writing Centers meeting. Sometimes it's especially good to get out of town. However, I was back in the office on Monday morning, where I submitted, again at the provost's request, a final memo (see "Some Final Reflections" in Appendix B). Then, like all the rest of the faculty, I waited.

On the morning of Thursday, May 6, I was called to the dean's office. The dean asked me to read a memo he had written, "Futures," which he said he was going to distribute to the English faculty on the next day. The third paragraph of the long memo read as follows:

> The conclusion I have reached and shared with the Provost is that it is time to create two distinct departments. While this may disappoint some, the comments suggested that opposition to creating two departments was less intense, that most faculty were resigned to change and some faculty looked forward to it.

It was over. The Department of Rhetoric and Writing was born.

The Devil's Not in the Details But in Not Attending to the Details

In his "Futures" memo, the dean also outlined a complex set of details for the transition to two departments. The key was a transition advisory committee (TAC), which was to be comprised of six faculty, three from each of the two new units. The committee was to be chaired by the associate dean. The dean asked for volunteers to serve on the committee, but he purposely chose to exclude anyone who had any administrative experience. After two meetings, I received a call from the associate dean. Since none of the faculty had had any administrative experience, none of them understood some of the institutional complexities they were dealing with. As a result, he asked me to serve as an unofficial staff member to the committee in order to provide him with the information he needed. My first duty was to send him a long note dealing with the specific issues of curriculum, staffing, and majors. Several days after sending him that note, he announced he had been named dean at another institution. He left UALR within the month.

The TAC continued to meet but never resolved any issues. The dean decided simply to have the faculty choose which department they wished to belong to. Finally, because courses had to be divided, I (then interim chair of rhetoric and writing) and the interim chair of English met in the student union over coffee and agreed to a division of almost all the courses in the curriculum. The several courses we disagreed on were assigned to units by the dean. The real sticking point was the budget. The dean was firm that he would make that decision himself. What seemed to me to be most important was that some of the money the department received had been specifically earmarked for the writing programs. The Quality Writing budget from the mid-1980s still existed and in 1993 was at $21,000 a year. In addition several years earlier, the M.A. in Technical and Expository Writing was named one of three "Centers of Excellence" in the university and as a result was given $10,000 a year, which was added to the regular English department maintenance (operations) budget. To begin with, a result of the budget problems discovered in January, all budgets were cut 15 percent. That meant that the main budget dropped from $51,479 to $43,757 and Quality Writing's budget dropped to $17,850. The dean's final decision was that both budgets would be split equally. He refused to listen to arguments that moneys earmarked by the university and the state specifically for writing programs should not go to literature programs. I lost that one.

The Chaos Continued

During all of this, I was trying to organize the new department. I was especially concerned that faculty begin work on curricular issues leading to a major and on governance. Perhaps because they knew money would be especially tight, the faculty wanted to focus on budget issues. In fact, some suggested that no money be spent without having the entire faculty approve the expenditure. They were also concerned with the schedule. I remember one of those early faculty meetings where the faculty kept insisting that their names be placed in the printed schedule next to the sections of composition they would be teaching instead of the generic "Staff." They refused to listen to my reasoning that the schedule was printed several months before the actual faculty assignments in composition were finalized. Meanwhile, the man who was acting as chair of the curriculum committee kept refusing to call a meeting. I realized we were in disarray, yet felt that every time I tried to bring us together, something else would get in the way.

Finally, while meeting with the dean on another matter, he simply informed me that two of the rhetoric and writing faculty had visited with him and told him that I had lost the confidence of the department. He said he saw no reason not to believe them so he had informed the provost that he was going to make a change in the interim chair. With that brief discussion, my more than eleven years of administrative work at UALR came to an abrupt halt.

While I had the luxury of returning to faculty life, the new department needed to progress. The man who had been recalcitrant about calling curriculum committee meetings became interim chair for the rest of the academic year. The department then went into "receivership" (being overseen by the new associate dean) for a year while we searched for an outside chair.

Despite its rocky start, the Department of Rhetoric and Writing at UALR seems to be in a good position. Though still underfunded, partly resulting from the dean's original decision, both its undergraduate and M.A. programs are strong. One of the healthiest signs is that in the last several years five new tenure-track faculty have been hired. These new hires, who have no history of the time of the split, are beginning to move into leadership positions in the department. I think that bodes well for the department.

THAT WAS THE PAST, NOW THE FUTURE

In the interim between Christmas and New Year's of 1999, when all good English faculty were attending MLA, I loaded up my SUV and literally headed westward. Then at the start of the new millennium, I began to lay the foundation for what would be a new independent writing department. (Please forgive me, but how many times do we get to invoke so many mythic allusions in our writing?) My first task at Arizona State University (ASU) was to draft the Proposal to Implement for the B.S. in Multimedia Writing and Technical Communication, which needed to be submitted to the Arizona Board of Regents (ABOR). Part of the process of writing that proposal was the creation of thirteen new courses—the curriculum that makes up the new program. That first step was accomplished, and the program was approved by ABOR on June 30, 2000. We taught the first courses in the program during the spring 2001 semester, but even before we ever taught one course, we had seven students signed up as majors.

In many ways, it's easier to start a new program from scratch than to try to piece together remnants of other programs. This is one of those times when not having a history can be a virtue. I had two other advantages as we developed the curriculum in the spring of 2000. First of all, I had a dean, David Schwalm, who not only understands the nature of writing programs but also understands the Byzantine administrative structure that defines ASU. His help was invaluable in getting the new courses through the system for approval. The other advantage was that there was already one other faculty member in place in the program, Marian Barchilon, a tenured associate professor of technical communications, whose previous homes at ASU were in engineering and technology. She has never been a member of an English department.

The Curriculum

As we were developing the new courses, we kept several principles in mind. Perhaps the most important was that we expected no one faculty member to "own" a course. While some faculty may be more likely to teach certain courses because of their individual expertise, we want ownership of the courses to belong to the program—not individual faculty. In addition, we created a set of issues that would cut through every course in the curriculum in order to stress their importance and to present a sense of programmatic cohesiveness. Some of these issues are ethics, the global nature of technical communication, and the appropriate use of visuals and technology. Finally, I modified the WPA Outcomes Statement so that it constituted an appropriate set of outcomes for technical communication courses. Doing so gives a beginning to later engage in programmatic assessment activities.

The other issue we faced and are continuing to face is our commitment to tie our program to local industry. Marian has been an active member of the Phoenix chapter of the Society for Technical Communication (STC) for years. Since I've arrived here, I've made a point to attend STC meetings regularly and work with the membership. While it is too early in the program to require an internship, we are already working on establishing the relationships that are required to develop internship possibilities. We already recommend all our students have some kind of intern experience. In addition, all graduating seniors will be required to take a capstone course. Part of that course will require them to prepare a professional portfolio to help them with their job hunt at graduation time.

The Faculty

At this moment we already have two tenured senior faculty. We advertised for another associate professor whom we had hoped to start in August 2001. Unfortunately, a protracted budget debate between the Arizona legislature and the governor prevented us from completing the search. Along with a new search (rank presently undetermined), our agenda for next year will be to draft promotion and tenure guidelines so that they will be in place when assistant professors come on board. While we've only begun the most preliminary discussions concerning the issues of promotion and tenure, we are all committed to drafting a document that will value a much broader definition of scholarship than is usually found in English departments. I fully expect that we will draw on Boyer and on Glassick, Huber, and Maeroff as we move through that process. I know from my experience helping to draft the tenure and promotion guidelines for rhetoric and writing at UALR, we will definitely draw on the WPA "Intellectual Work" document as well the MLA Commission on Professional Service report. In addition we will pay close attention to the CCCC "Promotion and Tenure Guidelines for Work with Technology."

While I, of course, can't guarantee a document that won't be written for another year, I am very confident that when we try to recruit junior faculty we will be able to show them that we will value a wide range of scholarly activities as they move towards promotion and tenure. I expect we will think it normal for faculty to coauthor articles and books, to write textbooks as well as scholarly articles, to use their professional expertise to help develop our curriculum (which will include helping to develop appropriate discipline-based assessment strategies), to regularly engage in consulting activities with industry, government, or nonprofits, to be active in integrating emerging technologies into their teaching—whether local or distant—and to publish not only in print but in electronic forms. In other words, we plan to evaluate writing faculty on the kind of work that is appropriate for writing faculty to do and for which they will be hired. By doing so, we hope to create an academic home for all our faculty, where they will be able to be creative as they work with students, develop the program, work closely with local practitioners, and engage in their own scholarship—a place where they'll feel comfortable enough and supported so that they wish to stay. Keeping an active, stable faculty is important to the life of any department; independent writing departments should be leaders in this endeavor.

HEADING HOME

Having invoked the metaphor of the home, I think perhaps that's the best way to close. I can remember back in graduate school in New England seeing the old, traditional homes there. Most were small. The rooms tended to be small, and the windows were usually heavily draped. There was, however, much history and tradition. Now, I find myself in the Southwest and see very different homes. Here, the homes tend to have large rooms with open spaces and fewer walls. The windows let in the sun, and when you look outside, the big western sky seems to go on forever. There's certainly nothing wrong with tradition. For many it provides much needed comfort. But for some of us, breaking away, building new, more open homes is not only all right, it's better.

NOTE

All original UALR documents concerning the split are now in the composition archives at the University of Rhode Island.

APPENDIX A

To: Joel Anderson and Lloyd Benjamin
From: Barry Maid
Subject: The Decision
Date: April 14, 1993

As you both know, I have spent much time over the past month or so communicating with people all over the country about our present situation and how it compares to other institutions. I have attached a narrative of my notes with some of the more important national figures and ane-mail response from David Schwalm, currently Associate Provost at Arizona State and former Writing Program Director there. I will be happy to continue the conversation, but the purpose of this memo is to try to give you a synopsis of what I've discovered. (I am focussing only on issues of separate Writing Units as opposed to large, whole English Departments. I understand that we have personality issues as well that cannot be ignored; however, I'd prefer to focus only on the positive, substantive issues.)

- What we see at UALR (the tension between lit and writing) is present in almost every program in the country. It appears to be most significant wherever writing programs have become large and successful. Writing Faculty almost everywhere see a separation as inevitable. Literature Faculty are desperately trying to hold on to Writing Programs because they are concerned that if they lose the Writing Program the only way to maintain the quality of academic life they enjoy will be to engage in activities they feel are inappropriate for academics (program building and professional service, perhaps even more teaching).
- Almost everyone in some way referred to the real distinctions between Writing Programs and English Departments were centered in what many called "Boyer Issues." It seems to be almost universal that English Departments are not likely to reward faculty for participating in the kinds of activities that are most appropriate for Writing Faculty to perform (i.e., teaching, pedagogical research, program development, and professional service). Indeed, most English Departments (and UALR's does this) create disincentives for faculty who chose to participate in those activities.
- To a person, everyone I have communicated with, once they understand the nature of the UALR situation (the fact that our graduate program is purely a Writing Program is a crucial factor here) recommended the creation of a new, autonomous unit encompassing the entire Writing Program (developmental to graduate, including the Writing Center).

- While it is theoretically possible for applied programs to remain in units with traditional academic disciplines, unless the traditional faculty are willing to allow the applied area to be rewarded and to grow, ultimately the faculty in the applied area will be forced to give up their applied work in favor of traditional research and publication. The UALR English Department has consistently not rewarded the work of the Writing Faculty, both tenure-track and non tenure-track. Indeed, it consistently places limitations on what they can teach and what part of their work can be rewarded. I do not see this changing without significant personnel changes which are unlikely to happen for the next ten to fifteen years.

COMMENTS FROM FORMER PROGRAM CONSULTANTS

I was frankly amazed at the enthusiasm and unanimity colleagues around the country expressed for the creation of a new unit at UALR. I think two of the most telling comments came from Bruce Appleby of Southern Illinois University and John Brereton of UMass-Boston. They had been consultants to our Writing Program three years ago before the creation of the instructor positions. I spoke separately, though they told me the same thing. Both commented on the strength of our program and emphasized that its strength came, to a great degree, from the fact that there is a programmatic whole from the developmental to the graduate level. They both pointed out that because our graduate program is a pure writing program we could maintain this whole in a new unit. Both said that this gives us a tremendous advantage over most programs in the country.

Based on my research and my own observations, I see the only logical option for our current dilemma to be the creation of a new completely autonomous unit (The Department of Technical and Expository Writing?) encompassing the entire Writing Program, developmental through graduate, and the Writing Center, reporting to the Dean of AHSS. In terms of the current options for solving the present crisis, it is the only solution which will prevent the present situation from recurring again over another issue in six months or a year. Perhaps, more importantly, it is the only way to confirm that UALR is now firmly committed to the model of the Metropolitan-Interactive University. Deferring to the voices of traditionalism at this juncture merely shows the faculty that traditional academic values, not new definitions of scholarship, are what really matter at UALR.

APPENDIX B

> To: Lloyd Benjamin and Joel Anderson
> From: Barry Maid
> Subject: Some Final Reflections
> Date: April 19, 1993

Surely, there were no unbiased participants in last Thursday's meeting. All I can hope to add, therefore, are my admittedly biased observations.

- I observed a group of people who really have very little in common with one another and who seem to want to stay together only because there appears to be something sacrosanct about the notion of an "English Department." I guess I now know how it felt to go through the Reformation.
- Russell's suggestion of two autonomous, parallel units joined only by a liaison but with a common title is, of course, intriguing. Actually, it sounds remarkably like my notion of around a year ago which when I thought it through seemed untenable. (If you have two separate units, both with a unit head reporting to the same dean, why don't you simply call it two departments? Unless, of course, there really is one unit head—then the issue of individual unit autonomy becomes questionable.)
- I am more and more convinced that most of the arguments we continue to hear evolve from mythic rather than real premises. (For example, the claim that if senior faculty no longer teach comp then the program will lose majors. The fact, as I assume you know, is that when most senior faculty were teaching in the comp program we had between 60–65 majors. Now when almost no senior faculty teach in the program, we have nearly 220 majors.)

Obviously, I can go on and on. I am convinced of the direction the writing program needs to take in order to better serve our students, the university, and the greater community. It will be most difficult, if not impossible, to accomplish these goals unless it is free to determine its own future.

A final word: It is not unusual for people sending e-mail messages to sign with an aphorism or quotation. Perhaps it's an attempt to interject a human touch in an electronic world. This morning while reading messages someone closed with the following quotation from Rabbi Hillel. I expect most of the writing faculty will echo his words.

"If I am not for myself, who is for me? And if I am only for myself, what am I? And if not now, when?"

9

WHO WANTS COMPOSITION?
Reflections on the Rise and Fall of an Independent Program

Chris M. Anson

In the summer of 1996, while at a conference in Europe, I was removed as director of one of the largest independent composition programs in the country—the Program in Composition and Communication at the University of Minnesota—by a temporary dean.[1] I returned to find that my administrative position had been given to a specialist in eighteenth-century literature, who had no scholarly background or training in the field of composition and who had expressed little interest in its work. As I withdrew to my regular status as full professor, the program was soon merged back into the English department from which it had been administratively dissociated fifteen years earlier. No satisfactory explanation was ever proffered to me or my colleagues for this sudden action—not by the dean who did it, not by the English department leaders who accepted it, not by the new director who welcomed it, not by colleagues in other departments who were surprised and shocked by it. To this day, the action remains shrouded in mystery, the subject of national outrage and intense investigations and analysis (see Boland; Shor 1997).

The unexpected takeover of composition raised many questions about motive. Nothing about the Program was a source of embarrassment or major concern: it boasted a first-rate training and development program; a strong team of teachers; a solid, nationally recognized curriculum informed by current work in the field and keeping pace with university-wide liberal education initiatives; productive faculty; and a consensus-based management system that helped to prepare graduate students in composition for possible roles as writing program administrators (WPAs) (see Anson and Rutz). A lean, fiscally responsible unit, the Program generated over a million dollars in revenues for the College of Liberal Arts after expenses. Composition teachers felt professionalized and respected, and placement into good tenure-track jobs was higher for graduate students in composition than for any other

English concentration. Data from student surveys showed a high level of satisfaction with the curriculum and instruction; only a handful of complaints (mostly about grades) came each year from over eight thousand students who took courses in the Program. We listened to suggestions, and we acted on the concerns of chairs and deans. We entertained and experimented with new ideas in faculty development and composition curricula: teaching portfolios and reflective practice, service learning and diversity-based courses, cross-observation programs, mentoring teams for first-year instructors. Like any program, we faced challenges and occasional setbacks. But we worked openly in a spirit of collaboration and a desire to solve problems. We had no scandals to hide.

Nor did the action seem targeted at me individually, the consequence of some unstated shortcomings in my capacity as director or as a member of the faculty. I had worked my way through the ranks to full professor very quickly. I had received a College of Liberal Arts Distinguished Teaching Award in 1992 and, in 1995, the Morse-Alumni Award for Outstanding Contributions to Undergraduate Education, which gave me a distinguished title. Just a few months before my removal as WPA, I had been the sole recipient (among several thousand faculty in the University of Minnesota system) of the State of Minnesota Higher Education Teaching Excellence Award, which was granted to me by legislative order of the Minnesota State House of Representatives on March 22, 1996. I had received a Governor's Certificate of Commendation in 1995 for my service-learning initiatives. My teaching evaluations were consistently among the highest in the English department, and I had accumulated so many merit points for publications, national service, and strong teaching and administration that the department couldn't pay for them all in my annual raises. My three-year reappointment reviews as director were highly supportive and filled with praise, even from leaders in the English department. I was well known across campus for my writing-across-the-curriculum (WAC) workshops and by all accounts was considered a highly productive member of the faculty.

Under the circumstances, it is not without cause to ask why a well-run, independent program was taken from the control of successful composition experts and reunited with a department that didn't really want it and had no other specialists to run it. The most plausible explanation concerns power and money, a subject I will turn to later in this essay. But the specifics of the case—already a subject of extensive research and analysis (see Boland)—are not as important for our purposes as is the broader issue of affiliation and control. The Minnesota case allows us to reflect again on the relationship between English and composition as disciplinary and administrative sites, because the differences between the two disciplines can—and, in the Minnesota case, did—reflect utterly different values and methods for the teaching of college composition.

A BRIEF HISTORY

The Program in Composition and Communication was formed in the early 1980s. After broad consultation, administrative leaders at the University of Minnesota-Twin Cities created a new, interdisciplinary composition program designed to offer writing courses for the entire campus. The move followed months of discussions in the English department (where writing courses were previously taught) and in various colleges of the university. The plan was strongly supported by the dean of the College of Liberal Arts and was endorsed by the university senate, which voted it into being.

Two English department faculty who created the plan, Professors Robert L. Brown Jr. and Donald Ross, were the first codirectors of the new program. Most of the courses were taught by teaching assistants (TAs), but they were now hired from different departments as well as from English. While this took away from English the control of TA appointments in composition, it had the effect of building a truly inter-disciplinary program that helped to train future faculty to incorporate writing into their own courses and disciplines.[2]

The Program in Composition and Communication, named after the Conference on College Composition and Communication (CCCC, which was seen as the national organization providing disciplinary leadership in composition) had no majors and was not a tenure home for faculty. Brown and Ross were both faculty members in English; the next two hires, one position in 1982 and then mine in 1984, also opted for English as our tenure homes, but the Program was designed to allow the transfer of effort from any other unit, including psychology, linguistics, cultural studies, education, or speech communication. In 1981, such a vision of a writing program was years ahead of its time.

While a few faculty members in the English department were opposed to the new program, saying that students were best served by writing in a literary tradition, most were, according to one source, "happy to see it go" so they would never have to teach freshman composition again. The literature faculty had little interest in composition teaching or scholarship (which some of them found "laughable") and preferred to focus on upper-level and graduate courses in literature.

In January of 1984, just as I was finishing my Ph.D. at Indiana University with a specialization in composition theory and research, I was offered a position at Minnesota as an assistant professor of English with a fifty percent appointment in the Program. Nationally, the Program was already known as a place on the cutting edge of the discipline. A growing graduate concentration in composition, supported by the Program's faculty and curriculum, had already produced some fine new Ph.D.'s—among them Robert Brooke, Marilyn Cooper, Michael Kline, and Dene and Gordon Thomas—and they'd been snapped up quickly by good universities. My position included opportunities to teach graduate courses for the likes of these students.

The Program's design reflected the brilliance of its founder, Robert ("Robin") Brown. Robin understood the need for students to learn about writing in different communities, even before the term "discourse community" had entered the composition lexicon or writing-across-the-curriculum programs had found much support nationally. There was still considerable respect for belles lettres and the literary traditions of composition; the Program even created a course for English majors that was designed to focus on writing in and about literary genres. But in keeping with its interdisciplinary goals, the Program did not limit its conception of writing, eventually offering upper-level composition courses in the arts, the general sciences, the health sciences, business, management, engineering, and the social sciences. Its curriculum served the needs of the entire campus; its scholarship looked outward to writing as a socially and contextually determined process.

The first-year composition course, required of most entering students, provided a solid if brief introduction to the process of writing and one's subject position as writer; to the concepts of audience, purpose, collaborative writing, revision, and peer response; and to some of the critical and textual skills necessary for students to do well in college, including attention to style and mechanics. Although some people have speculated that the coup had its genesis in a group of high-ranking, highly conservative university faculty and administrators with strong connections to right-wing organizations, little of what went on in the Program could have been construed as other than educationally well-informed and relatively apolitical instruction by well-trained, hard-working teachers.

The community that Robin had created was highly supportive and collaborative. New instructors took a ten-day pre-fall preparation seminar, where everyone wrote, talked about writing, considered research and theory in the field, and designed their own courses and syllabi in a structured setting rich in response and revision. We formed small teams of four or five new TAs and one faculty or a senior graduate student specializing in composition. Meetings continued throughout the year, and the most experienced graduate students in composition participated in some of the administrative work of the Program. The curriculum and its supervision were an enactment of the most promising and productive approaches informing the field of composition studies: an emphasis on collaboration, trust, seeing teaching as work in progress, seeing students as developing individuals who brought knowledge and experience into the classroom, thinking reflectively about instruction.

Soon after I received tenure and promotion to associate professor in 1988, I took over the directorship of the program. That role lasted for eight years, through two positive administrative appointment renewals, until the summer of 1996 and the subsequent death of the Program in Composition and Communication. During my directorship, two external reviewers in our field, David Jolliffe and David Schwalm, visited Minnesota by invitation of the provost's office to study and report on the various composition programs. Neither consultant wrote anything remotely recommending a merger of the Program into the English department, and both praised the excellence of the Program relative to the faculty resources the college had provided to it over the years.

POWER, MONEY, AND DISCIPLINARY CONTROL

Early in the development of the field of composition studies, conference rooms and journal pages were often filled with speculations about the future of the discipline relative to its historical association with English studies and its typical administrative location in departments of English. Important critiques of composition's growing independence appeared in issues of journals such as *College Composition and Communication* and *ADE Bulletin* and in collections of essays. One of the most vociferous calls for the intellectual autonomy of composition was Maxine Hairston's keynote address at the 1985 CCCC convention in Minneapolis (Hairston 1985). In that rallying cry, Hairston argued that the time had come for composition to formally separate from English literary studies and become an independent, freestanding discipline.

> I think that, as rhetoricians and writing teachers, we will come of age and
> become autonomous professionals with a discipline of our own only if we can
> make a psychological break with the literary critics who today dominate the
> profession of English studies. I agree that logically we shouldn't have to face
> this choice—after all, what could be more central to English studies than
> teaching people to write? But logic has long ceased to be a consideration in
> this dispute. I think for the literary establishment the issue is power; I think
> for us it is survival. (273)

While no national exodus from English departments ensued, the historical tensions between the two areas continued to grow as composition became an increasingly independent and interdisciplinary field.
The development of cultural studies and postmodern theory appears to
have created some renewed connections between the scholarly interests
of composition and literary studies, but the motivation, if not the exact
reasons, for responding to Hairston's concerns is as justified today as it
was almost two decades ago.

In this political context, we must ask whether the events at Minnesota
could have been prompted by the desire of the English department to
regain control of composition in a symbolic gesture of disciplinary
reunification. Was English so emboldened by its conviction that composition should be taught by literary scholars that it schemed to take over
an independent program run by composition experts? After all, concern about composition's "losses" if removed from the Burkean parlor
of literary scholarship were expressed throughout the years of the
Program's independence. Shulz and Holzman, for example, created an
artificial bifurcation between a series of disconnected but technical-
sounding composition "terms" and the "humanistic embrace" that characterizes the study of literature:

> As for the theory and practice of writing instruction, its fascination today
> with the paraphernalia of diagnostic testing, lab modules, primary trait scor-
> ing, rule-based systems, competency-based placement, composing and edit-
> ing processes, and computer reinforcement indicates that it would suffer a
> different but no less harmful degree of anemia by its separation from the
> study of literature. Divorced from the humanistic embrace of English, fresh-
> man writing is susceptible to domination by formalistic concerns. (28)

The speciousness of this argument is readily apparent. No one in
composition studies denies the importance of humanism or the need
for at least some literary study in all undergraduates' experience. But

the goals of most composition programs, as established and endorsed by the universities that have helped to formulate them, are not myopically limited to literary interpretation and criticism. Rather, composition courses help students to become effective, flexible writers who can analyze the way that writing works in a range of different disciplines and settings and who can critically interpret different kinds of evidence rendered in a variety of different modes of discourse. (See the Council of Writing Program Administrators' Outcomes Statement for First-Year Composition Courses.)

As more writing programs considered independence in the mid-1980s, the concern that composition was losing its connection with literary study was somewhat more condescendingly put in an essay by Sylvia Manning:

> The field of composition is likely to lose its heritage in the tradition of rhetorical studies that evolved into literary criticism and to lose touch with the finer workings of our language by which even the earliest groping efforts are tuned. (Do you know what happens to people who spend most of their reading time between the language of "remedial" students and the language of irremediable behavioral scientists?—Exit, pursued by a bear.) (25)

Not so subtly, Manning's point here is less a plea for keeping composition allied with literary study than a rejection of the very questions that composition scholars and teachers continue to ask in their professional work, chief among them how to help struggling writers, those "remedial students" whose writing no good literary specialist wants to read.

As the independent Program in Composition flourished, echoes of these authors' sentiments could be heard now and then among the literature faculty in the halls of the English department. But concerns about the consequences of independence were never particularly strong. In fact, there is almost no evidence that English plotted to take over the Program for purposes of disciplinary reunification. Had the English department believed it could provide better instruction in composition or improve its leadership, we might have expected to see some significant gains over the past few years. Yet since 1996, not a single composition expert has been hired among, at this writing, the ten new tenure-track positions filled in the English department; two of the four original faculty who ran the Program (Brown and I) have left the department, and a third (Ross) is on the cusp of retirement. Without a base of composition scholars to lead, inform, and innovate, it is not difficult to understand why there has been so little nationally visible activity in the composition wing of the English department.

Instead, more non-tenure-track and part-time instructors have been hired (and fired) than at any time in the Program's history (see Anson and Jewell); a nationally recognized teacher-development program (Lambert and Tice) is perceived to have fallen into mediocrity (Flash 1999); the teaching of composition has lost much of its interdisciplinarity; and there no longer exists a nationally competitive specialization in composition within the English graduate program.[3] The first new director has moved on, replaced by an excellent scholar of Victorian literature, who nevertheless lacks formal training or experience in the field of composition and who credits himself with teaching a composition course only once in the past decade ("Writing About Literature" in 1998).

For the leadership of the English department during the time of these events, controlling composition seems to have meant something other than a passion for the work of composition or the administration of a large writing program, which should have assumed the need for expertise. In the months and years that followed the takeover, investigations have concluded that the English department, in search of tuition revenues that would provide it with profit in a new university funding system known as "Responsibility Center Management" (RCM), wished to regain control of the independent program. RCM is based on the principle that every unit is responsible for generating its revenues and deciding how to spend them. Subsequent annual funding comes back more directly to each department, in proportion to the revenue it generates. Departments that teach many students at low cost, therefore, soon find themselves with increased funding. Those with a handful of highly paid faculty and few students are in trouble.[4]

Before the implementation of RCM, some departments were nervous that their funding would be reduced because they spent more than they garnered in revenues. English was not in serious danger under this financial scheme, but the faculty had already experienced some belt-tightening as its executive committee considered what to do about graduate seminars enrolling two or three students. A department that could generate large "profits" from student tuition could not only justify small graduate seminars but could use that profit as it wished— for example, to hire more faculty, bring in more guest speakers, get a bigger photocopying machine, carpet a main office, or put on catered receptions.

To many, the timing of RCM and the Program's demise appear somewhat more than coincidental. Ira Shor, reporting on his own independent investigation during a site visit,

> saw an apparent deprofessionalization of composition/rhetoric at Minnesota through the absorption of writing instruction into an English Dept. oriented to literature. This deprofessionalization seems connected to larger budget and policy issues . . . which have consequences for composition/rhetoric in general. (1996)

Sources explained to Shor that English was a "weak academic unit which needed to boost its courses and student contact hours," a matter of some urgency because of a "new cost-effective budgeting system imposed by the Univ. (a part of the 'U2000 Plan' known as 'responsibility-centered management' . . .)." Taking over an inexpensive program that delivered instruction to thousands of students a year could provide, according to one source Shor cites, a budgetary "shot-in-the-arm for the English Department" (Shor 1996).

WHY NOT ENGLISH? A PERSONAL ACCOUNT

In the many discussions prompted by the Minnesota case, some have asked why it was not possible for the Program to operate virtually unchanged within the English department, which was, after all, our tenure home and represented the mother-discipline that fed and nurtured the field of composition in its infancy. The revenues could have strengthened the entire department, whose status in the college could have protected the Program and even helped it to develop.

Clearly, the question of "why not in English" must always remain local, answered in the context of how receptive literary specialists may be to the principles of contemporary composition theory and instruction or how freely and equitably composition leaders feel they can work within a department populated by colleagues who do not share their expertise or particular values. Every composition leader making such a judgment brings to the task not only an analysis of the local political scene but a rich assortment of prior experiences that help to inform that analysis. Has the composition leader, one might ask, earned the right to judge whether a particular disciplinary location would be good for a writing program? In my opposition to an English-controlled composition program at Minnesota, I am answerable to this question.

In my role as a faculty member in the English department, I taught courses in literature, creative writing, linguistics, and literacy theory, as well as graduate and undergraduate courses in composition. I also routinely taught courses in writing about literature. I fully participated in the workings of the department, serving on committees and engaging in all the usual activities of a busy academic unit. While I didn't always agree with the faculty about some issues, I understood them because I am and always have been a member of the English profession.

My childhood and adolescence were marked by a passion for literature. I read everything I could get my hands on and wrote stories in imitation of great writers. By twelve, I imagined authorship: a hoped-for publication of the first pet-store pamphlet on how to care for gerbils (Anson and Beach 1999). I typed long letters to relatives on onionskin typewriter paper, crafted dozens of short stories and poems, memorized lines of literature and plays, went through a phase voraciously reading French writers (some even in French, which I had learned during my childhood years living near Paris). By high school almost all I cared about academically was connected in some way to literature and creative writing. As an English major in college I took every course I could in literature and audited or sat in on others. I felt no boundaries between creative writing, literature, linguistics, composition, and film studies. I sent essays to literary magazines, kept extensive journals, continued to write fiction. At Syracuse I completed my first M.A. in English literature and creative writing, became fiction editor of the *Syracuse Review,* read essays for *Thoth* (a journal of literary criticism), participated in an informal reading circle by invitation of some literature faculty, wrote a novel, and won the Alssid Prize for the best graduate paper ("Goddess Sage and Holy or *Balneum Diaboli?* An Anatomy of Milton's Melancholy"). I studied literary theory and continued to sit in on extra courses. I read Pope until I heard heroic couplets in my sleep.

Amidst this mélange of literate activities, I discovered a nascent field that was focusing on the ways that young people learn to write and how people write in different situations. As a teaching assistant at Syracuse, I was fascinated. Teaching was such a difficult and wonderful activity, and here was an area of study preoccupied with learning. Even the formative works emerging at the time seemed to reveal a possible bridge between English studies and the learning of language and literacy. But as I read Janet Emig and Peter Elbow, James Britton and Mina Shaughnessy, and as I reflected on my own education, I kept thinking about another experience I was having in a dusty classroom in an old Victorian building. Twice a week I would sit and listen to a freshly minted professor with a Ph.D. from one of the most prestigious institutions in the country. He would stand at the lectern and read his prepared text to us for fifty minutes at a stretch with five minutes at the end for controlled questions—read to us about literature, to all *five* of us enrolled in the course; read to us about his own reading; read to us as if to a huge audience of literary scholars in the only mode he knew, in the only venue for learning he could imagine. On those occasions a gap opened, then other gaps appeared, a long series of gaps stretching back into the recesses of my academic memory. I had done well in my schooling, but it was because I brought the disposition of an English major to it. Now as I struggled to help my classrooms of first-year students, I realized that very little of my college experience in English, not from the discipline or from the teachers, not from the hours of classroom instruction or from the communities of scholars I had tried to join, had shown real passion for understanding how people learn to become literate and thrive with their literacies. I had been blessed with some terrific teachers and scholars of literature, of course. But theirs was a passion for the arcane, a passion for sharing high-mindedness with high minds, not getting down close to the ground with young people who needed someone to help them discover literacy for themselves.

As I became more drawn to this new field, the distance between the interests and values of composition and the study of literature was becoming much clearer. When I began the Ph.D. program in English language at Indiana University, I still tried to make bridges between composition and literary studies. Yet in the late 1970s, most of the literature professors there seemed to look down on composition as an enterprise unworthy of their time. They talked with scorn or suspicion about both composition research and teaching, especially scholarship on teaching of any kind. I saw only scattered interest among them in pedagogy as an object of serious reflection or research. It became harder to find connections with them beyond the most erudite considerations of literary scholarship. I soon realized I had joined a kind of academic subculture, a community of compositionists and language scholars, who began introducing me to people in other buildings—people in education who were talking about issues of language and literacy development, theories of learning, research on reading, ethnography. It was easier to connect with cognitive scientists, who in spite of their empiricism really wanted to talk about learning. It was easier to connect with psycholinguists, who in spite of their behaviorism really wanted to talk about language and development. It was even easier to connect with linguists, who in spite of their formalisms really could talk about models of language behavior. Although the "comp" and "lit" people were all working in the same building, participating in the same departmental culture, we were asking entirely different questions. We were in different worlds.

When I accepted the position at Minnesota, the culture of the English department was very similar to Indiana's. Scorn abounded for the field of composition; many faculty didn't want to talk about teaching because they already knew how to teach; students got "dumber every year." But there was one important difference: the responsibility for teaching composition was no longer a source of tension, perhaps with the exception of control over TA appointments, and my colleagues and I could design and oversee a curriculum that was fully and freely informed by the developing field of our expertise.

Over the years, we tried (mostly in vain) to enlist some members of the English department to work with us on committees, in our teacher-development program, and in the teaching of our courses. We had greatest success recruiting faculty for our complicated and time-consuming TA hiring committees. But interest remained scattered. Eventually, I lost faith that my English colleagues could find even a fraction of the interest in and passion for composition that I had, and still have, for literature. Under those circumstances, independence seemed like a good thing.

My answer to "why not in English?" was not, then, uninformed or without experience and deliberation. Our predictions about the English department's lack of a collaborative spirit or interest in composition were soon confirmed. Once it had regained control of composition, only a handful of English faculty were willing to become involved in the enterprise. One person who taught a section of first-year composition ended up wondering "how on earth the instructors could survive" their multiple-section appointments. A glance at almost any small piece of composition administration often showed dramatic differences in approach. For example, in the old program, one of the faculty members would visit each new TA's class in the role of a mentor, discuss the class with the TA, and write up a descriptive, formative evaluation. More experienced TAs engaged in a program of peer cross-observations. Under the new leadership, the latter program was dropped, and the new director went to TAs' classes to write summative assessments. Several TAs, dumbfounded by the change in purpose, direction, and tone of the reports, shared them with me. The new reports were clearly designed to evaluate, the old to teach and coach. The new reports saw the classroom from the perspective of a Freirean banking metaphor; the old, as a contact zone. The new were preoccupied with demeanor and speaking angle; the old, with complex social relationships and pedagogical turns in the classroom. The new were brief, perfunctory, judgmental; the old were long, informal, and advisory.

Such differences, of course, can arise from simple nescience: perhaps the new administration was stumbling in the dark. But when the department might then have held out an olive branch and allowed us to help them reorient the Program, both Brown and I were kept at a distance from all composition-related work, and Ross's involvement was relegated to "computer consultant." The new director informed me personally that he "could not compete with me" for the allegiance of all the instructors and suggested that I "go off and write some more articles." From the fall of 1996 to my eventual departure in 1999, I was invited to run dozens of WAC and other workshops across the university campus and received a provostial invitation to be inducted into the Academy of Distinguished Teachers; but not one request for help or involvement in composition-related matters came from the administrators of my own department.

THE FUTURE OF DISCIPLINARY INTEGRATION

Across the United States, many outstanding composition programs operate smoothly and equitably within English departments. During my visits to dozens of these campuses, I have heard three refrains from the WPAs and other specialists in composition who are in charge of administering programs:

> they feel that the role and legitimacy of their discipline are respected and honored by their colleagues and by their administration;
> they are granted intellectual authority for making or helping to make decisions about the nature and delivery of instruction in composition; and,
> they are allowed some degree of administrative autonomy.

Ironically, the stronger these three principles are enacted, the less insular are the compositionists. Composition has always acted on its own beliefs in the power of collaboration and collective wisdom. Autonomy, therefore, may be desired only in proportion to the hostility or indifference shown by those who might otherwise be welcomed in.

These principles become all the more important given the present state of the English profession. Threatened by a sour job market for graduates, a declining interest in literary research, a growing skepticism by a public that equates literature with great books and is baffled by what now counts as literary scholarship, English departments are rediscovering composition as a neglected resource. The conservative public eases its criticisms if the department can "also" claim to be teaching undergraduates how to read and write. The discipline no longer appears to be in a state of decline if its productivity includes the work of composition. Graduate programs can thrive if there are teaching jobs for English students, jobs controlled, often as fellowships, by departments whose faculty rely on steady enrollments for their own specialized seminars.

But if the Minnesota case leaves us with an object lesson, it is for English departments to consider whether they accord their composition leaders the principles that characterize successful departmentally housed writing programs. Some English scholars have long argued that changes in the nature of English studies call for a new attitude toward composition. Laurence Poston, in a forward-looking essay with none of the condescending tone of Manning or Schulz and Holzman, suggests that English studies needs to begin accommodating new work in composition, widening its own scholarly horizons, and embracing literacy as a subject relevant to its work. In support of his claims, Poston quotes Jay Robinson of the University of Michigan, who wrote that "what is needed is not talk about bridging from literature to composition, but more serious talk about the human uses of language—the uses diverse humans make of language. We need not talk about 'composition' and 'literature,' but about talking and listening and reading and writing as centrally human and humanizing activities" (qtd. in Poston, 17). In its sustained focus on these activities, composition has branched outward to the point where it no longer is subsumed by literary scholarship but makes that scholarship the object of its own study, insofar as that study focuses on texts and contexts in all disciplines. Where once it was possible to have a marginal interest in the questions of composition and still know something about it, today composition includes subfields such as writing assessment that demand large investments of professional time and energy. It is no longer possible to run a writing program as a hobby, to be set aside whenever the stacks of nineteenth-century literary criticism or the latest *PMLA* beckon. Composition is embracing new, burgeoning areas strongly connected to learning and literacy: innovations in technology, service learning, and multifaceted forms of assessment; advances in faculty development, such as reflective practice and the scholarship of teaching; analyses of increasingly diverse writing communities; college/high school articulation. To be a WPA means to be passionate about and devote time to these interconnected areas. The maturing of our field, as Lee Odell has put it, has presupposed "the best efforts of each member of the discipline. Each of us has a responsibility to contribute to our individual and collective understanding of how people use language to communicate" (401). Those efforts cannot become newly mired in literary erudition.

Regardless of where composition is ultimately located administratively, its continued success will require that faculty and administrators across our institutions begin to think about it in new ways. No other discipline suffers the powerlessness, the deliberate divesting of authority and respect, that besieges compositionists. Members of departments of history, psychology, economics, nuclear engineering, food science, nursing—none endure arbitrary manipulation and control on the scale of composition. As composition leaders, we must develop principles and practices that insist on the scholarly, administrative, pedagogical, and professional status of our field. In so doing, we must think of ways to protect our pedagogies and administrative practices while continuing to invite others to share in the responsible management of our teaching and learning communities, just as we offer our own time and services to others. For their part, superordinate departments and administrative units must more often allow composition experts the administrative, curricular, and pedagogical freedom to make critical decisions about the nature and delivery of their instruction. In so doing, they will find themselves welcomed into the collective work of composition, listened to, and respected for their views.

CODA: DOING SOME GOOD IN THE WORLD

It is tempting to see the end of the Program as a symbolic loss to the discipline of composition studies, a subversion of our collective work. A few months after the dissolution of the Program in Composition, I wrote as much in a reflective post to the WPA-L (the national listserv of the Council of Writing Program Administrators), lamenting the way in which years of administrative work can be so easily erased. Part of my post read as follows:

> What strikes me . . . is how easily all the things that have taken so much negotiation, planning, and hard work are dismantled. Perhaps that's one of the

differences between administrative effort and scholarly work; one has the impression that one's administrative work is moving the world forward, at least locally and institutionally, but it can be undone in a matter of months. What's left is the *experience* of administration, but the "product," unlike scholarship, is gone. . . . A great writing curriculum can be "revised" into lectures on grammar. Or a really good teacher-development program can turn into the old 1950's practice of handing out a sample syllabus and the keys to a shared office. In the scholarly world, one of the criteria for the acceptance of new work is how and whether it builds on previous work. We don't have such criteria in administrative replacements—administration isn't necessarily intellectual as much as it is political. Regressive political agendas can land you right back to where you were ten, twenty, or thirty years ago—and then what? What has "moved forward?" Where has your work as an administrator gone?

Not long after this post appeared, Bob Connors, whose contributions to the list were always elegantly written and artfully reasoned, sent a rejoinder. In Bob's characteristic style, it was both abstractly intellectual and personally responsive. Much of his post focused on the "heartbreak" of administration represented by Fred Newton Scott, who was a great scholar but watched everything he had done to build an independent department of rhetoric at the University of Michigan fade into oblivion soon after his retirement. "And when he left in 1927," Bob wrote, "his department was within two years dissolved, the teachers and students folded back into the powerful and secure Department of English Language and Literature."

After Bob's tragic death in June of 2000, I retrieved his post and have reread it many times, in part because of what it says about our purposes. It reminds us that in spite of the politics and hierarchies in which we work as administrators of writing programs, it is the human moments, the connections we make and the lives we touch and improve, the ways we live and work *in* and *through* our places in higher education, that really matter. For Bob, administration was finally about people, not programs.

But are we to say that Fred Newton Scott wrote his name in water? Or that Chris Anson's effects on students and teachers at Minnesota are nugatory? We have gotten so used to the unilateral power over meaning that single-author writing and publishing provide that it can seem maddening to watch the way our influence diffuses throughout the social world of shared power (and enforced subordination) that administration is and creates. But though my individual writ may run forever unchanged in the dusty and uncracked pages of old journals, I hope my administrative efforts—minor, partial, imperfect, compromised though they are, and subject to partial erasure though they will be—may do someone some good in the world, too. (6 Nov 1996)

NOTES

This essay is loosely based on "(Re)locating Literacy: Reflections on the Place of Writing Programs in Higher Education," an invited plenary address I gave at the Annual Summer Conference of the Council of Writing Program Administrators, Houghton, Michigan, July 19, 1997. Many thanks to Carol Rutz for her helpful comments on earlier versions of the essay.

1. The composition program referred to in this essay has no administrative connection with two other writing programs at the University of Minnesota-Twin Cities, both of which are models of excellence and operate independently within their colleges. These are the writing programs in the General College, located on the Minneapolis campus, and in the Department of Rhetoric, located on the St. Paul campus. While there was and is articulation among the programs, neither of these other two units participated in the events described here.

2. About 70–80 percent of TAs continued to come from English, but rigorous hiring criteria made it possible for a promising scholar of literature to be denied an appointment on the basis of attitudes toward students, limited experience with undergraduates, or lack of promise in the classroom. Some of the very finest TAs ever appointed in the Program came from departments such as musicology, history, and comparative literature.

3. Instead, the English department offers an interdisciplinary minor in rhetoric, literacy, and language, presumably to help doctoral students in literature to prepare for the poor job market in their areas, but the department is not included in one of the major national lists of graduate programs in rhetoric and composition (Brown, Jackson, and Enos).

4. For a helpful introduction to the principles of RCM, see http://weathertop.bry.indiana.edu/mas/rcm/. For more on the effects of RCM in composition programs, see Anson, 2002.

10

REVISING THE DREAM
Graduate Students, Independent Writing Programs, and the Future of English Studies

Jessica Yood

If the last thirty years of deconstruction, feminism, and poststructuralist criticism have taught us anything, it is that our stories are not innocent, that every plot is political, and that histories are subject—and subjected— to interpretation and revision. If this belief has become a foundation for scholarly writing *in* English studies, it is surprisingly missing from the writing scholars do *about* English studies. While research on literature, student writing, and culture acknowledge the constructedness of language and discourse, in the stories we tell about our field, poststructuralist layering gives way to prescribed plotted narratives.

The tendency to write about the discipline one-dimensionally, most often as a cycle of "rising" or "falling" paradigms, of "crisis and panacea," or of "conflict and revision" is not unique to compositionists.[1] But the authors of composition's declarations of independence are especially prey to homogenizing the experience of disciplinary change. Some of the essays in this volume are a case in point. For every story told here about writing program transformation—including institutional and departmental histories, labor conditions, the structure of the university, and the philosophical concerns of administrators and faculty— there are tales left untold about how such revolutions affect writers and the production of knowledge related to writing. Narratives of "natural and appropriate" change (Deis, Frye, Weese), "self-definition" (Royer and Gilles), and composition as the "democratic" discipline (Aronson and Hansen), and the "hallmark of effective, enduring academic programs" (Deis, Frye, Weese) are scripted by the authors of change. What we don't know is how these progressive narratives potentially close off other considerations and ramifications of the separation of writing from English. What happens as writing program faculty and administrators seek an independent "self-definition," but teachers and students of such writing programs interpret "self" and "definition" in different ways?

Perhaps it is the many years of low status in the academic hierarchy that has prodded compositionists towards these histories with happy endings. But as we till the soil for the new field of dreams, we need to look at the variety of fruits from the labor. In what follows, I ask, how do certain interested and invested groups respond to new disciplinary structures, and how does this not only alter their institutions, but transform the system of making knowledge in writing and literature?

In this three-part essay, I first present a discussion of the importance of reception studies to contemporary disciplinary chronicling. I then provide a story of how graduate students in one changing writing program and English department responded to programmatic changes. As the boundaries of the program and discipline were shifting, graduate students were writing their professional identities through departmental memos, email exchanges, curriculum committee reports, and dissertation abstracts. I conclude by examining these lived products of our processes of change within a larger discussion about the future of graduate work in English studies.

THE READING, RECEPTION, AND SYSTEMIZATION OF CHANGE IN THE ACADEMY

Sociologists of knowledge and systems theorists argue that our historical moment is characterized by a level of complexity that makes observing, recording, theorizing, or narrativizing especially difficult. Knowledge of a discipline cannot be simply the outcome of one person, a group, or a school of thought, but rather is the "product" of "our collective lives," an ongoing activity of narrating, interpreting, and understanding our reception of ideas (McCarthy 17). We process change, adds systems theorist Niklas Luhmann, by connecting our observations of events with our experience of them. Intellectuals try to make sense of such processes through "second-order observations," describing "*how* others describe what others describe" (Luhmann 45). He argues that we cannot distinguish between our reception of change (our observations) and our representations of change—how we structure change into systems (like the essays written here).

Reception theory contextualizes the experience of systematic change and makes visible the reality that, even as we create separate structures or programs of "writing" and "literature," our observations and reflections create a new mix altogether. Reception theory changed the course of literary criticism and composition theory by placing the focus of textual interpretation on the reader or group of readers and on their historical and cultural surroundings. In the United States, work in reception has manifested itself most recognizably in reader-response theorists, who re-created the phenomenology of reception historians like Hans Robert Jauss and reception theorists such as Wolfgang Iser into a uniquely American form of pragmatism that engages readers in disciplinary meaning making.[2] An example of one well-known theorist who links reader-response theories to professional issues is Stanley Fish. In two of his books, *Is There a Text in this Class?* and *Professional Correctness,* Fish uses aspects of reader-response theory to make rhetorical arguments about the fate of literary interpretation.

Compositionists have adopted reader-response and reception theory because it emphasizes the role of the lay reader and writer and assumes that only with that reader can a text be interpreted or composed. Historians of composition studies integrate reader-response methodologies in their work on chronicling our emerging discipline. They see their discipline as a text and often provide what process theorists call a "movies of the mind" approach to reading this text: a step-by-step *exposition de texte* where personal and communal reaction dictate interpretation.[3] But as cultural theorists remind us, there are things outside of texts, and a reader-response approach is limited to describing a one-to-one transaction between reader (or faculty or administrator) and text (or department or curriculum). A one-to-one dialectic of reader and text and the evolutionary narratives of slavery and freedom, so prevalent in the disciplinary literature, do not address what writing means as an activity in our culture and as an academic subject in our colleges and universities. In order to understand how knowledge is made in a transforming cultural and disciplinary matrix, we need a dynamic reception-response approach that integrates experience and observation.

Rhetorically minded chroniclers of the profession have offered a more relational approach to reception theory. A reception approach to disciplines takes into account the society surrounding the enterprise of reform. In his book, *Reception Histories: Rhetoric, Pragmatism, and American Cultural Politics,* Stephen Mailloux uses aspects of reception studies to inform his experience as chair of a transforming English department. He explains the thesis of the book as follows, "I examine how particular tropes, arguments, and narratives contribute to historical acts of interpreting words, texts, traditions, and contexts" (ix). Rather than say "here is how something failed or succeeded where I work" or "here is a theoretical approach I subscribe to," Mailloux records the way different members of the department responded to change and enacted new forms of knowledge. These stories remind us that reception of disciplinary change is part of the new form of the field.

COMPOSING BEGINNING TEACHERS AND SCHOLARS: AN INTRODUCTION TO THE ACADEMY

The essays in the first half of this volume, and in most writing on the state of the field, tend to begin with institutional histories. But because my emphasis is on the connection between institutional change and new knowledge, I begin with student writing. It was the fall of 1995 when eleven other students and I began a graduate program at SUNY Stony Brook in what was (and had always been) an English department with a writing program. Before we arrived at the university, the director of the writing program requested that all future writing teachers compose brief sketches of ourselves as Ph.D. candidates and teachers. The biographies were to be put together and circulated to the eighteen new Composition 101 teachers, students from the humanities, social sciences, and the arts. I focus on eight Ph.D. students in English who remained in the department during the institutional shifts that occurred in the years to come.[4]

While the histories of writing programs discussed in this volume observe change through accounts of disciplinary reform, graduate student writing represents the experience of students whose place in the academy was outside of the profession's grander plans. In looking back at these statements, what stands out about the English graduate students is their commitment to teaching, to learning about teaching writing, and to sharing various pedagogical histories and philosophies. While all of the new teachers, regardless of discipline, express fear or excitement about teaching, the Ph.D. candidates in English characterize and theorize their place as future teachers of writing. One colleague begins this way: "I've been teaching for two years, while I got my Master's degree. I hope to continue to use some of what I learned in that Writing Program, though I know this program has a different philosophical approach. I hope to use popular culture as a rhetorical tool." Another writes, "I want to integrate my own intellectual interests into teaching writing this year, as I was unable to do that in the community college in which I adjuncted." In my own bio, I emphasize a "need to learn about college teaching, coming straight from college myself." My contribution expresses a desire to "see my own writing evolve with my students," a desire equal to wanting to become a "professional." One colleague likens her "insecurity about being in front of a classroom" to her decision to pursue the Ph.D.: "Part of what I like about this profession is its privacy and one's ability to specialize. I am nervous about teaching writing because I am not sure how to teach it outside of what I know about writing, which is writing about poetry." Another student, who had read about Stony Brook's program, writes that he "looks forward to hearing the philosophy of this program from the program creators themselves."

Most of us understood that there were existing political and philosophical realities in place before our arrival. The Stony Brook program had a national reputation for its composition practices.[5] But we believed we could write our own histories and philosophies into the program through our teaching. We expressed a need to "read and think and get 'tools' and 'secrets' of the trade all at once," writes one colleague. The potential recursivity of graduate school and teaching made us believe that the writing program would be revised with our participation in it. One of the eight English students describes this feeling: "I believe that I can share what I hold true about language and culture." Most of us viewed our emergent scholarly/teaching careers as separate parts of a larger whole, the whole culminating in earning the Ph.D.: "I know that teaching is one of the steps toward earning the degree—I look forward to it being a painless experience and not a time consuming one." A handful voiced a potential conflict between teaching and research and between teaching and learning. Yet we all say something about, as one of us puts it, "the love of language," "the importance of language," and wanting to "make a difference" through writing and teaching.

While these bios can be seen as naive sentiments of wide-eyed graduate students, they also stand as evidence that disciplinary shifts occur within a context of emerging identities and knowledge. In the middle of the 1990s, these graduate students in English had one thing in common: finding a balance between writing, teaching writing, and research. This commonality would lose balance as our bios would conflict with institutional plans.

PROGRAM INITIATION AND A RECEPTION
OF THE PROFESSION: 1995-1996

The early to mid-1990s was a time of recovery and reassessment for the humanities. The theory and culture wars, while no longer raging, were not quite over either. The new paradigm for English was not a new theory or canon but a commitment to "redraw the boundaries," as the editors *Redrawing the Boundaries: The Transformation of English and American Literary Studies*, a 1992 Modern Language Association (MLA) collection, put it. Post-culture-war efforts at collaboration and consensus, such as Graff's "teaching the conflicts," and programs in cultural studies attempted to revise and reinvigorate the boundaries of English. But morale was down. These efforts could not change the fact that the "crisis" in the humanities was not just a slogan nor merely a threat by a disenchanted public. The job market was at a low, and literature programs were retrenching.[6] On the other hand, while literature was redrawing the boundaries, composition's boundaries were rebuilding, "under construction," to quote the editors of another volume on the discipline (Farris and Anson). In the mid-1990s, new Ph.D. programs were started, more tenure-track jobs were created, and various writing-across-the-curriculum (WAC), writing-center, and technology programs were being built.[7]

This post-culture-wars climate of the humanities affected the curriculum for the eight Ph.D. students who began our degrees in the fall of 1995. The initial expectations and aspirations defined in our bios were reshaped in light of two required courses taken in the first semester of the program, the teaching practicum and the proseminar, subtitled, "An Introduction to the Profession." While one course's topic was the teaching of writing and the other course was teaching the conflicts of "the profession," both engaged students in thinking about the discipline as we were entering it. The practicum was taught at that time by the director of the writing program and was meant to introduce us to the philosophy of the program and to the general approaches to teaching writing. Readings were drawn from the textbook chosen for the first-year students, *A Community of Writers*, as well as *The Writing Teacher's Sourcebook*. The class counted for three credits, but not for a grade, and we were told that our main assignments were to share teaching strategies, lesson plans, and, on occasion, teaching and composition philosophies. The proseminar on the other hand was credit bearing. Faculty from the English department rotated their responsibility for teaching the course, and emphasis varied with each professor. The readings revolved around sample chapters from *Redrawing the Boundaries: The Transformation of English and American Literary Studies*, and we were expected to produce seminar papers testifying our allegiance to one of the twenty-one approaches to literary study presented in the book.

In the proseminar, we reflected on what the editors of *Redrawing the Boundaries* meant by English as a "field of rapid and sometimes disorienting change" (Greenblatt and Gunn, 2). For the practicum we were also asked to reflect on our place in the profession and in the academy, yet such reflection was for a particular purpose. As the editors of *A Community of Writers* say, "The main way you learn is by doing the unit's activities, not by reading theory" (Elbow and Belanoff, 3), and so we were to try out theories in the classroom rather than create position papers. While the proseminar was trying to "introduce" us to the "profession"—where the profession was something abstract and put off—the practicum saw the production of the profession as something immediate, always already happening.

The faculty did not try to link pedagogy and disciplinary theory, nor were we encouraged to do so ourselves. Yet the connections were made. As the semester progressed, the two courses in professional reflection became one activity in claiming a disciplinary identity. In the face of these two boundaries we were drawing bridges between crisis and reality and between coursework and our professional aspirations. I believe we fundamentally understood that literature was not so much "in crisis" as it was already exploded into many disparate pieces. And we knew that composition was rebuilding, "under construction," but the final structure was still uncertain. Graduate students read the writing on the walls of our institution and the discipline, which told us that we needed to sift through the building blocks and create a collective, productive plan for pursuing the profession in an age of change and disciplinary reconstruction. So after a few weeks, four of us started up a writing program newsletter, which included review articles on literature and composition conferences as well as a "Best Lesson Plans" column. In the spring cultural studies seminar, three of us produced collaborative projects on theories of language and cultural studies pedagogy. And the teaching-portfolio groups we joined doubled as study groups for other courses.

FROM COURSEWORK TO A CASE STUDY OF CHANGE: 1996–1999

It turns out that these efforts were purely academic—philosophical and pedagogical, but not pertinent to the prescribed programmatic plans of the administration. In March of 1996, the provost issued a report citing findings of a 1994 "Task-Force on Writing." This report claimed that there was not enough writing at the university and not the right kind of it. It was part of a long study on various programs at the university and how they were meeting or failing the new "undergraduate mission" of the university. The English department was singled out as ignoring needs of the school's new populations. Some of these needs were defined as "ESL tutoring, grammar, and mechanics." For most of the graduate students, the very existence of this task force was news, and our first instinct was to dismiss it as biased, for no writing teachers had been consulted before the report was written. But soon enough, parts of the report were found in mailboxes and emails, and the graduate student listserv circulated a rumor that the newly hired dean of arts and sciences intended to separate language "skills" from literature teaching. While it was only a rumor, committees and meetings began to spring up, and suddenly most of the work we did as graduate students was framed by the debate between language and literature.

Graduate students took the criticism of the writing program as our own. We wrote emails discussing our fears about losing our teaching-assistant appointments in composition should the writing program be removed from the English department. The writing program newsletter and our portfolio groups were put on hold for the while, and we began to write and study the fundamentals of our precarious positions in the academy. A memo that circulated in early spring, sent to the provost and dean and signed by the president of the Graduate English Society, sums up the situation as we read it: "We understand the [provost's] draft plan to be preliminary and . . . we are extremely concerned about the impact of these changes on graduate student workload, training, and representation." The chair of the English department followed suit, defending graduate students and writing program faculty. In one of his memos, he asked, "What does poor grammar and a writing program's location in English have to do with one another?"

Of course, as we were busy drafting memos, holding meetings, and awaiting news from deans and chairs, we also went on with our "progress toward the degree." That spring, I enrolled in an independent study with the former director of the writing program. The topic was "The History and Theory of Teaching Writing." Influenced by reading case-study and ethnographic research, I decided to include a survey of my colleagues as part of the final project. I asked ten questions in all, most of which were follow-ups to the concerns addressed in the biographies. But one question produced the most telling results about the dissonance between graduate student experience and programmatic change.

For the final question of the survey, I asked, "What do you think of the proposal to separate the writing program from the English department?" All eight students said that they were "opposed to the split." Two colleagues write that they "reject the very phrasing of the question," which, as one student puts it, "assumes that because a department can be split the act of writing and reading—literature and rhetoric—is in a binary opposition." And one student asks a question that connects "writing program independence" with the continuation of Ph.D. programs in English studies: "when there are no jobs for Ph.D.'s in English, what is the use of making more divisions in programs and divisiveness among humanities teachers and scholars?"

We began asking these questions in our courses and continued them in the context of actual curricular and disciplinary debates. The following semester, the fall of 1996, I was appointed graduate student representative on the "University-Wide Search Committee on Writing," organized by the dean. We were told that this committee was charged with "expanding the standards and offerings for writing at the university and hiring a new director of the Writing Program." Along with the interim director of the Writing Program, who had become my advisor, one other faculty from the writing program, and twelve faculty members from a variety of departments other than English, I attended the six meetings held that year. As part of this new role, I organized meetings of all the teachers of writing in order to create a community of compositionists who could speak about our practices. But it was the eight English students who were most invested in the philosophical and physical transformation of the writing program. We compiled evidence suggesting that graduate students should be trained as teachers and teachers of writing. As liaison between graduate student teaching and undergraduate education, I planned on presenting to the committee curricula we created and how our scholarship and teaching connected. Yet such issues proved at odds with the two charges of the committee; there was no time for cultivating soil for a field of dreams. Suddenly, at this research university, we were to make decisions without research or evidence; writing was an emergency, a crisis, and we were to change the course of literacy immediately. While it took three years to get a cultural studies certificate passed and two years to start a mentoring program at my university, this committee was told that the structure and function of writing were to change overnight.

And it did. While we discussed a long-term WAC program and theories of composition, in the end, the committee's deliberations resulted in hiring a new director of writing and in compiling an eleven-page report, published in June 1997. This report, written by representative members of the committee, recommended changes in the curriculum and staffing of the writing program but did not say anything about the graduate student/English/writing program connection. Decisions were made in five meetings and decided by majority vote; the writing program faculty, and I, were not in the majority.

After the vote, the committee disbanded. When we returned the following fall, the new director was in place, as were the new requirements. Graduate students worried about both the trivial and the critical facets of our future—we had to adjust to new mailboxes and new programwide curricula for the first-year writing course. But the real adjustment was not found in curricula or degree requirements. In the fall of 1997, the writing program became, without any discussion or meeting, the independent Program in Writing and Rhetoric, which would eventually grow, we heard, to a department.

THE STORY UNFOLDS AND CONTINUES: THE EMERGENT ENGLISH STUDIES

There are many ramifications of the move toward independence. It is too soon to say how these changes will affect undergraduates; most of my colleagues, who in 1999 and 2000 were still working in the writing program, claim that their students don't recognize the shifts. Yet the graduate program is completely transformed. Most new graduate students are not opting to focus on composition and rhetoric, and literature students don't get very involved in composition theory, conferences, or pedagogies. The composition requirement is now two semesters, and graduate students in English, who used to teach four to six writing classes, now average two to three. The few composition faculty who were teaching before the split now teach literature exclusively or have left. Six full-time lecturers have been hired, as well as two tenure-track faculty.[8]

I could end here, with a eulogy for the ending of a writing program as I knew it or a commencement speech for the beginning of a department that I will never know. But the changes I list above are structural. They represent only a simple transaction, a transfer of power. We need to ask what the lasting implications for knowledge in language and literature might be for the field.

For the remainder of the essay, I trace how three students produced dissertations in very different topics under the similar constraints of a fractured department. These students began their dissertations together, immediately after the writing program split. If dissertations represent the zenith of a graduate students' reading, research, and writing and the precursor for new knowledge in a profession, then we need to try to capture the process of these changes in light of current disciplinary reconstructions.

AFTERWARD: WRITING KNOWLEDGE IN A CHANGING DISCIPLINE, 1998–2000

In the spring of 1998, Stony Brook's Humanities Institute held a symposium on "The Future of the Profession." As third-year students in the English department, we began to realize that this "future" would be our present. It was at this time that two other graduate students and I began our dissertations and decided to form a writing group. We met a total of sixteen times over a period of eighteen months. What began as an activity to help us finish the dissertations became a study of creating knowledge in our present moment of disciplinary restructuring.

We were three students of very different aspirations and scholarly interests. I wanted to work at a university in composition studies. Another member wanted to be a modernist at a small liberal arts school, and the third member wanted to teach early American literature, "wherever I can," as she said. When we met for the first time our conversation focused not on American literature or composition theory or Joseph Conrad but instead on the perennial graduate student question, "How do you get the dissertation finished?" But such prosaic questions soon revealed themselves to be profound and unresolved conflicts in the structure and purpose of graduate study in English studies. It was at this point that I began taking notes on our meetings, a task we eventually all took up.

We came to the second meeting prepared with outlines of our proposed first chapters: I wanted to begin a dissertation on contemporary composition with a history of "process" philosophy. The member interested in early American literature also wanted to begin with an overview, in her case, of the role of women in the Revolutionary War, and our third member wanted the first half of her dissertation to provide a history of anthropology, to later connect it to the history of modernist literature.

We all agreed that completing the first chapter was crucial to getting us on the right track. But this "track," and the progressive histories we were beginning to write, stood in opposition to the lack of linear path our department and disciplinary affiliations were taking. We debated the chaotic nature of the state of the academy, in contrast to the stability we were supposed to create in highly specialized dissertations. We were writing in a professional vacuum. The writing program/English department split changed the way we saw our committee members, who were now labeled by their affiliation with the English department, with the writing program, or by their opposition to that labeling. The persons—and the profession—for whom we were writing had, in the scope of three years, disappeared.

Discussions on the struggles of writing a first chapter became conversations about the struggles of the profession and why representing ourselves in the form of a dissertation was difficult in ways other than the obvious strains of composing a book-length project. By the end of that first session, we had defined our first chapters differently. All of us decided to expand on our historical introductions. We created sections indicating where our big-picture overviews did not, or could no longer, correspond to any contemporary reality in the profession. For example, we realized that a chapter on the role of emerging women writers in early American literature related to our metadisciplinary discussions on the place of literature and writing. I acknowledged that a history of "process" required some discussion of my process of coming to this topic in the first place. The modernist of our group wanted to continue to write about anthropology and literature, but not without "explaining the issues that arise when two disciplines are working on similar questions and studying the same texts." We were trying to write dissertations, but we were also completing unfinished discussions on writing and literature begun three years ago.

My first chapter turned out to be on disciplinary theory, a topic that came out of the shifts in writing and English at my university. The dissertation on American literature began with a section on "print culture and women writers of the revolution" and included a long concluding paragraph about the importance of early American women writers to understanding more contemporary issues about culture, reading, and writing. She said she understood that the topic of her dissertation was "obscure, a hard sell" but that choosing this topic was "important to do, because it is not obvious why anyone would care about these writers." She linked this task to the task of any scholar/teacher in writing: "We need to stress the importance of what we do." She continued, "We need to explain our work to others and my topic helps me to do that."

The third member of the group researched on the modern novel and anthropology as planned. But through her research on cultural encounters and because of her encounters with, as she put it, "our graduate student dissenters" she came to also argue for the dissolving of the terms "modernism" and other period labels. She spoke about her decision this way, "I wanted to break down literary barriers, a result of the experience of arguing about theories in the proseminar and then living them out with the dean and the faculty." She told me that she had not planned, nor even wanted, to "delve into the whole 'what is English?' debate." But, she added, " I had spent so much time with you and at those search committee meetings and this stuff was in the air, so that is where my thinking went."

After we all had completed the first two chapters of the dissertation, the tenor of our group workshops changed. We were reading each other's work not just to ask questions or edit but to connect ideas and bridge our different issues, theories, and arguments. We didn't plan on integrating our dissertations in any way; indeed that task would, we thought, take us too far afield from the goal of finishing the degree. Yet we each felt as though completing our program meant making sense of how we began. Without the structural framework of one department or of a unified sense of a "Writing Program," these connections came in the form of layering our dissertations with one another's ideas and writing. When I finally did get to my third chapter on the history of the process movement in composition, the modernist in the group discussed the link between theories of process and the way ethnographic writers discuss cross-cultural encounters. The process that many early American authors took to become known had a striking resemblance to the way modern writers became "modernist" and to how literary critics or process thinkers became theorists. And so we discussed the connections, sometimes citing each others' sources, other times just noting the impossibility of segmenting out our particular dissertations as "free" or "independent" from the others'.

While I am mentioning only some of the shifts our dissertations underwent, I believe these examples provide material for asking essential questions about our stories of the discipline and about the way we are progressing in composition studies. This "integration" (of our group, our dissertations, and, by extension, our degrees) was a theme throughout the nearly two years of dissertation writing. Our dissertations were commenting on the pace and potency of change in our program as we earned our degrees. We could not imagine what writing that resulted from a more stable, unified disciplinary structure might look like. Are there any such dissertations (or disciplines)? And if we live in the age of synthesized, hybrid knowledges, why are we beginning to carve out "independent" and isolated writing programs?

FORWARD: DISSERTATING THE FUTURE OF THE PROFESSION

Tracing how graduate students receive, reinvent, and react to disciplinary transformations alters the dimension of our disciplinary narratives. An emphasis on the reception, however, not only changes the way we observe and narrate our discipline, it has the potential of altering the existing structure of our field.

Current literature on graduate studies generally focuses on three main issues: the discrepancy between graduate student training in theory and the more generalized teaching that graduate students will eventually do; the need for teachers to focus on literacy issues of our least prepared students, and the crisis in higher education and its effects on tenure-track jobs.[9] The recent Conference on the Future of Doctoral Education centered on these issues. In the over 150 pages of material produced at that conference and reprinted in the October 2000 *PMLA*, scholars continually recommend the shrinking of graduate programs, the need for greater attention to teacher preparation, and possibilities for alternate career opportunities.[10]

Important as these issues are, they do not address the current conflict between the production of knowledge by graduate students and the way our programs are reshaping knowledge. To make that connection is to acknowledge that the separation of literature and writing assumes a separation of writing about something (observing and critiquing) and creating something (producing new knowledge). But segregating parts of experience from the whole of disciplinary development runs counter to the realities of writing and knowledge making. The composition of our three hybrid dissertations is not something unique to my university but is part of our changing academic culture and interconnected world. This is what Niklas Luhmann and other systems theorists mean when they refer to contemporary society as multilayered. Luhmann explains that our world cannot simply be described as "modern" or "postmodern" or as "expressionist" or "constructivist," but rather as all of these things, as a "self-referential system" that "reproduces itself" through the very metalevel activities of trying to understand and place itself in this environment (42–46). The more we "progress" toward disciplinary independence, the more we come to rely on each other to change and adapt to new surroundings.

Stephen North and his collaborators acknowledge this environment in their book, *Refiguring the Ph.D. in English Studies: Writing, Doctoral Education, and the Fusion-Based Curriculum*. North writes that debates about the field occur in "real time" (260) and cannot be put off or staffed out to disciplinary theorists. He discusses the need for "refiguring" the Ph.D. towards a "fusion curriculum" that allows for flexibility in studying and practicing "writing, teaching, and criticism." This curriculum is an important contribution to the recognition that the discipline cannot just recolonize; it must move forward with the time. But what is most important about North's work in my mind is the recognition that we need to begin to make "doctoral student writing one of the primary means by which this refiguring of the Ph.D. will be brought" (260). I would add to that: we need to acknowledge the ways doctoral students are already restructuring the academy through knowledge making that integrates experiential observation, literary critique, and rhetorical and systematic analysis of knowledge production.

Composition studies can lead the way to making the connection between observation of change and its production. As the "teaching subject," to use Joseph Harris's phrase, composition has always been interested in the process of constructing texts. But we now need to focus on the process and products of disciplinary change. This change does not just happen in the space of one institution during one semester or within the margins of volumes such as these. It occurs in the material products gathered together—ever increasingly together—from a broken field of dreams.

NOTES

1.   The two genres of disciplinary discourse I describe here—the apocalyptic crisis narrative and the progressive tale—dominate much of the recent disciplinary literature. "The rise and fall of English" is Robert Scholes's phrase, taken from the title of his recent book. "Crisis and panacea" is Robert Connors's phrase, and I borrow "conflict and revision" from Gerald Graff's book, *Beyond the Culture Wars.* Other related books, written by scholars representing every field of English and composition include Bernard Bergonzi's *Exploding English,* Christine Farris and Chris M. Anson's collection, *Under Construction,* Alvin Kernan's *What's Happened to the Humanities?* and Mary Poovey's "Beyond the Current Impasse in English Studies."

2.   I am referring to Jauss's *Aesthetic Experience and Literary Hermeneutic* and Iser's *The Fictive and the Imaginary.* For a discussion of reader-response

and reception theory in terms of the history of literary criticism, see Terry Eagleton, 54–91.

3. Process theorists have integrated some of the reader-response techniques into their work on revision. I take the phrase "movies of the mind" from Peter Elbow and Pat Belanoff's textbook, *A Community of Writers.*

4. The bios, memos, and statements from graduate students are all taken from unpublished documents or from the author's personal notes.

5. See, for just two examples, Elbow and Belanoff, *Community of Writers,* and Elbow and Belanoff, "State University of New York: Portfolio-Based Evaluation Program."

6. Avrom Fleishman discusses the low morale in light of the theory debates in "The Condition of English: Taking Stock in a Time of Culture Wars." See also Michael Bérubé's *Public Access* ("Introduction").

7. See Farris and Anson's introduction to *Under Construction,* which discusses the progress of and public support for composition in the last decade. J. Hillis Miller's foreword to *Publishing in Rhetoric and Composition* discusses composition's growth in connection with literary studies' decline.

8. When I left the English department in the summer of 2000, the new curriculum in the writing program was focusing more on writing in the disciplines and away from a process-oriented approach to composition. A new writing center director has been hired as well as new associate director of writing. Such brief remarks don't address the more substantive changes in the program; my point here is to suggest that the quick structural reformations had long-term ramifications on the work of graduate students.

9. The *ADE Bulletin*s from Winter 1990, Spring 1995, and Winter 1998 include discussions on these issues. See Graubard's essay in *Daedalus,* which is devoted to disciplinary change. See also Michael Bérubé's *The Employment of English* and Robert Scholes's *The Rise and Fall of English.*

10. Jacqueline Jones Royster's talk from the April 1999 Conference on Doctoral Education, reprinted in the October 2000 *PMLA,* discusses this issue. Ten years earlier scholars were saying much the same thing, as reported in Lunsford, Moglen, and Slevin's *The Future of Doctoral Studies in English.*

11

LOCATING WRITING PROGRAMS IN RESEARCH UNIVERSITIES

Peggy O'Neill
Ellen Schendel

Typically those of us in higher education expect writing programs, particularly first-year composition programs, to be located within universities' English departments. At large research universities, there is a stereotype about writing programs: they are run by English faculty members with the first-year writing courses staffed by English graduate students (most of whom are earning literature degrees) and adjunct instructors, who experience substandard material conditions (not enough office space, little pay, poor access to technology, not enough support staff, etc.).

Unfortunately, this stereotype seems to be an accurate description of many programs. The Modern Language Association reported that in a sample of Ph.D.-granting English departments, 63 percent of the first-year writing sections are taught by graduate students, 19 percent by part-timers, and 14 percent by full-time non-tenure-track faculty (1997, 8). As James Sledd (2000) recently argued, many of these programs are run by "boss compositionists"—tenure-track faculty reaping rewards that include higher wages, smaller classes, bigger offices, and more advanced undergraduate and graduate courses. However, while this stereotype may describe the state of composition at a number of institutions, it doesn't accurately represent individual programs, which are much more complex, locally situated, and diverse, as Carol Hartzog found in her survey of writing programs at member institutions of the Association of American Universities (AAU).

Hartzog explains that she investigated the writing programs of this elite group of research universities because they are a small, definable group, yet very diverse; many of the writing programs have gained national recognition; and her home institution was a member of the organization. Another reason Hartzog cites for choosing to research AAU member institutions—and the primary rationale for our follow-up with them—is that "questions about the status and identity of composition have to do not only with teaching but also with research." She asks, "Is it possible to do substantial work in this field—and earn traditional academic rewards for that work?" (x). By examining the position of writing programs at these elite research institutions, Hartzog reasoned, we can get a sense of the value of composition within the academy and contribute to the debates about composition's academic status and disciplinarity. Hartzog described composition as a "field in transition" with writing programs "struggling not just for security but for dignity" (xii). Although composition studies has matured as a discipline since Hartzog's study was published and now includes over sixty doctoral programs, a strong job market, more tenured composition specialists, more peer-reviewed journals, and more work coming out in scholarly presses, its position within the university has not been completely defined and secured. With all these changes since Hartzog conducted her study, we wanted to find out what has changed or stayed the same in writing programs at premier research universities—and what, by implication, these changes might mean for composition as a discipline.

Although we have not embarked on a project as ambitious as Hartzog's, we did set out to explore the status of writing programs fifteen years after she conducted her survey to see if changes had occurred at elite research universities since the burgeoning of composition studies.[1] We began by looking at university websites, then sent email questionnaires to the AAU writing program directors or departmental chairs (usually in English departments), following up on some questionnaires with telephone calls or email interviews. Our focus was narrower than Hartzog's since we were focusing only on the institutional structure of writing programs—where they are located, who directs them, who controls the hiring and budget, and what courses/programs they offer. We were most interested in finding out how many writing programs at these elite research universities were housed within English departments and how many were independent units. We were also interested in determining what kinds of courses the writing programs offered: first-year, required composition courses and/or upper-level courses or even minors or majors in writing.

Based on our initial results—and the topic this volume addresses—we provide an overview of what we found and then focus on two independent writing programs: Harvard's Expository Writing Program and Syracuse's Writing Program. We chose to highlight the program at Harvard because it has always been an independent writing program, has been influential in the history of composition, and was one of Hartzog's case studies. We decided to highlight Syracuse's program for very different reasons: it was not an independent program when Hartzog conducted her research, and it contains a doctoral program in Composition and Cultural Rhetoric. We begin with some general observations from the survey before turning to the descriptions of these specific programs.

THE BIG PICTURE: RESULTS FROM THE SURVEY

We sent out sixty-one questionnaires via email, inquiring about the structures and curricula of the writing programs at AAU member universities. Of the sixty-one questionnaires we sent, we received responses from forty-one universities, for a response rate of 67 percent (see appendices for the survey and the list of AAU member schools we contacted). Of those forty-one responses, two were from writing program administrators who declined to answer our survey questions (it is against one university's policy to participate in such surveys, and the writing program administrator at the other university simply preferred not to participate). An additional four responses indicated that the questions we asked were too difficult to answer at that point in time, either because the writing program was undergoing major structural and curricular changes (in the case of three schools) or because the writing program was so unconventional that it was not easily described through the questions we asked. In these cases, survey participants wrote brief summary answers to our survey questions. When possible, we incorporated information from those summary answers into our tabulation of results.[2]

Our survey questions addressed a number of issues, including the size of the programs and their administrative and budgetary structures, teacher education opportunities for the people teaching writing courses, and the professional interests and qualifications of the administrators of such programs. What we found, while not surprising, was quite interesting: writing programs vary so much by institution that it is nearly impossible to present a clear summary of the answers to our questionnaire. Just to illustrate the wide differences among writing programs, we have chosen to highlight findings from four of the questions we asked on the survey.

1. *What unit (or units) directs or administers most of the writing classes on your campus?*

Of the thirty-five respondents who directly answered our questions (that is, respondents who did not provide us with summary answers), eight said that their writing programs were independent and administered by faculty or staff who reported directly to a division head or dean. The majority of respondents, a total of nineteen, reported that their writing programs were located within English departments, while four reported that their programs were located in a unit other than an English department (such as a rhetoric department or a teaching and learning center). Four respondents indicated that two or more departments shared in the administration of the writing program. In these cases, first-year writing courses were taught by faculty in many disciplines across the university; or English and another department shared in constructing and directing four-year writing-across-the-curriculum (WAC) programs, in which there may or may not be a first-year writing component.

2. *Who administers the unit and what is his or her academic degree, area(s) of expertise, and professional rank? If tenured, what department is the administrator tenured in?*

The information about who administers writing programs is just as diverse as the information about where programs are housed. Of the thirty-five respondents who directly answered our questions, twenty indicated that the persons administering their program were rhetoric and composition specialists or were specialists in other areas (such as literature) with rhetoric and composition training, experience, and/or interests. Other participants reported that the administrators of their programs are specialists in cultural studies (one response), linguistics or ESL or TESOL (two responses), or another area, such as literature (twelve responses). The majority of writing program administrators, twenty-six in all, are tenured or tenure-track faculty in their departments. Two additional respondents said that the writing program administrator was a senior lecturer, someone who was either "tenured" or granted renewable appointments that are in some way different from tenured/tenure-track faculty positions. Six respondents reported that the director of the writing program was not on the tenure track, but was an adjunct faculty member, a lecturer, or a postdoctoral fellow.

3. *What is the administrative structure of this unit? Is it a department, program, interdisciplinary center, or some other kind of unit?*

From the survey responses, we identified the following independent writing programs that are not departments:

- Columbia's Composition Program (formed in the mid-1990s)
- Cornell's John S. Knight Institute for Writing in the Disciplines (formed 1982)

- Duke's Center for Teaching, Learning, and Writing (formed in 2000 out of the University Writing Program, which was created in 1994)
- Harvard's Expository Writing Program (formed in 1872)
- The Princeton Writing Program (formed in 1991)
- The University of Colorado's Writing Program (formed in 1987)
- The University of Rochester's College Writing Program (formed in 1997)
- The Yale-Bass Writing Program (formed in 1977)

Besides these independent programs, we also identified several full-fledged departments—other than English—with tenured faculty and other signs of departmental status, as well as institutional recognition as a department that administered most of the writing courses:

- The University of Iowa's Department of Rhetoric (achieved departmental status in 1988)
- Michigan State's Department of American Thought and Language (formed in 1946)
- The University of Minnesota, St. Paul's Department of Rhetoric
- Syracuse University's Writing Program (formed in 1986)

All of these departments administer core, required composition programs as well as other courses or programs. Through our web searches, we also identified other writing units independent of English, such as the University of California-Berkeley's College Writing Program, Massachusetts Institute of Technology's Writing Program, and the University of Texas-Austin's Division of Rhetoric (none of which responded to our survey).

These independent or interdisciplinary units responsible for teaching writing all have very different histories and reasons for coming into being. One respondent noted that the independent writing program at her university was formed because of "the desirability to have one department responsible for first-year writing instruction." Other respondents indicated that their independent programs were formed as interdisciplinary units because there was widespread resistance on those campuses to one department being solely responsible for the teaching of writing. One respondent, for example, wrote that her program began because "College faculty felt that writing should belong to all programs, all departments, and that this could not happen if the program were located in only one department." Another respondent wrote that her program "is stand-alone because it was not effective for the English department to try to run a large, interdisciplinary program. A decentralized-center was required." Moreover,

The structural development (administrative and operating) [of the program] has been determined by the university's and the [program's] wish to make the teaching of writing an interdisciplinary and integrated effort throughout the university. [The program] has wished to emphasize writing as an integral part of learning and of effective teaching. The developments have been greatly aided by successful endowment-seeking efforts.

Still another respondent listed a number of reasons why her university's writing program is independent, reporting directly to the dean of arts and sciences. Her response illustrates a number of complexities leading to the campus's formation of an independent writing program:

- The politics of teaching courses satisfying graduation requirements in several different colleges, while being funded through only one (A&S);
- Administrators' consistent refusal to allocate any tenure-track lines or roster any tenured faculty in the program, even to provide for eventual replacement of founding co-directors;
- (In earlier years) perpetual pressure from administrators to increase class sizes and add sections at the last minute;
- (In recent years) the university's increasing tendency to move long-time part-timers into contract instructorships;
- The increasing pool of adjuncts nationwide; partly as a result, increasing professionalization (or at least credentialization): a rise in the percentage of writing program teachers with a Ph.D. (from seventeen percent in 1986 to forty-six percent in 1996 and still rising), a fall in percentage of writing program teachers having the B. A. as highest degree (from thirty-six percent to five percent over the same period, and now almost zero), and a fall in annual teacher turnover (from forty-nine percent to fourteen percent over the same ten years);
- The politics of student evaluations and grade inflation (a serious concern here, with PR repercussions);
- The politics of operating under state higher ed commission (indirectly affecting colleges' design of requirements and the design of courses, therefore student "demand");
- (Very recently) pressure from various administrators to return to a somewhat more traditional structure, teaching mainly freshmen and staffing much more with graduate students.

Yet another respondent explained that the university's writing program came into being because

Previously, when under the English Department, increasingly the Composition Program was ignored. English faculty did not teach our courses and had little or nothing to do with our program. Getting action or support or advice was difficult, if not impossible. . . . Our primary connection with the English department was (and remains) through the grad students in English, all of whom (with very few exceptions) teach for 2-3 years in our program.

Clearly, there are a number of ways in which independent and interdisciplinary writing units came into being, namely, a need to centralize writing instruction; a need to build a base of interdisciplinary support for writing across the university; and administrative, structural, and logistical problems in working with a department fundamentally disinterested in the teaching of writing.

4. *Who teaches most of the courses within that unit (TAs, adjuncts, full-time instructors, tenure-track faculty)?*

Also varying from institution to institution is the makeup of the writing program faculty. All but one of the thirty-five respondents who directly answered all of our questions reported that their programs employ adjuncts, fellows, lecturers, or graduate teaching assistants to teach in their program. Of these thirty-four, all but one reported that *most* core courses in the writing program are taught by adjuncts, fellows, lecturers, or graduate teaching assistants. Only fourteen, or 40 percent of the thirty-five respondents who answered our questions, reported that tenured or tenure-track faculty teach core writing courses in the program. However, twelve respondents made the following stipulations about faculty involvement in the writing program:

- Tenured/tenure-track faculty teach honors courses only
- Tenured/tenure-track faculty teach freshman seminar courses only (with other instructors teaching "regular" first-year writing classes)
- Tenured/tenure-track faculty teach writing-intensive courses other than first-year writing
- Only "a few" courses a year are taught by tenured/tenure-track faculty (two respondents noted this)
- One percent of all writing program courses are taught by tenured/tenure-track faculty
- Five percent of all writing program courses are taught by tenured/tenure-track faculty
- Forty percent of all writing program courses are taught by tenured/tenure-track faculty

- Fewer than ten percent of all writing program courses are taught by tenured/tenure-track faculty
- "Some" writing courses are taught by tenured/tenure-track faculty

Based on the results of this survey and our reading of information located at these universities' websites, we drew several conclusions. First, what "counts" as a writing program is very different from institution to institution. For many universities, a writing program is synonymous with "first-year composition program," while at other institutions a writing program might include upper-level courses in composition, professional writing, and creative writing, or it might indicate interdisciplinary ties with departments other than English or writing. In other words, writing programs are contextually defined according to institutional mission, university goals for writing, graduate programs, WAC programs, and many other factors. Second, the teaching of writing takes place in many different locations, from English and writing departments to science and history departments. Third, composition research and the administration of writing programs seem to be valued, since the majority of directors are tenured/tenure-track; however, the teaching of writing, especially first-year composition, is still often relegated to part-time faculty, graduate students, or instructors who have little power in the programs/departments in which they teach or who are "passing through" and therefore have little investment in the writing program. And fourth, composition studies is still in transition, both within local settings and the field as a whole. That four of our survey respondents indicated their programs were undergoing major changes surprised us; the changes in writing programs since Hartzog first published the results of her study indicate that universities and faculty who teach writing are engaged in finding better, more contextual ways to respond to student needs.

Responding to student needs in the classroom, however, is not necessarily distinct from participating in the research and scholarship of composition studies. Robert Connors argued in favor of keeping the teaching of writing as an essential part of composition studies' identity, as he suggested possible directions for the field: "Most centrally, teaching writing and working with writing teachers are and remain the fundamental functions for specialists in composition studies. . . . working rhetorically in the world with writers is the continuing key to defining the field" (1999, 20). Writing programs that exist outside of the departmental structure, with few if any tenure/tenure-track faculty are essentially outside of the knowledge-making community valued by the research university. Professionals working in these programs can still be active members in the scholarly community of composition (and many are), but how does their status affect the way the scholarship is valued by the larger academic community? And, more importantly, is recognition and acceptance by the academic community something composition studies needs?

Of course, being outside the tenure system without departmental status can make programs and instructors much more vulnerable to institutional politics. Two of the independent programs that Hartzog identified—the University of Michigan's Composition Board and the University of Minnesota, Minneapolis's Communication and Composition Program—are now defunct, having been reappropriated by the English departments at their institutions (see Anson this volume for the Minnesota story). Tenure, although it is under attack and revision at many institutions, still confers privilege, status, resources, and benefits on those who receive it. Not having tenure clearly marks writing instructors, administrators, and scholars as somehow outside the academic mainstream of the university hierarchy.

To more concretely discuss issues associated with independent writing programs, we profile two independent programs: Harvard's, which is interdisciplinary, and Syracuse's, which has recently established a doctoral program in Composition and Cultural Rhetoric.

THE EXPOSITORY WRITING PROGRAM AT HARVARD

Expos 20, Harvard's first-year writing course, is described as one of that university's oldest traditions: "A one semester course in expository writing has been the one academic experience required of every Harvard student since the writing program was founded in 1872" (Harvard Expository Writing Program, n.d.). The Expository Writing Program, which is independent and interdisciplinary, is also one of the oldest and most influential writing programs in the history of American universities. English composition was first introduced into the undergraduate curriculum at Harvard, according to most scholars, by Harvard president Charles Eliot in order to achieve several purposes, including promoting English as the language of learning and pressuring preparatory schools to teach English composition.[3]

Composition quickly moved from a second-year course to a first-year requirement, and it spread to other Ivy League colleges, to elite private and public universities, and eventually into the general education curriculum of almost all American postsecondary institutions, where, for the most part, it has stayed firmly rooted. With the spread of the first-year writing requirement, Harvard's composition teachers also enjoyed a measure of influence through the development of textbooks and pedagogy. What didn't spread so rapidly, however, was the administrative structure of its writing program, which has remained interdisciplinary and independent from a department since its inception, according to a pamphlet published by the program, although it has been closely aligned with the English department at times.

In 1984–85, according to Hartzog, Harvard's program was directed by Richard Marius, a Ph.D. in history and an accomplished writer, who was a senior lecturer (which is a yearly renewable faculty rank, not a tenured position). As director, Marius handled the day-to-day activities, reporting to the dean of undergraduate education and a standing committee comprised of interdisciplinary faculty. Besides offering the required first-year course and an advanced expository writing elective, the program also included a writing center that tutored students and offered workshops for faculty across campus.

Based on her survey, site visit, interviews, and review of materials, Hartzog concluded that the program was "successful in these ways":

> it is based on a clearly formulated philosophy that writing should be taught by writers and that students in writing classes should learn "how to observe sharply and think clearly" (Marius, Informal Notes 1); it is directed by a forceful leader and recognized scholar committed to his teachers, to his program, and to writing; it is staffed by articulate, intelligent, and energetic writers committed to teaching; and it has been carefully evaluated by those responsible for teaching in it. (126)

Although Hartzog applauded the program's independent and interdisciplinary status and its philosophy that writers should teach writing, she expressed concerns about its future, especially in terms of its staff. The teachers were adjunct faculty who could be renewed only up to five years, compromising the evolution of the program and making the instructors—and in some ways, the program itself—marginal to Harvard's academic community.

Today the Harvard Expository Writing Program is thriving, having survived some difficult years after Hartzog's visit. Although it retains many of the same basic features since its inception, the program has developed and grown under the leadership of Sosland director Nancy Sommers and her assistant directors. Sommers, who joined the writing program in

1987 as Marius's assistant director and took over as director in 1993, is an accomplished composition scholar. In recent interviews, Sommers and Gordon Harvey, associate director of the program (who joined the program in 1986), identified several major changes that have occurred in the program over the last seven years:

1. Instead of six different courses that satisfied the requirement, there is just one course, Expos 20, with a variety of special topics for students to select from. The courses are designed by the instructors on a topic of their choosing (jazz and literature, famous trials, and the culture of consumption were three of the more than thirty different topics offered in fall 2000), but all focus on academic writing and preparing students for the types of writing they will encounter in their careers at Harvard. Students write four essays, between five and ten pages long, that require the writer to make an argument using different strategies and sources. There is also a "basic" writing course for students who need more practice before taking Expos 20, and an advanced expository writing elective is offered every other year.

2. The instructors in the program are still temporary appointments (with the exception of four permanent assistant directors). However, instead of being teaching assistants (TAs), they are all hired as preceptors, which is a faculty appointment with a higher pay scale. Along with the change in title, the hiring philosophy changed: today most preceptors are accomplished *academic* writers, either Ph.D.'s or doctoral candidates, although they represent a wide range of disciplines. According to Harvey, the program has rigorous standards for hiring instructors and devotes much time and many resources to professional development. For example, every year he goes to the Modern Language Association convention to interview candidates.

3. The program has developed an official WAC program, the Harvard Writing Project, which was founded by Sommers in the spring of 1995 "in an effort to make writing a more vigorous part of Harvard's undergraduate education" (Harvard Writing Project website). The WAC program, which has a writing-in-the-disciplines (WID) emphasis, offers workshops and individual faculty consultations, sponsors a lecture series, publishes student and faculty resources, and offers other services across the campus.

4. The program has become more research based and more research oriented. Research, according to Sommers, is at the heart of a university, so she feels compelled to be knowledgeable and active in the research community. For example, Sommers explained that, shortly after taking over the program, she did a preliminary study that involved interviewing faculty across campus and examining the types of writing required in their courses. This preliminary research, along with other factors, has influenced the

direction of the program in recent years, contributing to a more academic focus in the courses and pointing to a need for a WAC/WID program. The Harvard Study of Undergraduate Writing, currently being conducted by Sommers, is following 25 percent of the Harvard Class of 2001, or about 420 students, "through their college years in an attempt to draw a portrait of the undergraduate writing experience" (Harvard Study of Undergraduate Writing). This large, longitudinal study is supported by the writing program as well as through the office of the president and a Mellon Foundation grant.

5. The physical facilities for the program have been upgraded and consolidated. In 1997, the program moved into its own building, a renovated, three-story Victorian house in the center of campus. All forty staff members are housed there, and although Sommers admitted that space is still at a premium, she sees the "beautiful, warm, friendly Victorian house" as a sign of "gratitude and respect" by the Harvard administration, especially since there is such limited room on campus.

According to Sommers, most of the changes have been made with students' best interests in mind. In the interview we conducted, Sommers repeatedly focused on how the program better serves students now than it did in the past. These changes, explained Sommers, have also contributed to the development of a more professional, more academic program that is integrated into the Harvard community. For example, Sommers described the program as "a virtual publishing house," generating high-quality, professional documents for students and teachers, including the *Harvard Writing Project Bulletin, Exposé,* and *Writing with Sources: A Guide for Harvard Students,* all of which are used across the campus. She also noted that the writing center has a solid reputation, with many professors linking directly to its online resources. According to Harvey and Professor Patrick Ford, a member of the standing committee that oversees the Expository Writing Program, Sommers's leadership style has made a substantial contribution to the program's development. While Sommers downplayed her own role and praised her staff's dedication and hard work, noting that she sees herself as a low-key delegator who has worked to build alliances, Ford identified Sommers as "a person of tremendous energy and ability," whose appointment as director is the single biggest change in the program over the last ten years. He also noted that the Harvard Writing Project initiated by Sommers "has changed the face of writing at Harvard."

Sommers also attributed her ability to enact so many changes in such a short time to the program's independent, interdisciplinary status. Because it is not aligned with an academic department, it is not directly involved in the departmental politics that are familiar in academic communities. And, because the expository writing courses are staffed completely with non-tenured instructors with five-year renewable appointments, the program administrators are able to maintain consistency of writing pedagogy across sections. As Sommers said, and Harvey confirmed, people "are not hired if not with the program," and she admitted that it would have been impossible to accomplish such a consistent program if they were dealing with tenured/tenure-track faculty. Harvey noted, however, that one can't help feeling somewhat marginal since none of the staff are professors and therefore have no real voice in the university's decision-making process. Another benefit associated with their independent status, explained Sommers, is that the program operates its own budget and can engage directly in fundraising. It has, in fact, secured several endowments and grants during Sommers's tenure. For example, the Harvard Writing Project has its own endowed faculty grants and an endowed lecture series that focuses on professors as writers; and the study of undergraduate writing has been able to obtain grants from the Mellon Foundation for research. Sommers's position is also an endowed directorship although not a professorial chair.

Overall, Sommers said that she thinks that advantages of being an independent program, even though not a full-fledged department, far outweigh the disadvantages. She sees several ways that Harvard's program can contribute to the discipline of composition studies. The research she is conducting, for which she already has support for a full-year sabbatical in 2002, is the largest longitudinal study conducted on undergraduate writing, and Sommers believes it will make a significant contribution to the field's understanding of the role of writing in undergraduate education. She also mentioned that the program's publications—which she sends to people across the country—are influential in what happens in writing programs on other campuses. She noted, however, that perhaps their most important contribution is in the preparation and training of writing instructors, who often leave Harvard and enter departments and programs at other universities or colleges, taking with them knowledge about effective writing pedagogy. Although they might be informed writing instructors, the preceptors are not necessarily members of the scholarly community of composition studies or active contributors to the field. The program's influence will also be extended to secondary education teachers through an outreach program that Sommers and her staff are developing. This summer program will provide Cambridge and Boston public school teachers with fellowships to take two courses at Harvard over the summer, one of which will be a course on teaching writing.

Although Harvard's Expository Writing Program is flourishing, it is telling that Sommers, the winner of two Braddock awards and an important voice in composition studies for over twenty years, is not tenured and is not a member of the professorial faculty. As Ford said,

> In one respect, Expos is not unlike the situation of writing in many universities. It is not a department and its faculty are called by the strange name 'preceptor.' I support changing this to 'lecturer,' but that doesn't seem likely to happen. Fortunately, salaries have improved somewhat for preceptors but are still below that of lecturer. Teachers of writing have been professionals for some years now, but there remains almost everywhere a suspicion on the part of 'real' scholars that writing and writing pedagogy lie outside of the main preoccupations of the academy. This is not likely to change, in my view. The best defense for writing programs are strong directors and a core of faculty who care.

Sommers is by all accounts a strong director, and she has built a solid program grounded in composition research and theory that has much to offer the field. She has also learned how to work within a university structure in savvy ways, garnering endowments and grants to finance research and services that the program sponsors.

THE WRITING PROGRAM AT SYRACUSE UNIVERSITY

The freestanding Writing Program at Syracuse University began in the fall 1986 "in response to internal and external evaluations of the freshman English program," according to Faith Plvan, Deborah Saldo, and Beth Wagner, all full-time staff of the Writing Program. The internal evaluation consisted of the investigations of the 1985 Ad Hoc Committee to Review Writing Instruction, which reviewed current scholarship about composition theory and pedagogy, along with samples of writing by Syracuse students. The committee also surveyed faculty about their opinions of student writing instruction at Syracuse. In addition to conducting its internal investigation of writing, the committee consulted James Slevin and Donald McQuade of the Council of Writing Program Administrators.

The recommendation the committee made, based on these internal and external evaluations of the then current writing program, was the establishment of a "broader program more clearly informed by current theories about how students learn to write," as well as the formation of "a four-year writing curriculum with students taking a 'studio' in writing" in each of their first two years and one at the upper-division level, explained Plvan, Saldo, and Wagner. The university then conducted a search for a scholar in composition and rhetoric to develop and direct the Writing Program; ever since its formation as an independent program, it has been administered by a tenured faculty member with a specialization in the field. Three of the program's directors have been full professors.

The new Writing Program at Syracuse evolved rapidly toward departmental status, acquiring its own jointly appointed tenure-track faculty in the first year. Although budgetary and managerial autonomy came with the founding of the program and the administration soon recognized the director as a department chair in the College of Arts and Sciences, in practice becoming "departmentalized" was a more gradual process. Today, while still called "the Writing Program," the department has built up a tenure-track faculty of ten (one choosing to remain jointly appointed in English) and has tenured several junior faculty. The faculty offers a freestanding doctoral degree program in Composition and Cultural Rhetoric (approved in 1997) and in 2001 began implementing an expanded upper-division curriculum, with plans for building a writing minor.

In its first year, the Writing Program initiated what was conceived as a multiyear developmental curriculum, although its early focus was on the lower-division writing studios. Shortly after it began, by moving one semester of the previous first-year course to the sophomore year, the program created a two-year sequence, Writing Studios 1 and 2 (WRT 105 and 205), required by most schools and colleges, while offering two upper-division courses. Recently, the writing program has reformed and expanded its upper-division curriculum, including four studio courses and four content electives, which give students the opportunity to investigate the kinds of writing done in the workplace and community and to explore writing and rhetoric as it pertains to technology, identity, and literacy. The program has therefore achieved its original goal to have course offerings available at all levels, so that an interested student could take writing classes throughout his or her four years at Syracuse.

The Writing Program also administers a campus writing center staffed by professional writing consultants (although a small number of peer consultants also tutor in the center). Even though the writing center has always been a part of the Writing Program, it has recently become "very visible" on campus, according to Plvan, Saldo, and Wagner. The open physical structure and location of the writing center, which is housed in a glassed-in building in the middle of an academic quad, gives it a "real presence" on campus. At the inception of the Writing Program, when the program lacked space for a writing center, the director created a new teaching role of "writing consultant" and invited the teaching staff to explore its possibilities inventively in various forms of "consultative teaching." Many teachers have since rotated through this role as part of their teaching loads, forming a corps of experienced consultants, who developed an array of extracurricular services. Such services include not only one-on-one tutoring for individual students, but also consultative teaching and professional development for faculty, teaching assistants, student groups, and other disciplines, carried out in classrooms, computer clusters, and sites across campus, as well as through interdisciplinary projects. Undergraduate peer writing consultants, trained in a practicum course, later joined the consulting staff. These functions are now being centralized and reimagined in the new writing center.

The Writing Program's courses have always been taught by part-time, professional writing instructors, teaching assistants (until recently, drawn largely from the Department of English), and full-time, tenured and tenure-track faculty. In recent years, with the establishment of a doctoral program in Composition and Cultural Rhetoric (CCR), there has been an influx of graduate teaching assistants, who are wholly invested in the program's activities.

To discuss the benefits and drawbacks to the program's status as an independent unit, we have gathered the views of experienced staff members and the personal perspectives of several faculty administrators, past and present. The following points represent a range of perspectives about the Writing Program, expressed by Plvan, Saldo, Wagner, Eileen Schell (a recently tenured faculty member of the program as well as the director of graduate studies) and Louise Wetherbee Phelps (professor and founding director of the Writing Program). As their administrative responsibilities and histories within the program are very different, each staff and faculty member articulated different benefits of the program's status as an independent unit.

A hiring process aimed at finding the best teachers for undergraduates has been established. The program is in charge of all program-related personnel decisions. There is an established process for hiring graduate teaching assistants and part-time professional writing instructors: applicants must submit teaching statements along with evidence of their other qualifications. The English department's and CCR program's graduate committees recommend graduate students for positions in the Writing Program, but the Writing Program's director has final approval for awarding such assistantships.

An independent budget allows full-time staff to help administer the Writing Program. The three staff members we interviewed work with the Writing Program in a number of ways. As the assistant director of the Writing Program, Faith Plvan oversees the professional development of instructors in the program. Among her many duties, she coordinates both online and face-to-face discussion and teaching groups and organizes two teaching conferences a year. As the program's financial coordinator, Deborah Saldo works with every aspect of the program's budget. Beth Wagner works to schedule teachers and classes and handles registration and grading issues related to the program. Two administrative staff meetings a month are held to oversee the smooth functioning of the program and a very large teaching community; the Writing Program currently includes eleven full-time faculty, fifty-one teaching assistants, and forty-three professional-writing instructors. Over half of the administrative staff teaches in the program.

The program has attained a respected position within the campus community. Phelps believes that the program is more visible and better able to function effectively on campus because it is situated as a department in arts and sciences and reports directly to its dean. Within that framework, it exercises autonomy in budget, hiring, and curricular decisions. Its departmental status, tenure-track scholarly faculty, discipline-based curriculum, and now the doctoral program have opened the way to playing a role alongside other academic units in the intellectual life of the college and campus.

There exists a commitment to viewing the work of the Writing Program as scholarship. Because the tenure-track faculty within the program are invested in producing scholarship in composition studies, rhetoric, and literacy, because part-time faculty practice teaching as a form of scholarship, and because the doctoral students in the CCR program also share these scholarly commitments, the Writing Program is able to foster and benefit from a sense of teaching as scholarship. Eileen Schell cites this focus on making knowledge in the classroom as the primary benefit of being an independent writing program: there is a focus on truly understanding students and student writing and an assumption about teaching writing that is not based on a deficit model. Students are not in a writing class to be "fixed," purged of bad writing habits. Rather, the focus of teaching and scholarship within the Writing Program is based on a fundamental respect for all writers. Schell believes this concentrated focus on the professional and intellectual issues of writing and language can, at times, be lost if writing is housed within another department (such as English).

The ambiguity of being both a program and a department gives the Writing Program flexibility. Phelps believes there are advantages to keeping the ambiguity between a program and a department that arose from the unit's historical evolution and mission. She argues that the Writing Program can operate on multiple levels in these two modes. The programmatic nature of the unit allows for a focused mission that has encouraged the formation of a teaching community out of a diverse group of instructors. The departmental status gives the faculty a voice in campus governance, control over the tenure and promotion process, and membership in the research community. She thinks that at a research institution like Syracuse, only a unit with a tenure-track faculty can "have full access to all that the university offers and be part of the academic mainstream." She sees the Writing Program as having the potential to work with colleagues across the institution "to help students make sense of their undergraduate education."

The Writing Program is positioned to make significant contributions to the field. According to Phelps, the unique structure of Syracuse's program provides one strong model—not the only one—for how rhetoric and composition can work in the university structure. It also increases the visibility of the discipline because it has attained departmental status and a doctoral program at a private research university. When instructors who teach in the undergraduate curriculum leave (whether they be graduates of the doctoral program, professional-writing instructors, or teaching assistants from other departments), they take with them "the customs of being part of a teaching community and the practice of talking and writing about their teaching," which contributes to the culture at their new institution. Finally, Phelps sees the doctoral program as having real potential to influence the field because it "strategically focuses" on composition as a discipline through a very diverse group of scholars.

Phelps and Schell, who frequently collaborate with each other, expressed different personal views regarding potential drawbacks to housing writing within an independent unit.

A smaller, more focused tenure-track faculty makes for fewer cross-overs among the many fields of English and can reduce the power that collective bargaining of a large faculty can enjoy. Schell herself completed her Ph.D. in English with a concentration in rhetoric and composition. She has come to value and enjoy talking with colleagues in literature and theory whose professional interests intersect with hers. As a faculty member in a writing program, she must work harder to maintain those professional ties with members of the English department. As the director of graduate studies, Schell is also concerned that CCR doctoral students may not be completely prepared to work in English departments. She and other faculty—and the doctoral students themselves—are always conscious of the fact that the majority of CCR program graduates will work in English departments and will need to be prepared to interact with (and present tenure cases to) fellow colleagues who may not understand their work. Although, within the program, the formation of an intellectual community focused on writing and language is a very positive element of being a stand-alone unit, the novelty of writing as separate from English can be confusing to people outside of the program. Many people—students and faculty alike—do not understand why writing should be separated from English.

Phelps, however, doesn't believe "that composition and rhetoric is intrinsically part of English Studies"; rather it is an "interdisciplinary mélange" with roots in several different fields, and it was "a historical accident" that it was located with literary study in English departments. She thinks that its relations to the many parts of English studies remain conceptually and politically important, but not exclusively so. She also explained that by being separate from English, the unique needs of the writing program are not subordinated to competing concerns and needs of a large English department.

Separating from English departments does not mean that the resulting Writing Program will be free of the same "problems" facing composition within English departments. One of Schell's own scholarly interests is the position of part-time faculty within composition programs. By separating into a freestanding department, the working conditions for part-time faculty are still an issue. Moreover, with the addition of the CCR doctoral program in 1997, there have been other tensions that have arisen, as yet another constituency was added to part-timers, tenured/tenure-track faculty, and English department graduate TAs.

Tensions exist between the benefits that are associated with being independent and maintaining our non-traditional disciplinary features. Phelps explained that in working to fit within the traditional expectations of a discipline and department in a research university, there has been a struggle to maintain the nontraditional aspects that we value in composition, such as an emphasis on teaching and the scholarship of teaching.

What is clear from our discussions with Plvan, Saldo, Wagner, Phelps, and Schell is that the writing program is still changing. Rebecca Moore Howard, the current director, plans to continue developing the Writing Program in four key areas, according to Plvan, Saldo, and Wagner:

- coordinating the program with the American rhetoric and African American studies programs
- sponsoring a diversity speakers series;
- recruiting more minority faculty; and
- developing support for non-native teaching assistants.

The features that most distinguish the Writing Program at Syracuse from the Expository Writing Program at Harvard are the inclusion of a doctoral program dedicated to composition and rhetoric and the tenured/tenure-track faculty. The CCR program, according to Schell, shifted the culture of the unit. There is certainly the addition of another constituency—that of graduate students—vying for resources and recognition within the department, and that has been a complication. Doctoral students "pass through" the program in four years. The professional-writing instructors often stay much longer and are concerned that their teaching assignments will shift as the program attempts to give doctoral students the opportunity to teach a variety of courses and take administrative roles within the program. At the same time, beneficial partnerships have emerged among the different constituencies around programmatic and curricular projects like the new upper-division writing curriculum, which was recently revised, and the service-learning collective, which is a group of faculty, graduate students, and professional writing instructors.

The Syracuse Writing Program has had a long history of forming a community of scholars and writers dedicated to the study of language, learning, and literacy; the establishment of the doctoral program continues the development of that community in a new direction.

IMPLICATIONS AND CONCLUSIONS

Although the results of our exploratory study indicated that there has been an increase in the number of independent writing units in these research universities, it doesn't mean that composition studies is becoming more of a mainstream academic discipline. The fact that most of the independent units are programs, employing contingent labor, with an emphasis on teaching, seems to locate them outside the primary mission of their institution. Thomas Miller articulated this recently in an electronic discussion:

> A political reality check: the "elite" universities that have been cited in this context—Duke, Princeton, Cornell, etc—have writing programs that are basic service units, right? None is connected to an English or another academic unit that has a research mission or is in other ways connected to the intellectual work that is generally identified with that mission, right? The units tend to be run by non-tenure-track administrators, and the courses are taught by adjuncts or grad students, and in the latter case there is far less relationship between that teaching and the grad students' other work than there might be if the teaching was done in their own departments, right? (2001)

Katy Gottschalk, director of Cornell's independent, interdisciplinary writing program, responded that

> locating the teaching of writing outside the traditional structure of an academic department doesn't relegate it to second-class status. An independent writing program that draws its major resources (faculty and courses) from a wide range of disciplines can play a significant role in fostering the attitude that teaching of writing is the responsibility of the college or university, not just one department . . . So the Knight Institute has benefited, I believe, from having been separated, administratively, from the English Department back in 1982, because it is now more than ever part of over 30 departments who think of their writing seminars and writing in the majors courses as very much their own curricula. (2001)

In her response, Gottschalk doesn't address Miller's critique that these types of programs are not part of the knowledge-making structure of the university. In the excerpt above, Miller is not criticizing the teaching of writing that these programs do, but rather, questioning how they participate in the scholarly community as producers of academic knowledge. In other words, Miller highlights the marginal position that independent programs occupy at research universities when they are outside the research agenda that distinguishes these universities from other post-secondary institutions. And, although Gottschalk detailed the quality, professionalism, and status of instructors in Cornell's first-year seminars (and Rebecca Howard from Syracuse University testified to it), most instructors of freestanding composition programs are non-tenure-track, according to a recent survey conducted by the Conference on College Composition and Communication (in conjunction with the Coalition on the Academic Workforce). In fact, freestanding composition programs have the lowest percent of tenured/tenure-track instructors out of all the academic fields participating in the survey:

> Composition programs, and English departments, which teach large numbers of required introductory writing courses, have the smallest proportion of full-time tenured and tenure-track faculty members. Freestanding composition programs (those outside of English departments) report that only 14.6 percent of their teaching staff is full-time tenured and tenure-track, while English departments report that 36.3 % of the faculty is full-time tenured and tenure track. (Coalition on the Academic Workforce)

Although this survey is not specific to AAU institutions, it does accurately represent what we found, especially at Harvard and Syracuse. Harvard's program has no tenured/tenure-track faculty, and while Syracuse does have ten tenure lines (and one joint line), most of the writing studios are taught by graduate students. In both of these programs, however, there are composition scholars making substantial contributions to the field of composition studies (Sommers at Harvard and Phelps, Howard, Schell, and others at Syracuse) even if the majority of teachers aren't. Richard E. Miller sees this situation as part of the corporatization of the university, in which adjunct and graduate student labor is increasingly responsible for moving students through the first two years of coursework and where most people earning a Ph.D. in composition and rhetoric will be required to manage a writing program—performing such managerial tasks as overseeing labor, interacting diplomatically with chairs and deans, handling budgetary concerns, and writing grant proposals (1999, 98–99). Miller argues that writing programs should embrace their service role by staffing their courses with instructors who "demonstrate a commitment to learning how to read and respond to student work with care, to assisting in the revisionary process, and to applying local assessment practices evenly" (102). Instead of advocating that all courses need to be taught by tenured/tenure-track Ph.D.'s in composition and rhetoric (in other words, certified knowledge-makers), Miller contends that we should focus on improving the material conditions of the instructors. The traditional structure of the university, according to

Miller's argument, is already breaking down, and composition is positioned to take advantage of the corporate structure—much as Sommers seems to have done at Harvard. He explains that

> it is a mistake to abandon the ethic of service that defines the field in the hope that doing so will bring about broader respect for the intellectual work done in the discipline. While it is certainly true that composition can replicate the very kinds of research that one finds being pursued in other disciplines . . . the record shows quite clearly that work of this kind, no matter how skillfully executed, is generally judged to be derivative by those not involved with writing instruction. . . . in attempting to achieve the signs of disciplinary success that accrued in the past to those who labored in the University of Culture, composition will be preparing itself only to live in some bygone era, when no one questioned the merits of researching the history of the paragraph or of building a superconducting supercollider. In the University of Excellence, however, all research projects, from the use of the comma to the makeup of subatomic particles, are increasingly scrutinized, assessed and frequently funded on the basis of their utility—on the basis, in other words, of the service they perform for society. (103–4)

As Miller argues, composition can be a preeminent force in the future if it embraces the new university structure and capitalizes on its service mission. Miller's colleague at Rutgers, Kurt Spellmeyer, makes a similar point, arguing that writing programs' marginal status affords opportunities to make a real difference in students'—and by extension the community's—lives. According to Spellmeyer, in all of their classes, students are required to "play a familiar and enervating role—as dutiful consumers of expert knowledge." But, he continues, "Only in writing class, so far as I know, might they [students] have the chance to discover what it feels like to be the maker of one's own truth, the maker of one's own life" (180). If we give up our marginal position in pursuit of traditional notions of disciplinarity, argues Spellmeyer, we run the risk of reproducing the same structures and values as other disciplines. Sledd also endorses a rejection of the traditional disciplinary rewards in favor of strengthening the commitment to serving students and improving the working conditions for teachers and learners. He proposes abolishing rank and tenure, forming militant unions that include faculty and staff, and "serious teaching of general purpose prose" instead of continuing "compositionists' struggle for upward mobility in the academic pecking order" (2000, 11). In short, Sledd, Spellmeyer, and Richard E.

Miller advocate resisting the seduction of traditional disciplinary trappings in favor of the potential inherent in working with students and working to improve the conditions for teaching and learning.[4]

In response to the initial question that Hartzog posed and that we have pursued, "Is it possible to do substantial work in this field—and earn traditional academic rewards for that work?" (x) the answer seem to be "It depends." At Syracuse several professionals are indeed reaping traditional academic rewards—tenure, promotion, graduate programs and courses—but in many other places, such as Harvard, they are not, which in itself might not be a bad thing, according to Spellmeyer and Miller. If the university is changing, as many people argue, focusing on traditional academic rewards may not best serve compositionists or their students.

NOTES

1. We are most interested in the administrative structures of writing programs at these institutions. In her "Administrative Structures" chapter, Hartzog reports that four universities, out of the forty-one who responded to her question about the administrative home of English composition, had independent writing programs: (1) Harvard University's Program in Expository Writing, (2) the University of Minnesota's Program in Composition and Communication on the Minneapolis campus and the Department of Rhetoric on the St. Paul campus, (3) Massachusetts Institute of Technology's Writing Program, and 4) the University of Southern California's Freshman Writing Program (14). She also noted that the University of Texas at Austin had just formed the Division of Rhetoric, which split the writing program from the English department, but, as Hartzog explains, they did not participate in her study. She also noted that there were many programs not housed within English departments. For example, at the University of California, San Diego, independent writing programs exist in each of the university's four residential colleges (14). At twelve institutions, including the University of California-Berkeley, Michigan State, the University of Iowa, and the University of Nebraska-Lincoln, more than one unit was responsible for coordinating composition (15). Over twenty universities, however, identified the English department as the unit responsible for instruction in composition, with great variation in the structures of these programs (14).

2.　Although we are pleased with the response rate, we realize that mitigating factors may have decreased the number of responses we received: (1) We were not always sure to whom the survey should be sent. Because writing program structures vary greatly from institution to institution and because a writing program's administration can change from year to year, we often could not find a name associated with the writing program through a university catalog or website. In these cases, we sent survey questions to the chair of the English department, the director of the campus writing center, or the head of the arts and sciences (or humanities) division—whoever *seemed* to be someone who either administered writing courses or worked closely with the writing program director. (2) Although email is an efficient and inexpensive method of administering a survey, it may not yield as strong a response rate as telephone surveys or even mass mailings. (3) WPAs or department chairs may choose not to participate in such a study for fear of being identified in an article that portrays their schools or writing programs in a negative light. (4) It is certainly not our intention to point out "bad models" of writing programs or critique structures or curricula in place at specific universities, but the people who received our email inquiry may have felt some anxiety about releasing information about their program to researchers they did not know personally. As the results of our survey indicate, the WPAs at some universities are untenured or not on the tenure track. Therefore, they may be especially concerned about participating in a survey without knowing exactly how the results would be used.

3.　Kitzhaber argued that although Eliot did succeed in making English the language of learning, Harvard's composition program—and more specifically A. S. Hill—overall had a negative influence on writing instruction during the nineteenth and early twentieth centuries. Kitzhaber, Donald Stewart, and other historians conclude that Harvard's program and its people reduced writing instruction to a concern for mechanical and superficial correctness promoting a fixation with error, dissociated writing instruction from the meaningful social context, and contributed to the split between composition and literature and the subsequent privileging of literary scholarship and teaching.

4.　Of course, all of these are speaking from a position of privilege as tenured faulty—or in the case of Sledd, emeritus faculty—at prestigious research universities; this fact does not discount their arguments, but does need to be acknowledged.

APPENDIX A

Survey Questions

1. What unit (or units) directs or administers most of the writing classes on your campus?

2. List all the courses and programs administered by this unit and the approximate number of sections taught of each per academic year.

3. Who administers the unit and what is his or her academic degree, area(s) of expertise and professional rank? If tenured, what department is the administrator(s) tenured in?

4. What is the administrative structure of this unit? Is it a department, program, interdisciplinary center, or some other kind of unit?

5. Who teaches most of the courses within that unit (TAs, adjuncts, full-time instructors, tenure-track faculty)? What kind of preparation/education do those teachers have or receive?
   Who makes decisions about hiring and teaching assignments?

6. What is the mission or philosophy of your writing program?

7. Who (or what university agency) does the unit report to?

8. Who allocates the funding for the unit and who controls the budget?

9. If your writing program is a stand-alone unit (not part of another academic unit), how long has it been independent?
   Why is it a stand-alone unit?
   What factors have influenced the development of this unit's administrative and operating structure?

10. Name, title, and email address of person completing this survey.

11. Would you be willing to participate in a follow-up phone interview? If so, please include your telephone number.

Thank you for your cooperation.

APPENDIX B

List of the members of the Association of American Universities

Brandeis University
Brown University
California Institute of Technology
Carnegie Mellon University
Case Western Reserve University
The Catholic University of America
Columbia University
Cornell University
Duke University
Emory University
Harvard University
Indiana University
Iowa State University
The Johns Hopkins University
Massachusetts Institute of Technology
McGill University
Michigan State University
New York University
Northwestern University
The Ohio State University
The Pennsylvania State University
Princeton University
Purdue University
Rice University
Rutgers, The State University of New Jersey
Stanford University
Syracuse University
Tulane University
University of Arizona
University at Buffalo-State University of New York
University of California, Berkeley

University of California, Davis
University of California, Irvine
University of California, Los Angeles
University of California, San Diego
University of California, Santa Barbara
University of Chicago
University of Colorado, Boulder
University of Florida
University of Illinois, Urbana-Champaign
University of Iowa
University of Kansas
University of Maryland, College Park
University of Michigan
University of Minnesota, Twin Cities
University of Missouri, Columbia
University of Nebraska, Lincoln
University of North Carolina, Chapel Hill
University of Oregon
University of Pennsylvania
University of Pittsburgh
University of Rochester
University of Southern California
University of Texas, Austin
University of Toronto
University of Virginia
University of Washington
The University of Wisconsin, Madison
Vanderbilt University
Washington University in St. Louis
Yale University

12

WAGERING TENURE BY SIGNING ON WITH INDEPENDENT WRITING PROGRAMS

Angela Crow

Subject: Job Opportunity
Date: Dec 1, 2000
From: Bill Condon
To: Writing Program Administration List

Victor Villanueva (my Department Chair) asked me to post this notice:

Imagine being a specialist in composition studies and rhetoric where your chair and your dean are also comp and rhet folks, where there's a writing-programs administrator who handles WAC and assessment and writing center concerns so that the Director of Composition doesn't have to, where there's a separate administrator, also rhet and comp, who handles cutting-edge digital equipment, with programs that include 3D animation. Imagine being a junior professor but pretty close to tenure time and knowing that a third of the department's faculty are rhet and comp folks, that there are four full professors in rhet and compn within that third. And imagine that when you go up for tenure, you're at a research university where teaching really counts, where collaborative work is valued, as is work with technology. Then imagine dissertations on The Rhetoric of Removal: The Case of the Cherokee or The Political Economy of Language, Land, and the Body or The Rhetoric of Race Representation on the Web.

Well, none of this is a fantasy. It's Washington State University.

Villanueva's ad seduces. To a composition scholar, working collaboratively and focused on technology, such an ad suggests a fantasyland worth visiting, particularly given the familiar histories unspoken within this ad—the devaluation of composition labor within traditional literature departments (e.g., Anson in this collection). The ad works because Villanueva plays on fears and desires: the fear that one's labor will not be valued because of the differences between composition and literature scholarship and the desire to land in the midst of composition faculty who celebrate and explore the possibilities for composition research and teaching. Who wouldn't want to examine the role identity plays in rhetoric (or one's own version of fantasy dissertations)? Who wouldn't want a faculty sympathetic to one's labor, a structure of upper administration and colleagues who both understand and support collaborative labor and, perhaps more importantly, understand what composition and rhetoric scholars study? And who wouldn't hope to land where administrative labor will be valued, supported, and clearly demarcated? Why not stack the deck in favor of composition? Tenure concerns are shaped by the ways one's labor will be valued and supported with resources, by the kind of labor one will be encouraged to explore, by the other faculty members' perceptions of one's work, and by the systemic support for endeavors, particularly when one is called on to participate in administrative roles that require sophisticated awareness, analysis, and interpretation of discipline-specific scholarship.

The question, for the purposes of this collection, is why one would choose Villanueva's land over a position within an independent writing department? The unspoken aspect of Villanueva's ad, that one is still within an English department, where numbers of full professors still can outvote the numbers of senior composition faculty, remains an issue for those of us who seek the panacea Villanueva describes. The positive aspects of independent writing departments could easily be the fodder for an ad that would compete with Villanueva's. Dan Royer and Roger Gilles could describe a department comprised of teachers who value first-year writing courses. Or technical and professional faculty might be seduced by Louise Rehling's narrative of being outside the gaze and influence of the traditional English department. Aronson and Hansen might emphasize the opportunities they have to shape other institutional affiliations as a result of their independent status. However, as Hindman suggests, along with Turner and Kearns, the institutional structure isn't necessarily set up to accommodate change, and one is often engaged in time-consuming public relations and document production not typically required within an established department. Or the political and economic factors of university education may shape administration decisions despite composition theory to the contrary and regardless of the impact on students, as Anson's text reveals. In addition, "family" systems are not necessarily erased simply because structural divisions have taken place, as Agnew and Dallas's essay indicates.

But these are programs that are, for the most part, in their infancy, and perhaps the wager is greatest in such a location.

Given the positive and negative realities, which is the better gig? An independent writing program in its infancy or a English department with an increasingly strong composition and rhetoric voice? The answer depends on many factors, not the least of which is each individual's ways of making sense of the relationship between literature and composition/rhetoric. The reality is that few panaceas exist for composition faculty. As O'Neill and Schendel demonstrate, the wager also must take into account the actual system in place for addressing first-year and vertical courses, and many institutions have addressed composition concerns with a service mentality that leaves scholars in the field in precarious employment positions. Nonetheless, if a colleague or a graduate student is weighing the option of wagering tenure in the departments discussed in this collection, what kind of counsel should we give? This is a complicated location for response. What these various programs demonstrate is that the process of establishing an independent writing program/department/center is largely dependent on the location and its institutional history, and might have much to do with the ways institutions address local contexts in building the structures for change. In terms of addressing the instruction of composition, Royer and Gilles tell a vastly different story than Agnew and Dallas. Maid's and Rehling's experiences also reveal how central systemic structures are to the battle for tenure and promotion. While these programs have many similarities, the political climate of each institution affects the degree to which one should wager tenure in a particular location. For all of us, the hiring process is, to some degree, a crapshoot, but in this text, I hope to suggest some of the factors one might consider in the tenure wager within an independent writing program.

SITUATING THE WAGER WITHIN TENURE LITERATURE

No wager is ever a "sure bet" because multiple challenges are at play in each institution. In general, advice to new tenure-track hires includes the suggestion that one expect a time of adjustment, that one be sensitive to the issues and values of senior faculty, and that one anticipate a time of socialization (Schoenfield and Magnum 37–38). In high-consensus fields such as chemistry and physics, fields in which participants share "theoretical orientations," similar research methods, and "importance of various research questions to the advancement of the discipline"

(Braxton and Berger 244), faculty may have less difficulty adjusting. In low-consensus fields adjustment may be more difficult. Because of the diversity in our field, we are a low-consensus environment in which composition scholars likely face competing and perhaps disparate messages about what "matters." Gebhardt, for example, points to the "diversity of scholarly approaches"(4), and that is but one area of contention for our discipline. The high-consensus/low-consensus split is made more difficult because composition and rhetoric faculty have been housed in literature departments, where disparate values are even more marked; as Anson argues in this volume, within traditional English departments, "historical tensions between the two areas continued to grow as composition became an increasingly independent and interdisciplinary field" (158).

When we enter specific institutions, we face the additional task of local socialization. Experts suggest that tensions occur when an entering colleague has more allegiances to "cosmopolitan" issues than to "local" issues: "Those faculty more committed to their discipline than to the institution are described as cosmopolitans, whereas faculty committed to the institution are described as locals" (Tierney and Rhoads 17). In the socialization process, the focus may include an expectation that the gaze shift from disciplinary issues to local institutional issues. Such an expectation can be particularly complicated if one is in the midst of attempting to establish an independent writing department, one that reflects discipline-specific expectations that directly conflict with institutional level traditions for the teaching of writing. In addition to socialization to the local environment, sources suggest that for many, the adjustments from graduate students to faculty, with accompanying increases in teaching load, scholarship, and service make for difficult shifts. As Robert J. Menges indicates, "junior faculty feel tremendous pressure from obligations that compete for their time and energy" (20).

While these general issues affect faculty across disciplines, compositionists also are usually warned about additional concerns. Expectations for publication can be difficult, access to resources and mentoring may not be available because of the relative newness of the discipline, the tepid enthusiasm some literature faculty have for composition can be a concern, specific gender-based issues (Enos) and attitudes towards technology are frequently delineated as potential areas of conflict (Lang, Walker, and Dorwick). While strategies for and warnings about gaining tenure and promotion are the subject of publications within our field, those conversations are repeated in the larger discussions of tenure and promotion designed for faculty who suddenly find themselves on tenure and promotion committees within their college. Those kinds of sources argue that academic traditions of tenure and promotion have created universities that are profoundly conservative and slow to change (Schoenfield and Magnum). New disciplines face particular challenges (Diamond) and need to be particularly careful about articulating clearly and fairly the tenure guidelines (Richard I. Miller). The main point for composition studies or for new departments of writing is that tenure and promotion committees outside the new discipline should be familiarized with the complications peculiar to new disciplines.

While we may want to make sure that tenure and promotion committees are aware of our concerns (whether in an independent writing department or within a literature department as compositionists), we also must examine our assumptions and perspectives on what we think tenure signifies. Tenure seems designed to accomplish two agendas—academic freedom and economic considerations. Tenure protects and encourages alternative scholarship that helps us rethink dominant ways of seeing and creates the possibility that we, scholars and citizens in the world, might live more ethically aware/appropriate lives as a result of our research. The American Association of University Professors (AAUP) 1940 Statement of Principles argued that "the common good depends upon the free search for truth and its free exposition." While we certainly want people to question "accepted theories" and "widely held beliefs" (Malchup 23), the game of tenure is not an "anything goes" set of principles. In the AAUP 1970 interpretation of the 1940 Statement of Principles, cautions and limitations were articulated. Teachers could not, for example, expect academic freedom to protect them "when persistently intruding material" that had no relation to their subject was a part of their courses. However, AAUP differentiates between "persistently intruding material" and controversy: "The intent of this statement is not to discourage what is 'controversial.' Controversy is at the heart of the free academic inquiry which the entire statement is designed to foster." Nonetheless, in the current climate, tenure will not necessarily create an armor against controversy; tenure, however, at the very minimum ensures us due process (Van Alstyne), and in this economy, that may be all we can expect.

Second, tenure is founded on economic motivations. In its statement, AAUP cites academic freedom, but they also indicate that tenure gives "a sufficient degree of economic security to make the profession attractive to men and women of ability." Tenure and promotion guidelines sway in response to the changing structures of university funding and sway as a result of market needs. Several authors have marked the changes in university structure and financing that have occurred due to shifts in government funding (Soley). Any discussion of tenure must assess both the institution's strategies for funding and the individual market value of various degrees. In tenure discussions, we may be reticent to articulate job security based on market forces, but the traditions indicate that economic factors play a role in the university tradition of tenure. The troubling and complicated issue for us within the university is how much economics plays a role. One has only to look at the ways salaries are driven by market conditions to know that bottom-line decisions are affected by economic considerations. For literature and composition faculty who know that compositionists currently are more marketable, the question of market force and appropriate responses to it in the tenure and promotion process are crucial. How do departments negotiate uneven standards for tenure and promotion that reflect market-driven demands, particularly if department traditions include an uneasiness regarding the articulation of capitalist ideologies driving university decisions and particularly if that which has traditionally been seen as "women's work" (i.e., compositionist's labor) suddenly has more market value?

Finally, tenure guidelines are within the purview of the individual institution to establish and to modify as its aims and missions inevitably shift. Each institution chooses people for tenure that it believes are a good fit at a particular time in history. As the institution of the university undergoes profound changes, the decisions about tenure made prior to shifts and changes in universities create tensions about what kinds of people are best suited for its new directions. The awarding of tenure, then, reflects shifts and trends that universities take and reflects sources for income with which to maintain and develop programs. Academic freedom, in the midst of private and public funding, becomes articulated by institutions that serve multiple constituencies. Perhaps like donations to campaigns, we can worry over academic freedom when our primary contributors hold ideologies contrary or even repugnant to our own. Certainly, the game of tenure becomes more tenuous in late capitalism, where traditions of long employer/employee experiences are no longer the norm, as the rise of post-tenure suggests.

Given the current struggles for tenure within the field of composition and given the current climate for tenure and promotion more generally within the university, one might assume that counsel would be difficult, at best. Nonetheless, if we want to counsel someone new on the market or new to the concept of an independent writing program, given all of the issues and complications associated with tenure and promotion, what would be appropriate strategies for surviving and gaining tenure and promotion? Suppose, for example, that a graduate student receives several offers and is trying to imagine having a career in Villanueva's land or in an independent writing department/program/center. How might we counsel that colleague? For either job, what questions would we suggest the person ask? What concerns would we raise? Given the stories in the first section of this collection and the issues raised in the second section, some obvious questions emerge; and this text attempts to address some of the factors that can help an individual know the risks, so that a decision to sign on with an independent writing department fits with his or her comfort level for the inevitable gamble that we all face in taking positions, particularly when deciding on an independent writing program. In addition, because we are in a tight labor market, this text implicitly suggests concerns for departments, chairs, deans, provosts, and presidents who wish to support independent writing programs, namely the agenda of clearly articulating and valuing the labor that goes beyond the auspices of service and is not comparable to the experiences junior or senior faculty encounter in other departments within the college. What follows are three areas for candidates to assess when considering a position with an independent writing program, with my own experience at Georgia Southern University as one example.

GENERAL CLIMATE ISSUES

We wager at the institutional and state level in terms of the possible ways that politics will play, but we should also try to get a sense of the local politics. At the college level, we need to gather a sense of the dean and his or her ability to negotiate effectively for liberal arts interests. When focusing on the dean, we want to see what kinds of departments are most treasured and what kinds of strategies the dean employs to gather resources for departments and individuals interested in developing and maintaining talents. But we also want to know how effectively the dean meets the challenges of diversity within the faculty and student body and diversity in terms of the kinds of programs he or she encourages. Centering on the dean allows for certain issues to come into focus, from faculty and student retention to innovative program design and rates of success with funding. For general climate issues, that gaze should not only focus in on the dean, but should also look to broader and more narrow factors. In terms of general climate issues, the following areas should be explored:

- institutional and college histories/structures and strategic plans
- department histories and consensus about its mission statement
- department positions on composition studies
- available resources and commitment to maintaining faculty development
- numbers of composition scholars available to share administrative responsibilities
- numbers of composition scholars and availability of desired courses
- department positions on identity politics

Each of these factors may not be available within the typical scan of a department, college, or university website, but asking specific questions about these issues can give the candidate a better sense of the risks involved.

GEORGIA SOUTHERN UNIVERSITY AND GENERAL CLIMATE QUESTIONS

When I took the job at GSU in 1998, the president was acting, and it appeared that a different president would be hired. As someone who was not familiar with the Georgia University System, I looked for information about the way the structure worked and tried to guess what might occur with the change in leadership. It was a wager, but it seemed that the institution was changing, and likely in ways that were familiar and positive, so at the large levels, the climate seemed promising. At the level of general climate, I made certain wagers based on the trends of other universities in Georgia and based on the chancellor in charge of the Georgia University System, a man who recently argued eloquently for the need to fund education, to go against the national trend of dumbing down. Those wagers were profitable. We have a new president and a new provost, both of whom have significantly changed university structures and procedures. At the dean's level, I was most concerned about the likelihood of the department actually having a major, and all indications pointed to support of the department doing more than first-year writing courses. The hiring of tenure-track composition specialists also indicated that commitment. I was hired, along with another composition specialist, and the total number of composition and rhetoric specialists in the department then was six. In my first year, three additional composition specialists were hired, bringing our total numbers to nine. The difficulty, and the wager, has come in the dean's decision to take another position at another university. We have taken two years to secure a dean, and in that time, we have experienced the profound effects of limbo. In the last year, many of the family systems in place have been disrupted as members of the upper administration have chosen to gain employment elsewhere or to step down from their positions of authority. While we understand and support the university's newly adopted strategic plan, we're not quite sure whether the new provost understands our department and supports the former dean and former provost's desire to see a major in our field. We hope; however, indications are not yet clear.

It's possible that within the next months, all of the major institutional shifts in higher administration will settle, and we can begin to really see the shape that this institution will take. It is an institution in profound change. Values are shifting, and top administrators under the former president are resigning or changing jobs within the university, making systemic change possible. When I first came here, for example, faculty with master's degrees could have tenure-track lines and could gain tenure but be ineligible for promotion. That policy has been eradicated. The university plans to hire only faculty with terminal degrees. The new president is taking the university from a regional to a comprehensive university, so issues of scholarship are shifting, values for teaching are changing, ways of funding are reflecting trends across the nation, and in some ways, Georgia Southern is becoming the kind of university that I find familiar. We all face the gamble that a university will change profoundly, and not necessarily in directions we admire. None of us know when the university president will decide to seek another position. Nonetheless, in our department, we still have significant climate questions that are unanswered to this date because of the radical changes in upper administration.

At this institution, the risks were pretty high for someone entering the independent writing department. The college histories and structures were undergoing change; the strategic plans were up for review. In the college and in the department, there were histories that would impact consensus (as Agnew and Dallas indicate in their essay), and the local department had conflicting positions on composition studies. However, the general climate indicated that there were resources for some kinds of faculty development, and there were enough composition faculty that a composition specialist would not need to participate in administrative duties prior to tenure. In addition, the department has a passionate leader with a vision, one that I found palatable, so it seemed a wager worth making, despite the tenuous issues.

With general climate questions, I've come to think that it can be the site of the most and the least stability. In some ways, we can predict generally, from what trends we watch across the nation, the relative stability of institutions—and we can see patterns for how composition scholars will be treated. However, the change in presidents can have a rapid and profound impact on the institution. Because of the chancellor in Georgia and his leadership style, we see institutional patterns shifting. At the same time, the chancellor may not stay in Georgia, and a change in leadership at that level would radically impact the local terrain. One makes one's wagers—especially in regions where systems can easily be changed. The positive aspects of independent writing programs are clear: one may gain in salary, institutional design, rearticulation of one's field. The negative aspects are also clear: one may lose out on the predictability associated with unionized lands or established departments, which brings up the next area of concern: how one's labor will be rewarded.

LABOR ISSUES

Composition faculty always must be careful to negotiate labor concerns for tenure and promotion, particularly when a good portion of their efforts will include administrative work. In traditional literature departments, especially ones that have limited numbers of composition colleagues, one must be careful to establish the boundaries of one's labor so that tenure and promotion are possible. The same is true for independent writing programs in their infancy, though the labor may not be administrative, as much as it is "start-up" work in a new department. While we may enthusiastically counsel a colleague to consider a position in an independent writing department where the following issues are clearly articulated and will be valued at tenure and promotion, we should also consider the complications of re-entering the job market. If the local institution decides to grant value to documents and labor in nontraditional ways, that value may not transfer. Many of the issues for a department in its infancy should be negotiated, including considerations such as these.

- Expectations for creation (or radically shifting the focus) of a first-year writing program, which can be compromised by the following variables:

- The population that teaches first-year writing and possible complications based on the local population of workers
- Training of the first-year writing faculty
- The voice first-year writing faculty have in program development
- The degree to which collaboratively produced program outcomes will be considered publications in terms of scholarship,
- Histories of the department's formation and potential labor to resolve existing tensions and conflicts.
  - Who made the decision, how were faculty placed in different departments, are people happy with their placement? How do the literature faculty perceive the split?
- Interdepartmental alliances/education (whether through writing-across-the-curriculum [WAC] or other initiatives, whether through sitting on external committees or consulting as a form of public relations).
  - Can documents produced in these interdisciplinary alliance-building activities be seen as publications?
- Document creation or reformulation for new major(s).
  - Can the documents be counted towards scholarship?
- Marketing and recruitment.
  - Can documents and success in attracting students count in the tenure and promotion criteria?

Each of these labor issues has an impact on the viability of a wager. The odds are not good for a candidate if most of these issues are not established. If, in fact, a candidate chooses to make the wager despite these odds, then that person should negotiate at the time of hire for clear articulation of how these particular elements will be valued. A savvy participant will ask to mark labor in familiar terms. Perhaps the different documents/negotiations can be placed under the auspices of administrative labels; perhaps some of the material production can be marked under publishing and scholarship, but a newly formed department must consider the labor and provide incentives to those who choose this wager.

GEORGIA SOUTHERN UNIVERSITY AND LABOR ISSUES

The more one can gather a sense of the history of the institution, the college, and the department, the better. If I had known some of the histories at Georgia Southern with regards to composition faculty, I think I would have been in a better position to understand my wager. The split at this particular university, as Dallas and Agnew have indicated, was not amicable. Faculty did not make the final decisions, and the department did not share a mission when I arrived; nor did I realize many of the structural complications that would affect our ability to become a department with a major. In retrospect, I don't think I could have known how to ask questions that only later became apparent. For example, I was naive to the ways that structures outside the norm of the university would undermine the department. We had a structure in place that doesn't happen in universities often: a large number of faculty were joint appointees, serving in our department and in the learning support department. What I've learned, in looking back, is that the more the structure is dissimilar within the university, the more cautious I would be because the wager is significant.

Ironically, one of the reasons I really liked Georgia Southern initially was because teachers of writing had full-time jobs, and they were able to gain tenure with a master's degree. We were able to have these full-time opportunities, in part because of the joint-appointee option. I believe in job security, in treating people with dignity, which includes a living wage and benefits. However, I hadn't thought about the implications of a large number of tenured faculty whose training was predominantly in literature and whose allegiances were sometimes with the literature department, sometimes with the learning support program, and who didn't necessarily welcome the split of the two departments. Many of us, trained in composition and rhetoric and in writing program administration, have learned how to negotiate with other composition teachers using strategies that are based on the reality that these teachers are without substantial job security. While composition scholars may want to advocate for decent living conditions for colleagues who predominantly teach composition, I think many composition scholars have enjoyed the ease with which program change can occur because the dominant group teaching composition are graduate students and adjunct labor. If one is expected to help shape a program, the population who teaches the first-year program is crucial to assess because it impacts the program's development and, by extension, the amount of unmarked time one must contribute to the creation of documents. At our institution, program development includes many people who have tenure are not necessarily interested in shifting those positions, again as Agnew and Dallas indicate in their essay. These negotiations, and the time they take, have implications for program development and also for tenure and promotion.

In addition to considering the relation of the labor pool to the program's development, the other issue that we often consider is the degree to which we will have administrative duties prior to tenure and promotion. One of the best reasons to consider Georgia Southern, for me, was that it allowed me time without administrative duties, where I could focus on my own research concerns. There are enough composition specialists here to share administrative tasks. While that concern loomed large in my initial consideration, in retrospect, having administrative tasks might have been wiser because that kind of marking will travel from institution to institution. Here much of the labor remains unmarked; for example, the work of negotiating for programmatic change that will aid in the formation of an excellent writing program cannot be tallied in ways important for tenure and promotion.

Labor questions are crucial, and as independent writing programs were not something that we discussed extensively in graduate school, I didn't think to ask particular questions that are now always in my consciousness as I prepare for tenure and promotion. If one is expected to contribute to the shaping of the first-year writing program not only in terms of lending expertise but also in terms of debating issues with faculty who may be resistant to changes that would more adequately reflect trends and issues in the field, I think there has to be some way to document that labor beyond the service category (because service remains a substantially less valued component of the evaluation process and ever more so as the university changes). In addition, complications emerge when junior colleagues with Ph.D.'s in composition and rhetoric are put in the role of advising faculty who see themselves as having seniority because they have gained tenure (with master's degrees in literature).

At Georgia Southern, I have come to believe that we cannot have a valuable major if we don't have the first-year program working in smart directions. At the same time, as we shape our major, I have started to realize the extremely time-consuming aspects of creating a degree that I had not imagined. As a new person, I should have asked the following questions: How much will I be expected to contribute to the shaping of a major, and what kinds of recompense would be given? How much public relations material needs to be created? How much work needs to be done between departments to establish alliances? Will the document created count for scholarship? How will research for the document be rewarded? Ironically, this work currently counts as service, but if one's expertise is needed to create the proposals, to develop the public relations documents, and to argue for alliances, shouldn't the reward be significant when it comes to counting for tenure and promotion? Doesn't this labor benefit the university more concretely than many of my other tasks?

At Georgia Southern, we have worked extensively, as a department, in creating agreed-upon program outcomes. Much of the labor for the first-year program remains unmarked. The hours spent in discussion/conversation with colleagues, the debates, the attempts to create meaning when words signify differently based on disparate training—all that labor remains outside the gaze of the documents one brings to tenure and promotion. In the last eight months, we have created a program proposal for a major in professional and technical writing. That labor requires not only providing expertise but communicating with others not familiar with the field, in ways that create consensus about possible directions for the shaping of the major within the department and college. While a document is created, in the current scheme of tenure and promotion criteria, its "publication" will count only towards service. Finally, in the creation of that major, it became apparent that we needed to work on alliances both within our college and within the university. Those kinds of negotiations are extremely time-consuming and are crucial for the success of the program but won't be worth much when it comes to tenure and promotion. While each of these issues could just be abandoned, the problem for many independent writing programs, in the formative stages, is that hiring often happens at the junior colleague level, and the tasks would be more easily negotiated by senior faculty. However, the catch-22 is that if one decides to focus on tenure and promotion to the exclusion of the department needs, when tenure and promotion are achieved, there really wouldn't be a point in staying; however, if one attends to the first-year program, the public relations, and the major, one risks tenure and promotion on two fronts: first, the kind of scholarship required may suffer, and second, one risks the animosity of faculty who vote on tenure and promotion. I don't think I would argue against signing on with an independent writing program, but I do think that we need to prepare graduate students (and junior and senior faculty) in negotiation, in the art of gathering promises about how labor will be rewarded prior to signing on.

EVALUATION OF LABOR ISSUES

In independent writing programs, particularly in their infancy, many documents must be created, and many issues must be explored and discussed, including establishing the guidelines for tenure and promotion.

The process of determining criteria is incredibly political, as it shapes the direction a department takes; and if criteria are not in place, a person would be wise to ask not only about procedures for establishing criteria but also to find out who will have a vote in the criteria. The degree to which an independent writing department can create a new direction may depend on the population of voting members, who may or may not want to shape a program in directions that are promising simply because a department is independent of the traditional literature department. A colleague, considering the possibility of taking such a position, should evaluate the following issues:

- What are the existing criteria and potential alterations to criteria used to evaluate tenure and promotion?
- Who votes on tenure and promotion?
- What are their qualifications to assess credentials?
- What will the tenure and promotion committee understand about composition as a discipline?

A candidate should never assume that he or she knows the answers to these questions, and it's best to have not only existing criteria in mind, but signals from upper administration. In addition, terms should be defined, particularly what is meant by tenure and whether tenure is separate from promotion or whether promotion is implied in a discussion about tenure.

GEORGIA SOUTHERN AND EVALUATION OF LABOR

Some scholars who write about tenure and promotion point to the frustration that can occur for a junior colleague, trained by the research university but then placed in a teaching institution (Braxton and Berger; Tierney and Rhoads). I think my own training at a research institution precluded questions that I should have asked when interviewing at Georgia Southern. While I asked the question about what criteria will be used to evaluate tenure, I assumed that tenure and promotion were joined together. The assumption came from the traditions of my graduate education. Faculty who were tenured were also promoted. The two went together for all the professors I watched encountering the process. I didn't think to ask the question differently. When I asked what I needed to publish for tenure, the answer was a minimal requirement. For promotion, however, the publications required are more substantial.

The other question that I should have asked, and one that might have revealed an issue I would have considered more carefully, runs as follows: "Who will vote on my tenure and promotion? What are their qualifications to assess my credentials? And what will the tenure and promotion committee understand about composition as a discipline?" It never occurred to me to ask who would vote on my tenure because I had the paradigm of junior and senior faculty in my head, and only senior faculty would vote on such matters. At Georgia Southern, all the faculty with tenure can vote on my tenure, regardless of whether the individuals with tenure can be promoted and regardless of the credentials of the participants. I could have figured out, from books in the field, that the tenure and promotion committee was likely not to know much about my field, but I should have asked.

I've learned, from being in this kind of department, that one needs to assess the department one enters in terms of its ability to mirror other departments. In our department, I've already mentioned the contingent of faculty who were, until this year, joint appointees. That paradigm doesn't often exist within the university system. Second, the majority of tenured faculty in our department cannot be promoted. These colleagues do not consider themselves junior faculty despite the fact that, across the university, they are seen as junior colleagues. They also vote on tenure and promotion issues. This paradigm likewise doesn't often exist within the university structure. The concept of junior and senior faculty may not be the issue that a person needs to consider when wagering tenure with an independent writing program, but one needs to be able to assess the departmental structure by comparing it to institution and university traditions and determining similarities and differences. The more one understands the differences one finds, the more accurate the sense of the odds.

Tenure is always a wager, and one hopes that a fit exists between the individual and the community, but composition traditions complicate the ability to wager tenure. Given the general climates, the kinds of labor, and the populations who evaluate tenure, I believe that colleagues should counsel a person to ask very specific questions of independent writing programs, questions that can at least give individuals a better sense of what kind of wager they are making. But I also think that we need to be advocating for composition faculty when they are in the position of creating new departments/programs. Upper administration needs to be cognizant of the labor involved in attempting a new department, and that labor should be rewarded in ways that can travel for the individual. Currently composition scholars can migrate relatively freely, in this market, if their vitae mark their labor. In tight markets, keeping employees means considering methods of maintaining a position's appeal.

Even in markets that are not so tight, administrators want to keep quality employees, and in independent writing programs/departments, upper administration would be wise to create incentives that aid in employee retention. Easy strategies start by negotiating tenure and promotion concerns with the college tenure and promotion committee. Time-consuming work that contributes so much to the local institution should be adequately recompensed at tenure and promotion time; it may mean developing titles that accurately reflect administrative or scholarly duties (currently under the guise of service), thus marking that labor in ways that make it possible for other institutions and the local tenure and promotion committee to understand the work completed. In addition to educating local administrations, we need to discuss, as a field, ways of understanding the labor involved in creating independent writing programs. Then, if one wagers tenure in such an institution but later determines that a better fit exists at another institution, those within the larger field of composition studies can adequately appreciate work that does not easily become marked within the traditionally higher valued categories of scholarship and teaching.

III

The Big Picture

IMPLICATIONS FOR COMPOSITION, ENGLISH STUDIES, AND LITERACY EDUCATION

13

A ROSE BY EVERY OTHER NAME
The Excellent Problem of Independent Writing Programs

Wendy Bishop

Perhaps I shouldn't have started writing about independent writing programs immediately after returning home from a two-hour English department meeting on hiring needs, tenure criteria, and the election of the next year's evaluation committee. My department is staffed at these approximate faculty levels—60 percent literature faculty, 35 percent creative writing faculty, and 5 percent rhetoric/composition faculty—yet offers a Ph.D. and M.A. degree program in *each* concentration.[1] However, I did. I thought about and began writing about such programs using all the essays in this collection at some point, mapping one narrative and argument after the other against my own experiences, my readings in composition and institutional history, and my own academic situation. Quickly, these thoughtful essays became markers and checkpoints in a game of "What If . . . ?"

What if, as a female assistant professor writing program administrator (WPA), instead of choosing an exit option when the First-Year Writing Program (FYW) grew too large for me without adequate institutional support, I had let the program grow *slightly more out of control* and then gone to upper administration with a plan for forming an independent unit? (See Bishop and Crossley.)

What if, as an associate professor in rhetoric and composition, when the first female assistant professor WPA after me[2] was denied tenure (primarily due to lack of department faculty support), I had proposed an independent writing unit?

What if, as a full professor of rhetoric and composition, when the next female assistant professor WPA, who had just seen her predecessor experience the same, was also unfairly denied tenure (this time at the College of Arts and Sciences level), I had proposed an independent writing unit? (See Leverenz.)

What if I had prevailed in the discussions during my ninth through eleventh years at this institution in convincing the department chair that it was essential to support a tenure-line WPA position? If I had done so, might I have been prepared to use the economic strength of the FYW program under the direction of a tenured WPA to help leverage an independent writing unit, something that now seems triply difficult due to the WPA line's staff status?

What if I had done none of those and instead done . . . ?

WHAT IF?

My story is one of trying to remain connected, aligned, a valued part of an English department. But Chris Anson in this collection considers the degree to which housing writing outside the English department seems inevitable:

> Clearly, the question of "why not in English" must always remain local, answered in the context of how receptive literary specialists may be to the principles of contemporary composition theory and instruction or how freely and equitably composition leaders feel they can work within a department populated by colleagues who do not share their expertise or particular values. (161)

At the time any of my own what-if scenarios might have been investigated, I either knew nothing about independent writing programs or only had talked with colleagues who were having initial difficulties beginning theirs (and exhibiting bravery and energy beyond what I've felt I've managed from day to day in my own work). Until 1999 I had not visited such a program. When I did, speaking at the University of Central Arkansas, I greatly admired what I found there—composition and creative writing faculty running a coordinated writing program, teaching together, discussing reading for writers; yet I also felt, well, a continuing discomfort, overall, with the idea of such efforts and what something similar might mean for my institution. As rain wears stone, I've been forced to start thinking differently. But I've been as slow in this change as have those in my English department in their attitudes towards composition studies.

As a former English major and creative writing degree student before I moved into composition, I continued romantically (and no doubt self-servingly) to fight for inclusion and acceptance and—let's face it—admiration within the traditional English department. This was the place where I'd been bred, ignored, hurt, sometimes nurtured, infuriated. This is the place where literary texts still figured, in my limited experience, as the initial stepping-stone toward any further study in the field. In short, I was always (and in one chamber of my heart still am) unable to imagine divorce, no matter how hard the marriage so far had been.

Finally, I can imagine it—change, separation, divorce. However, I fear my own decade-long departmental stance (late-adopter-rebel-who-loved-her-cause-so-much-she-was-unable-to-envision-change) has now made such a decision impossible. I did not explore alternative routes because I'm model-oriented and had no models; because I was unwilling to take on the work of such negotiations and pay the academic prices of such change; and because I was unable to imagine where such actions would land me and the program with which I work. Hubris to imagine it was up to me, but who knows how the what-ifs would have played out. Or still will?

While I may have taken the right steps for my own story—something I'll never know—reading these essays lets me consider the rich complexity of the decisions I made. Just as I did—want to collaborate, change from within, get along—so too (and often to its own disservice) does this field we call rhetoric and composition. "Composition has always acted on its own beliefs in the power of collaboration and collective wisdom. Autonomy, therefore, may be desired only in proportion to the hostility or indifference shown by those who might otherwise be welcomed in" (Anson, this volume, 166). Programmatic initiatives, experiments, narratives, progressions like the ones described in *Field of Dreams* are wonderful "factions," to use anthropologist Clifford Geertz's word for narrated fact-based writing. They offer readers the chance to reverberate, compare/contrast, test the cut of their own programs, calculate, gauge, plan, plot.

A collection like this—reporting on the state of contemporary stand-alone writing units—pools knowledges, adds to the wealth of testimony required to share transformative naturalistic research, each case adding to the next case, each raising cautions and questions, each celebrating possibility for systematic reflection that can lead to productive change. These cases illustrate the benefits of individual and collective decisions, but all the decisions came at a price. Just as we claim in our writing classrooms—that a writer can't write a better draft without learning about the failures of good attempts—so too we can't learn to design better programs without experiencing problems on the road to improvement. *Field of Dreams* offers narratives of tumultuous progress and of needed additional progress.

Reflecting on such progressions, my personal and program list of what-ifs readily begat offspring. Are independent writing programs the inevitable, the desirable future? For individual programs, for composition as a field? Should we continue to move toward the model? How could we? What is gained? What is lost? What is next?

SHOULD WE HAVE . . . ?

For the essayists in this collection, the answer appears to have been a solid yes. Yes, we should have started an independent writing department, center, program, or unit. Daniel Royer and Roger Gilles, argue that curricular and programmatic and disciplinary change should be pursued because a program design, as Royer and Gilles initially experienced it, that forces reluctant English literature faculty to teach first-year writing is problematic. At the same time, exempting non-composition-trained faculty from such courses allows this majority faction of the faculty to remain at a disciplinary distance from composition. Equally, when rhetoric and composition specialists alone run such a program, often as not they are not "spent" teaching first-year writing. By virtue of these units' small sizes, newness, need to reform and administer, and/or need to produce convincing scholarship, a move from the traditional English department structure often requires that faculty who develop independent writing programs not assign themselves to teaching first-year writing. This pragmatic and no doubt necessary development continues to reproduce an English department hierarchy within composition studies. Literature scholar–administrators are to graduate, part-time, and adjunct writing teachers what writing program leaders must be to the instructors, adjuncts, and campus teaching assistants they hire into their programs—bosses rather than colleagues (though we might try to claim that there are Bosses and then there are Program Directors).

Royer and Gilles highlight another double bind. When departments of "writing" consider forming, it seems natural to suggest uniting all writings: composition, professional, and creative writing. "Clearly, most of the noncomposition faculty preferred not to teach composition, but neither were they eager to see writing faculty take the program and build a new department, especially with the creative writing majors in tow" (this volume, 31). Not only are departments of literature variously loathe to lose creative writing (though a few are eager to eliminate it), but those who teach writing for different purposes (technical, business, creative, journalistic) come from and have allegiances to different historic, academic, and pedagogical traditions. They don't necessarily speak the same language or grow in the same garden. That is, if they are allowed to leave together at all and in good health.

As I've found in my own program, a "separate but unequal" rule generally applies. We are told the concentrations of literature, creative writing, and rhetoric and composition will all get money for speakers, receptions, and so on. We have the freedom to spend "our money" as we wish. But we are not encouraged to pool those programs or monies, and there are separate directors for the first two programs but not for rhetoric and composition because we attract many fewer students since my sole composition colleague and I have found it unethical to recruit until (if ever) our program stabilizes with a minimum of four faculty members or increases beyond that number.

Department policies that encourage writing specialists (creative writing, professional writing, journalism, composition) to remain separate and to compete predict that the minority field like composition is nearly always at a disadvantage, having no numbers to fight the numbers and having, equally, to compete for professional status from a one-down position. Compositionists are deemed "younger" than journalists and creative writers and, compared to literature faculty, are "in trade," as several essays here point out. For other concentrations to join us means they would be combining theory with "practice," and in that combination theory is always assumed to be tainted and harmed, inevitably diluted. Like popular writers compared to academic writers, compositionists *do* something. Popular literature entertains, and often authors of the same make money; both effects are considered suspect in literary and creative writing circles.

Compositionists use their intellect but often in service of action-oriented projects; they too often (unfortunately) do not entertain anyone or make money (except enough to fuel an entire literature curriculum). Worse, compositionists participate in a world populated by educators, anthropologists, computer specialists, folklorists, linguistics, undergraduates, support sites, university administrators, and so on. They strike off across party lines, across class lines; and they fail to communicate primarily (or solely) by the book. Because of this, the field of composition has been misrepresented as anti-intellectual, atheoretical (so much so that we in the field now accuse each other of being the same) and lacking in rigor, ever always already an upstart or nondiscipline, malcontent, and even downright scary. It is not a simple move then to unite all writing instruction, within or without the English department.

HOW DID WE PROCEED . . . ?

Independent writing units—program, center, department—all have merit, but all have thorns. Over sixty programs exist, and more are, no doubt, being planned. Composition is in a new era, and it appears there *are* options:

- Let all faculty choose to (a) truly support integrated English/composition or (b) let the program leave. At Grand Valley State University the program left.
- Firm up and improve an already separate but as yet undefined structure, as at Metropolitan State University.
- Form a graduate and undergraduate professional-writing program with no service component, as at San Francisco State University.
- Like the University of Winnipeg, form a center, not a department, and negotiate the problems inherent in such a program structure.
- Stay separate within the English or communications department *with English faculty support* (I'm assuming that some of the many programs that might have changed in the last decade decided not to, due to a better department response after suggesting such a strategy).
- Separate; join other skills-oriented programs; have few faculty and many adjuncts, as at San Diego State University.
- Make a change, but later have it reversed. At the University of Minnesota, the independent program is returned to the English department while the director of the program is on leave.
- Form a new program, but give up the protection of tenure, as several programs have done and as is discussed in particular in light of the Georgia Southern University program.
- Form a new program by university decree and work around this limitation as at the University of Arkansas at Little Rock and SUNY Stonybrook.
- Form a new program and make (expected) mistakes that may be thoroughly rectified only by applying failures at one site to inform the development of another site, like Arizona State University East.

And so on.

WHAT WAS GAINED?

The first thing that comes to mind is improved program morale. Ultimately, first-year and possibly all undergraduate students who take courses in an independent writing unit may not notice a great deal of change when a program moves from department to independent unit. These sites—particularly at large universities—are often staffed by the same individuals (graduate teaching assistants, adjuncts, term-faculty) who would previously have staffed a program lodged in the English department. Students may notice that they are no longer being taught writing by those who profess literature and who feel underprepared and uninterested in teaching writing. What seems to change is instructor morale due to greater autonomy, of sorts.

Within independent programs, instructors generally have more voice, if not the only voice, in choosing texts and shaping program and course rationales and evaluation. At Hampden-Sydney College, which created a program of rhetoric, including a writing center, the program designers believe that "all graduates . . . shall have demonstrated the ability to write and speak clearly, cogently, and grammatically"; and this is done through "(1) a required course sequence; (2) a program of testing; (3) a writing center for tutorial support; and (4) cross-curricular faculty participation" (Deis et al, this volume, 76). Developments like this may allow trained faculty to reconsider the issue of grammar instruction, and, in this area, university community support may prove easier to gain than was English department support.

The faculty of independent programs also, by name, assert their professionalism, becoming not the "writing concentration" *within* the English department but the "Writing Program" (Center, Department, and so on). Louise Rehling explains, "Of course, our focus and our independence also keep us small, yet we have managed to turn that quality into a virtue, with benefits ranging from staffing flexibility to creating a supportive, networked community for our students" (this volume, 62). Administrator/faculty also receives a greater degree of (or complete) budgetary autonomy, although some of these programs experienced bait and switch along the lines of "Yes, you have autonomy, but your program is so small and new and unknown you only have this much (i.e., not much) of a budget."

While the drawback of the center, support site, undergraduate-only writing unit would seem to be the loss of tenure for incoming faculty (those developing such sites usually retain tenure in their originating department), for those who develop independent writing departments, the move seems to strengthen tenure cases, as happened at Metropolitan State University:

> [T]he structure of independent writing departments works toward resolving some of the professional development and tenure issues that have plagued

composition specialists. In a separate department, faculty have a much greater opportunity to help establish criteria for tenure and promotion that differ from those of English departments. In a practice-oriented field of study, faculty are more likely to be recognized for practice, particularly for writing practice outside of the academy and for teaching practice. (Aronson and Hansen, this volume, 61)

To the degree that tenuring in composition in general continues to be a site of struggle (see Leverenz), it will be wise for us all to watch the variations in the process that do and might occur in stand-alone programs.

WHAT WAS LOST OR CONTINUES TO BE DIFFICULT?

I mentioned earlier that one chamber of my heart still longs to develop or participate in a united English department, stronger for embracing and supporting—not merely absorbing—different areas and knowledge, braiding together writing, reading, linguistics, and folklore (see, for instance, Gerald Graff's *Professing Literature* for a discussion of the ways English studies accepts but does not "digest" challenges to the core curricula). I found this longing for an improved rather than a new model is embedded in the narratives of even the most successful independent programs: "Our experience confirms that the independent department was best for us, in our situation at Grand Valley State University. *Other English departments might have rallied around the first-year course, choosing to recommit to it as a regular part of the job. With a genuine commitment, such an arrangement would likely succeed*" (Royer and Gilles, this volume, 37, emphasis added).

At times, movement from an English department site to an independent site does not "solve" problems, it resituates them. At Metropolitan State, faculty found teaching/administrative loads increased rather than decreased because "the chairs have the double burden of [being] writing program administrator . . . and department chair" (Aronson and Hansen, this volume, 53). And assumptions about the "prestige" of different genres of writing continued at Grand Valley State University, where uniting types of writings allowed for the formation of an independent department because such a combination formed an argument for separation from literature. Still, these faculty members had their own personal and historical vested interests, which, of course, they brought with them to the new unit. "One of the most difficult 'marriages' in our department is that between the most vocational and application-oriented of writing activities—technical communication—and the most creative and impractical of writing activities—poetry, fiction, and other creative genres" (Aronson and Hansen, this volume, 57).

In all the narratives, I detected a not unexpected sense of "damned if you don't, damned if you do." Give up English, fine. Give up tenure, fine. But. . . . And these were exactly the scenarios I had spun out vis-à-vis my own program—the scenarios that made me proceed in my secessionary movement with little speed. For instance, at the University of Winnipeg the discussion over "department" or "center" recasts the practice/service issue. "It did not take us long after separation from the English department to discover just how vulnerable a new academic unit can be, especially when it lacks the prestige of a strong and *known* disciplinary tradition, as is the case with composition and rhetoric (especially in Canadian universities)" (Turner and Kearns, this volume, 93). Without a perceived disciplinary tradition (the reason, perhaps, compositionists so firmly link themselves with rhetoricians), tenuring here proved as difficult as or more difficult than it was within an unsupportive English department.

And, of course, we in composition may tend to forget our own territoriality when working together to stake new territory. Though small in number, we too are prone to academic pettiness (usually big fights over small prizes; or, the smaller the prize, the bigger the fight?). Finally having achieved autonomy and larger faculty numbers (in some cases), there is more at stake, more to imagine we are winning or losing: "As the number of composition/rhetoric specialists grew in our department and discussions about our new mission evolved, this veneer [over ugly feelings] quickly evaporated, as shock waves of discord rippled through the department" (Agnew and Dallas, this volume, 39).

Equally likely, in the secession and separation wars, there are multiple casualties. Barry Maid describes his decision to move from the University of Arkansas at Little Rock where he developed a university-mandated independent writing program over a struggle-filled decade and then left, eager for the renewal offered by the chance to develop a new program in Arizona, based on what he had learned in Arkansas. His is a story of hope renewed, but that is not always the outcome. The journey to a new program design often results in designer alienation, burnout, even dissatisfaction with both the old *and* the new program. At San Diego State, several of these eventualities occurred. "[The Department of Rhetoric and Writing's] first seven years brought several new tenure-track hires. However, several tenured faculty also departed.

In fact, of the original five proponents of the proposal for establishing an independent department, only one remains as an active member of the department, and her appointment fluctuates from zero to .50 FTE, depending on the semester" (Hindman, this volume, 113).

Though not as often discussed in this collection as the issues above, developing an independent program strongly affects graduates and adjuncts who entered under one system and may be worried about exiting under another. These individuals may be excluded from the administrative discussions that impact their present situation and their future undertakings. At Stony Brook, for example, "Graduate students took the criticism of the writing program as our own. We wrote emails discussing our fears about losing our teaching-assistant appointments in composition should the writing program be removed from the English department" (Yood, this volume, 177).

These represent just a few of the many issues that future independent writing programs will want to try to account for in their plans.

WHAT SHOULD, COULD, OR WILL BE NEXT?

As mentioned earlier, I believe that it is inevitable, given the material conditions in English departments across the country, that the programmatic solution of forming an independent writing unit is going to be given regular, serious consideration. This will happen within a newly minted Research I institution, like my own, that is striving hard to measure "excellence" in a manner that will justify a larger, revenue-producing campus population. Such a change places a renewed focus on traditional research over necessary teaching and increases pressures within a literary culture that is at war within its own ranks and that is cohesive primarily in its disdain for writing and praxis of any sort. At other institutions, this will happen within a more convivial department that is lobbying for its first M.A. or Ph.D. program. This will happen at four-year colleges where there is a strong argument for combining "service" programs and support sites into one unit.

What I fear in each scenario is a diminishment of the quality of academic life for those in composition: "leaving that earlier position to accept a post here at SDSU has suited my enthusiasm to work in a more independent writing program. But it definitely did not improve my material labor conditions. On the contrary—it has greatly expanded my administrative tasks and my teaching load and greatly reduced my time for writing and reading" (Hindman, this volume, 114). For me, the big continuing issues of communication and integration remain. I believe that even independent units need the support from English and communications departments, as well as from other departments across the university. Independent units need to be known to be accepted and accepted to be known.

Once again, as seen in the turbulent history of composition, this recognition continues to fail to occur, as at two strong programs studied by Peggy O'Neill and Ellen Schendel. For instance, program director Nancy Sommers at Harvard is not on a tenure line despite being a renowned scholar (such a line would assure a strong measure of tacit and explicit respect at such an institution, not to mention job security). At Syracuse University, a separation from the English department may mean a separation from one's roots or multidisciplinary interests and may create problems for those graduate students with degrees in composition who end up teaching not in stand-alone programs but in more traditional English department structures. O'Neill and Schendel report from personal interviews that

> [Eileen] Schell herself completed her Ph.D. in English with a concentration in rhetoric and composition. She has come to value and enjoy talking with colleagues in literature and theory whose professional interests intersect with hers. As a faculty member in a writing program, she must work harder to maintain those professional ties with members of the English department. As the director of graduate studies, Schell is also concerned that CCR doctoral students may not be completely prepared to work in English departments. (this volume, 204)

Again, this experience does not predict the same will happen at other sites, but it does remind us of some of the losses a person, a program, a department, or a university might expect to incur when redefining structures.

WHAT REMAINS?

These essayists offer detailed program histories, highlight key choices, point to checklists for future program designers, and share profoundly depressing and profoundly transformative experiences. They also point to a great deal of good will, generosity, and hard work done by composition change agents.

Reading this collection, considering my own situation—which all the authors urge their readers to do—I can't help but wonder what college and university size predicts for future independent units. Since the State

of Florida dissolved the statewide board of regents—effective July 2001—
and we enter an era of corporate management, I have to question how
this move will affect each institution's first-year writing program. Had our
program developed into an independent unit, I have many reasons to
assume we would never have been given department status, since department progress is now measured against national rankings and organizations—measures unavailable to composition "departments." What would
the corporate university design mean to that imagined program? Would
it have destroyed it, supported it, complicated it, and/or altered the program's faculty teaching load and production outcomes? Speculations of
this sort lead me to wonder too about the beneficial results of working at
a smaller institution? Might I have felt better prepared to be a change
agent because I had faces I could link to all those involved and a limited
number of faculty and administrators to contact and try to influence?

Early programs now provide documented histories, are growing in
numbers, may be surveyed and turned into case studies and borrowed
from; they can offer the needed touchstones to support those who are
generating new models. They can do this to the degree that they report
their successes *and* failures, while identifying crucial issues, such as fac-
ulty/staff working conditions and assignments to "service" functions.
Such discussions will remind a potential planner like me to ask if I have,
personally, resisted the "service" label for my own programs (as WPA, as
rhetoric and composition faculty) primarily because I intended to seek
tenure and security? Will "service" designations come to matter less, or
will they continue to shape discussions for stage II programs—those that
continue or those developed in a new era, based on past models?

Such discussions will remind a potential planner like me to ask how
English studies discussions of the relationship of theory to practice translate into composition discussions and how those discussions translate
into independent writing unit program discussions? Should they? I don't
know. Do they? I suspect so. The service issues that I mentioned earlier
include the issue of whether service (practice) and scholarship (theory)
are different, even distinctly separate. My own experiences (and my argument for keeping WPAs on tenure lines within the English department)
have made it clear to me that I can't undertake and never have undertaken a practice without systematically thinking about it (theorizing)
ahead of time and that all my practice leads to theorizing and retheoriz-
ing. Scholarly training and discipline teach me how to do both more
effectively and systematically. However, most institutions perpetuate the

notion that there is a deep unbridgeable division between research, service, and teaching (in a way that makes service sound neither theoretical or practical, merely a romantic giveaway to different "publics"). An assignment like mine of 45 percent research, 50 percent teaching, and 5 percent service is a structural delusion. In a daily sense, I do 100 percent of each; in a real sense, I am evaluated 80 percent on research, 19 percent on teaching, and 1 percent on service. How can my university display its status otherwise, because currently no national scales are in place that allow it to be "highly ranked in teaching." And a corporate model mandates such a ranking before an administration feels justified in providing more money for teaching (in pursuit of higher rankings).

Clearly our systems—selves, disciplines, departments, administrations—are slow to evolve. And this is because processes provide few measurable traces of themselves, at least given current accepted measurement devices. I can learn new wisdoms and cultivate a new attitude toward independent writing programs; my department might learn to support me in proposing one; and a program could be put in place, all to be dismantled by corporatization, by a department falling on hard times, by the loss of a key faculty member—who knows, perhaps me—looking for imaginary greener pastures. Then, with Chris Anson, we'd have to observe:

> What strikes me . . . is how easily all the things that have taken so much negotiation, planning, and hard work are dismantled. Perhaps that's one of the differences between administrative effort and scholarly work; one has the impression that one's administrative work is moving the world forward, at least locally and institutionally, but it can be undone in a matter of months. What's left is the *experience* of administration, but the 'product,' unlike scholarship, is gone. (Anson, this volume, 168)

The product of curricular change is regularly lost in English departments. Those seeking change start to feel silly carrying stacks of memos around or holding them for years on email, as Chris Anson was smart enough to do. Curricular documents are valueless unless they are contextualized in a valuable way, and independent writing programs have the best chance of innovating in this area. Certainly only those involved tend to archive and historicize curricular developments (along with a few graduate student historians seeking dissertation subjects), and that is the usefulness of a collection like *Field of Dreams.*

Here is evidence of the "experience" of administration. Such evidence first brought me joy, then depression, now I'm at steady state, sobered, yet somewhat recharged. I fired off a long letter to my department chair talking about how the climate in the English department regarding my program has too long been ignored and claiming I won't let it be so any longer. I've been encouraged to speak up—and plan to do so regularly and forcefully, hoping to shake off an encroaching sense of weariness. Such a reaction is evidence in the power of shared knowledge. The voice I'll speak in will be richer from the thinking and questioning engendered by what-ifs, and I hope will lead to more reasoned "what-abouts." The problems don't go away, but can be better digested. Imaginary gardens with real roses in them. Some programs it seems already have cultivated them.

NOTES

1.   At my institution, we have approximately 120 instructors, adjuncts, and teaching assistants—at least 100 of the latter—directed now by a full-time, nontenure-line, Ph.D. associate in English (twelve-month contract) and a second associate who coordinates the computer classrooms and department writing center and assists the WPA.

2.   I was the second of two assistant professors, my male colleague, a tenured associate professor, who I expect will go up for promotion in the near future, having been hired two years before me to resuscitate a Ph.D. and M.A. program that was already on the books in the 1980s. After that, we hired two female assistant professors, who were qualified for but denied tenure in 1998 and 1999, respectively. During the 2000–2001 academic year, we were again down to two faculty members, as we had been in 1989 when I arrived. We have hired a third female assistant professor with four years toward tenure to begin fall 2001 and have lost our bid to hire a fourth assistant professor, a replacement, to begin fall 2002. For the near future, we are expected to offer a degree program with three rhetoric and composition faculty. In the last four years in the same department, a female literature faculty member was denied tenure, another female African American literature professor was not given a counteroffer and took a position at an historically Black university across town, and a third female literature professor was denied promotion to full professor. To my knowledge, no male candidates have been denied tenure or promotion or lacked for counteroffers in the same time period: hence my emphasis on gender in this narrative.

14

KEEPING (IN) OUR PLACES, KEEPING OUR TWO FACES

Theresa Enos

Reading through the chapters in this collection, I keep thinking how far we've come and how much we've stayed in place since we professed that we do indeed have a discipline, whether we call it rhetoric and composition, composition and rhetoric, rhetoric and writing, or whatever. But in our various namings, I think we have been careful to capture by these yokings our Janus-faced nature.

In a study I did some ten years ago of those who "live" rhetoric and composition, I reported that about twenty percent of the faculty I surveyed made a distinction between *rhetoric* and *composition, rhetoric* being associated with theory and history, with "rigorous scholarship," with graduate programs and courses; *composition,* with "service" courses and the undergraduate curriculum (78). For those who see a distinction between the two terms, rhetoric is the theory that drives practice, more of an intellectual distinction than a programmatic one. Rhetoric draws us into the theoretical and historical study of texts while composition draws us into the theory and practice of the writing process. A number of respondents distinguished the two terms along the lines of intellectual versus personnel/administrative work: rhetoric is theory-driven, and composition is service-oriented. Indeed, the responses mirror the long history of rhetoric with two joined-yet-separate faces: subject and method.

Since the 1960s, we've tried to preserve the conjunction between the two words in light of the ever increasing tendency to surrender to the disjunctive *or.* Because I may be the Romantic Idealist that some have tagged me, I strain always to preserve the linkage of rhetoric and composition because it captures what for 2,500 years rhetoric has been—the oldest of the humanities, a true metadiscipline with both a body of knowledge and a methodology.

Indeed, I recognize my preservationist tendencies here, the tendencies that make me uneasy about separating ourselves from our traditional English department home, however dysfunctional this familiar home may be. We don't need to be told again those old horror stories of both gender and disciplinary bias, of the tenure famine of the 1970s and early 1980s, of the dawning realization that yes, our field is a "feminized" one in terms of salary equity and real power. One needs only to look at the surveys of doctoral programs in rhetoric and composition studies from 1985 to 2000 and the Modern Language Association's *Job Information List* since 1993 to see the growing strength and recognition of rhetoric and composition studies.

And we have made significant progress: in the 1980s doctoral studies in rhetoric/composition grew rapidly; by 2000 such programs are defined by their consolidation, diversification, and maturation. The biggest change in graduate studies has been the interdisciplinary breadth of course work and dissertation areas, leading to a new kind of generalist rather than the specialist that helped define us in the 1990s. The majority of doctoral students in rhetoric/composition are female (70 percent), and this majority will be reflected in faculty positions in the near future. Study and analysis of all these changes can help us write, or rewrite, the future direction of doctoral programs in rhetoric and composition studies. The chapters in this volume will help us all think about future directions, whether it will be more writing programs separating themselves from the traditional home in English studies or whether it will be the majority of us keeping our places—even if it means "keeping in our places."

Because I have no direct experience with independent writing departments, I can respond to this collection only within the framework of the above paragraphs. What the various chapters do make clear to me is that no definitive guidelines exist for creating independent departments of writing. Each independent department or academic unit evolved from particular circumstances such as local politics, funding fights, the ubiquitous gap between literature and composition, part-time labor issues. How an independent writing department is defined differs from institution to institution, each unit being adapted to its particular institution.

What is less clear to me, and more troublesome, is how or if independence would strengthen or weaken the gains we've made in redefining our intellectual work, the kind of scholarship of integration that Ernest Boyer has argued for, which makes connections across the discipline and which places work and knowledge in a larger context of knowledge making. Our discipline has modeled this reconsideration of scholarship, so I am troubled by what I see as the almost total exclusion of rhetoric in independent departments of writing, troubled by what I fear is a regression in the gains we've made in getting tenured, troubled by what might be even more marginalization of the field by even more intense disciplinary and gender bias, troubled by the thought of erosion of our newly achieved solid base of doctoral programs in rhetoric and composition, troubled by a wider gap—real or perceived—between public-supported universities that have large, structured programs of writing remaining in their disciplinary home and independent units with perhaps less political exchange value in the institution at large.

I have no ready answers; I do find myself asking lots of questions in response to my reading of *Field of Dreams*. My questions, reflections, and responses that follow seem all tangled up, connected by major issues about which we've been conversing for years. So the issues themselves are not new, but we may lose precious ground we've managed to gain over the last ten to fifteen years. (When I say that the issues themselves are not new, I recognize that with only a few changes here and there, my comments could be about rhetoric and composition studies housed in English departments, not separate departments of writing.)

Would continued formation of independent departments of writing create yet another binary analogous to the ever spreading binary between the civic and knowledge-making characteristics of rhetoric and the career-oriented, service-providing characteristics of a narrowly conceived perception of "composition"?

How is "rhetoric *and* composition studies" being defined through and by the formation of independent departments? Although there is some mention of trying to keep the conjunction *and,* most identify themselves, and the departments, as being defined by composition, not rhetoric. (Some independent departments of *rhetoric,* however, are mentioned, but these references are tangential to the volume as a whole.) With few exceptions, the independent departments offer no "rhetoric" history, theory, praxis, even though they might include "rhetoric" as part of the department name. One unit that is named the "Rhetoric Program" has as its published outcomes/goals "the ability to write and speak clearly, cogently, and grammatically" and its principal elements "a required course sequence," "a program of testing," "a writing center for tutorial support," and "cross-curricular faculty participation." The program is primarily motivated by the "growing national attention to writing and writing pedagogy" (see Deis, Frye, and Weese, this volume). "Composition Studies" is part of this volume's subtitle, and I would argue that in this term, which many of us have adopted as naming our discipline, reside the theory and history of rhetoric; that is, the term *composition studies* evokes praxis in its fullest sense. Most of the independent departments described herein, it seems to me, do not embrace the more inclusive meaning of "rhetoric," but rather "composition" in its narrowest sense of "service"; what is lost is the concept of rhetoric and composition as knowledge making and conscious civic participation.

Will the too narrow focus that most of the independent units describe lead to even more marginalization than we now experience for writing programs housed in traditional English departments? Almost without exception the independent departments are career oriented, offering a curriculum in "academic" writing, business writing, technical writing, scientific writing, expository writing, perhaps journalism, along with the traditional first-year composition curriculum—and possibly creative writing. Most of the independent departments exist without a major (some do have tracks or majors in technical or professional writing); there are no curricula or tracks whereby undergraduates in rhetoric and composition could feed into either M.A. or Ph.D. graduate programs in rhetoric and composition. Thus, too often the writing instructors are seen as "discourse technicians" or "tenured remediators" (see Turner and Kearns, this volume). Such a curriculum seems at odds with what many rhetoric and composition programs are working to put in place: undergraduate tracks in rhetoric and composition that include history, theory, research, and pedagogy—not just text production. I don't think there is another discipline where students can enter its graduate level with no course work in the discipline itself. Yet this is mostly true of rhetoric/composition. Imagine entering graduate studies in literature with not one undergraduate course in literature.

Will independent status exacerbate familiar problems we all face: underfunding (in large part more work being done by fewer faculty under heavy workload/light power conditions, low status, salaries not commensurate with other faculty); our image as mere "service providers"; problems with promotion and tenure (especially over definitions of intellectual work, how administration "counts," and insistence on "traditional" kinds of scholarship); overdependence on adjunct and part-time labor, even though several of the independents draw mostly on a faculty that is permanent non-tenure-track? Maybe working conditions would change over time for faculty in independent departments; it seems to me, however, that the onerous burden of administrative work we all carry seems even heavier for the few ranked faculty in independent units, mostly staffed by adjuncts, teaching assistants (TAs), and/or permanent non-tenure-track faculty.

Will the dependence on permanent non-tenure-track and part-time faculty mean even fewer senior faculty, which would likely lead to further problems in the few tenure-track junior faculty getting tenure, as only, usually, full professors serve as voting members of promotion and tenure committees? In addition, the lack of senior faculty means not only a heavier burden of committee work for junior faculty—both non-tenure- and tenure-track—but also perhaps expanded time lines and constricted progress with committee work.

How might the tenure process be further complicated by a faculty member's unique status in being part of an independent unit housed outside the English department? Some if not most of the independent programs seem outside the institution's promotion and tenure system in that they are outside an established and accepted disciplinary tradition, making the new academic unit and its faculty vulnerable to problems with getting tenure. Of course, there would be the usual problems, such as how to recognize and value much of writing program administration as discipline-based intellectual work, but outside the hard-fought discipline base we now have, the problems most likely would be exacerbated. Many if not most of the essays mention problems with getting tenure—those familiar problems for us old-timers in rhetoric/composition. There's a sense of déjà vu in that some of the hard-fought-for understanding of who we are and what it is we do seem to be the same old fights—but on a new field.

What are the implications of independent programs or departments primarily being housed in small liberal arts colleges and in some four-year universities? With few exceptions, such independent departments are not housed in comprehensive or research universities (see the description of Syracuse's independent department, this volume chapter eleven, for the most cogent exception). This question, of course, is a big one; subsumed in it are many of the other questions I muse over in my response to the fields of dreams, some already built.

How will independent writing programs affect graduate studies in rhetoric and composition? As far as I can tell, only three of the separate departments described in this volume have a graduate program in rhetoric or rhetoric/composition, and, of those three, only one has a doctoral-level program: Syracuse University. Will there be no course work in history and theory of rhetoric (already there is no place or space to present research and scholarship in these areas, it seems, at the annual meeting of the Conference on College Composition and Communication)? Will Ph.D.'s in rhetoric/composition—or "composition specialists" as they'll no doubt be named—be turned out only to become permanent non-tenure-track instructors? At my own university, the rhetoric, composition, and the teaching of English graduate faculty are committed to the stewardship of the composition program. If rhetoric is shorn from composition (some say it's already been shorn), will we be posturing either as those who place themselves within one of the traditions of rhetoric or as those who face themselves toward composition?

A final assertion and another question: We can ask these same questions about writing programs staying *within* English departments. With such an apparent, and final, split between "rhetoric" and "composition" in the way separate departments of writing are formed and in the majority's career-oriented mission, what will be our future place, and face? We can build our fields of dreams, far away from the playing field we've tried so hard to level—and with considerable success—and players will come. But who will lose—or win—the most?

15

MANAGING TO MAKE A DIFFERENCE

Thomas P. Miller

As we grow older and lose the ability to see the immediate world in vibrant detail, many of us are forced to put on bifocals to read and see. Those of us who were nearsighted are left unable to see what's in front of our face as well as things coming at us from a distance. We shift our gaze back and forth across that line between nearsightedness and far-sightedness, creating areas of striking acuity separated by a distorted boundary zone, usually centered on exactly what we are looking at. In popular books and films on academe, and often in our own depart-ments, we have encountered the caricature of the bespectacled profes-sor who abstractly rocks his or her head back and forth to negotiate the discontinuity between the page and the world beyond. The absent-minded professor who looks somewhat askew is a popular image for the sort of myopia that generally befalls professions when left to their own devices. Of course, bifocals can enable us to see our surroundings more clearly, in a sort of divided and distracting way. By making the disconti-nuity between our object of study and field of vision no longer seem quite so natural, bifocals force us to attend to the zone separating near at hand from further afield. As a rhetorician who works in writing pro-gram administration, I believe that such a bifocal perspective has prag-matic value because it can help us reflect on what it means to be farsighted and nearsighted about what we do and the boundaries our profession imposes on what we see.

Writing programs create a rush of daily challenges that can keep us perpetually in a crisis management mode. If we can take the time to look up from the stacks of papers on our desks, we may be able to take a more long-term perspective that can be strategically useful in assessing the positions of writing programs. Some of us have maintained that it is unprofessional to set up an independent writing program without ade-quate research-oriented faculty, because a program comprised of lectur-ers will tend to be defined as merely a service unit. By not making research part of what writing teachers do, such a program undermines the disciplinary standing of composition studies and reinforces the dysfunctional dualism of skills and content that positions teachers of writing as assistants to faculty who teach more substantive bodies of knowledge. Nationally, independent writing programs have significantly higher percentages of nontenure-track and part-time instructors than those that operate within the boundaries of the discipline, suggesting that independent programs may be bad for teachers as well as researchers (*MLA Survey*, 1999). This line of analysis seems generally valid to me, but my institutional perspective is rather limited—confined as it is to large public universities. In many institutions, local factors can make an independent program a compelling pragmatic alternative even without a critical mass of tenure faculty. In making such practical judgments, we need to acknowledge that research-oriented faculty speak from privileged vantage points that are often removed from the positions of writing teachers, who as a class have about the worst working conditions in the higher education system. This system perpetuates itself by keeping such teachers focused on keeping the paper mill running and reserving time for critical reflection to those with more standing in the profession, who tend to be vested in the hierarchies that structure it.

Some of the basic hierarchies we work with arise out of the historical contradictions between the public positions and professional functions of American colleges and universities. Writing is everyone's concern and nobody's responsibility because prevailing reward systems devalue teaching in general and the teaching of writing in particular. In fairly systematic ways, college faculty have failed to come to terms with the fact that they teach for a living, because they have been rewarded for thinking otherwise. Ironically, writing programs and colleges of education may have helped disciplinary specialists to think in such ways by making writing and teaching distinct fields of professional specialization rather than part of the shared work of college educators. Some of the prevailing misperceptions of what we do arise from the institutional workings of professionalism. Professions generally ignore how they are rhetorically constructed because they gain authority by teaching practitioners and the public to see them as autonomous fields of expertise (see Russell 1991). When a profession attends to how it is composed, it opens itself up to questions about its public responsibilities, and the opening that often gapes for attention is the initiation of new members into the field. Not surprisingly, when a field of work becomes professionalized it formalizes the processes of credentialing new members and creates codes of conduct that consolidate the internal workings of the discipline in order to make it self-regulating (see Thomas Bender). After access and interventions have thereby been limited, a profession tends to ignore these processes as much as possible, enabling it to blame individual initiates if they cannot master its expertise and to download more onerous responsibilities onto marginal members of the profession, such as paralegals, nurses, technicians, and lecturers.

A rhetorical stance on such tacit processes can foster critical thinking about how they work and how we can help them work differently. Work with writing makes learning visible, creating opportunities for critical reflection upon the purposes served by a profession's hierarchies and the methods that perpetuate them. In our collaborations on the teaching of writing, we have witnessed those eye-opening moments when a disciplinary specialist comes to see that a student's composition is not simply a faulted version of what they know but a competing vision of what they are about; and we have seen the epiphany that dawns on students' faces when they realize that they can write their experiences into the work of the academy. As learning becomes visible at such moments, people come to see knowledge making at work. Such moments present rhetorical situations of tremendous pedagogical potential. Such a moment faces our profession with the composition of independent writing programs, and it is useful to step back and look at what we are making of it.

To provide a model for how a rhetorical stance on writing can help our students and colleagues see the critical potentials of their situations, I will offer a rhetorical analysis of the political possibilities and institutional constraints that need to be considered in assessing independent writing programs. The studies in this volume present a rich set of case studies that is aptly complemented by the scenarios in Linda Myers-Breslin's *Administrative Problem-Solving for Writing Programs and Writing Centers*. I want to move dialectically from their practical insights to the historical issues that rhetoric might help us to see in these situations. I believe that some of the disabling dualisms that constrain our efforts can be effectively mediated by rhetoric, if we view it as a pragmatic philosophy of social *praxis* and not simply a set of techniques for writing. When understood as a civic philosophy of deliberative action, rhetoric can help us to bridge the gaps between professional discourses and personal forms of writing, between belletristic and utilitarian value systems, and between research and service missions, if we can put on our bifocals and shift our gaze back and forth between its immediate practical applications and more long-range reflections on the situations, audiences, and purposes that confront us. Rhetorical concepts such as *phronesis,* or practical wisdom, provide a historical alternative to the modern tendency to model practical understanding on the logic of scientific inquiry, which assumes the stance of the critical observer removed from the perspective of the agent always and already in the situation of having to choose how to act. This alternative can be of practical value now. Beyond the immediate pressures facing us, we can see converging historical transformations in the technologies and economies that shape how knowledge gets made, used, and valued. Computers are obviously not simply new tools for writing, and the service economy is more than a vague abstraction for the changing socioeconomic functions of universities and colleges. It can be hard to keep these complex transformations in focus when the pressing needs of writing programs take up so much of our field of vision; but if independent programs are to make a difference for teachers and students, we need to think dialectically about how they can help us to achieve the potentials of historical changes in literacy and learning.

ON BECOMING PRAGMATIC ABOUT SERVICE

One of the basic challenges that confront independent writing programs is to harness the power of providing an essential service without becoming defined as essentially a service provider. Such contradictions can tear a program apart by pulling people to identify with opposing values; but a rhetorical stance recognizes that such conflicts in prevailing assumptions or *topoi* are sites where alternatives can emerge out of oppositions and hierarchies that are ceasing to make sense of the needs of a group or institution. We often experience such competing identifications as pressures to advance research or devote ourselves to teaching. The challenge is to redefine the opposing terms to create more dialectical and holistic ways of understanding the inescapable contradictions that writing faculties need to manage to work together. One rhetorical strategy for confronting a divisive dualism is to shift focus to a third point of reference. The obvious third category for definitions of academic work is service. In evaluations of academic work such as annual reviews, service tends to become the lowest priority, but this value system is becoming unstable as universities and colleges are pressed to give new accounts of the services they provide. These pressures can be put to good uses by redefining the purposes of composition programs in broader terms. A comprehensive writing program needs to be networked with schoolteachers as well as college faculty. Our outreach responsibilities arise from our positions as "bridge" programs charged with teaching entering students how to write their way into the academy, and many programs offer teacher development workshops, sometimes under the national Writing Project or as parts of articulation or assessment efforts. These collaborations expand the power base of composition programs in pragmatically useful ways, as is evident in the model discussed by Parks and Goldblatt. Similar partnerships with alumni associations, business organizations, professional associations, and civic groups can expand our base still farther, giving us leverage in dealing with administrators concerned with fostering such relationships.

These collaborations can also help us make productive use of another contradiction that confronts writing programs: while everyone has an opinion on how to teach writing, most would prefer to tell somebody else how to do it rather than do it themselves. Writing programs need to have deliberative forums where people from across the university and beyond can be brought together to discuss writing instruction and be educated about what it entails. If managed well, faculty and other advisory committees can be used to support reforms and slow down administrators who want to do things quick and dirty. Such forums are crucial to educating public constituencies about our work so that they can support it more effectively. Of course, we need to avoid defensiveness and be willing to explain over and over that teaching writing entails more than correcting errors, but when a writing program embodies a more comprehensive sense of its duties, the differences between correcting papers and supporting student writers can be made evident. Through such deliberative forums, those who work with writing can make learning visible not just in individual classrooms but in the general institution as well. A comprehensive writing program needs to be networked with student life offices, faculty and graduate student development programs, and teaching with technology initiatives. A full service writing program can help develop coherent networks out of overlapping and ill-defined systems for supporting students and teachers. Writing is a converging concern for reforms of assessment and instruction, and writing programs present broadly persuasive models for peer tutoring, performance assessment, and student-centered instruction oriented to learning by doing.

We need to develop collaborative networks to expand our service mission, as discussed by other contributors to this collection (see, for example, Turner and Kearns), but many programs are so overwhelmed with the demands of staffing first-year composition classes with reasonably trained teachers that taking on such expanded responsibilities can seem impossible. First-year composition requirements provide the justification for many, though not all, independent writing programs (see Rehling and Aronson and Hansen). Some of us have spent years defending such requirements as essential to meeting the needs of students, especially those who come from disadvantaged backgrounds and who may not connect with faculty in larger, more impersonal classes. We have struggled to make such courses central to English departments' sense of their mission and faculty's sense of the development of student writing. Such struggles have gotten us so deeply invested in first-year composition courses that we often do not have the time to develop more comprehensive programs for supporting student writers. While I oppose the general abolition of first-year composition requirements, abolitionists such as Crowley have made arguments that are quite compelling. They have convinced me that where a composition requirement has created indefensible staffing and training standards, administrators and teachers need to deliberate upon reducing or even eliminating it, if for no other reason than to negotiate the resources needed to teach writing well. First-year composition requirements can instill a misleading confidence that we are taking care of our core responsibilities. However, students can now conveniently purchase college credits for high school courses through dual enrollment programs that provide at best a distant sense of what it is like to write and do research in college. These courses have become a common distance-learning offering; and any composition program that unduly depends upon them could be outsourced, which would be but a logical extension of the historical tendency to temp out writing instruction as marginal to the professional responsibilities of disciplinary specialists.

Such trends bring to the surface another basic contradiction: writing courses seem unimportant because they are seen as marginal to scholarly disciplines, even though universities are being pressed to develop different accounts of the services they provide to the public and, within many disciplines, critical intellectuals are arguing that the margins are places of power where dominant ideologies can be called into question against broader needs and values. Rhetoric provides a set of categories that can help us to put these institutional needs and interdisciplinary trends to good purposes. Rhetoric has historically functioned as the art of mediating between learned and public spheres of discourse, though it has traditionally served to give virtue to power by making educated, property-holding, white males the voice of the public. If it is reconceived to treat differences as resources for imagining alternatives, rhetoric's historical engagement with the arts of citizenship can be used to focus writing courses on techniques for applying received beliefs to changing needs. Such an orientation can help us to make common cause with other outreach programs, with national efforts to make civic duties a part of general education, and with critical studies of gender, race, and class issues, which are too often uninvolved at a practical level with the communities that are being represented. More than perhaps any other course, composition occupies a public space in the curriculum by virtue of the fact that it has been required of all students, all the faculty have an interest in it, and the public identifies it as essential to all educated citizens. We need to exploit the civic potentials of our position by developing public outreach, making political rhetoric part of the teaching of writing, and creating forums where specialists can speak to public debates, as we do in our program by integrating interdisciplinary colloquia, rhetorical analysis, and local issues into our curriculum.

ON BECOMING RHETORICAL ABOUT PRAGMATICS

My analysis of how networked programs can fulfill their public duties has thus far concentrated on the principal analytical categories of rhetoric: situation, audience, and purpose. This rhetorical trinity sets out the commonplaces of the discipline and thus encapsulates its philosophy of practical understanding—a philosophy oriented to making productive use of the sort of constraints and opportunities that face us here and now. From the basic assumption that the contingencies of a situation define its possibilities, rhetoric looks to purpose as the guiding concern in deliberating upon what should be done. Rhetoric concerns itself with the resources of situational contexts as the means to realize such purposes and treats the transactional relations of authors and auditors as fundamental to dialogical forms of collaborative reasoning toward shared purposes. Of course, rhetoric does not have sole purview over these concerns. Linguists invented pragmatics to reinvent rhetoric when it came to seem anachronistic from a scientific perspective, and postmoderns have made the precepts of rhetoric foundational to critiques of foundationalism, without invoking rhetoric as more than a trendy term for discussing how knowledge is socially constructed through discourse.

Some have gone so far as to argue that in an era of "rhetoricality," rhetoric has become merely an object of nostalgia for the ideal of the good man speaking well for the common good (see Bender and Wellbery). In my estimation, such critiques demonstrate the need for rhetoric, while denying it, for they are characterized by a disengagement from practical agency that is all too common in contemporary critical theory. Rhetoric's traditional concern for the situated, purposeful, and dialectical dynamics of communication maps out a field of study that can help us reorient ourselves as we move beyond the traditional boundaries of English departments. Indulge me for a couple of paragraphs, and I will briefly survey the oldest of rhetorical questions: what is rhetoric and what good is it?

A rhetorical stance is oriented to purposeful action, not merely criticizing or theorizing, but applying critical understanding to the question of what and how one should act in this situation here and now. Rhetoric's objects of study are the controversies that issue from arguments about such questions. Such arguments embody the methods, hierarchies, and purposes that define a domain of discourse, traditionally categorized into the three genres of classical rhetoric: judicial reviews of what has been done, epideictic celebrations of the values that shape what can be done, and deliberative arguments over what should be done. Such controversies are defined according to whether the arguments turn on questions about facts, definitions, evaluations, or procedures (for example, was someone killed, was it murder, was it defensible given the situation, and is this the appropriate place to make such a judgment?). Looking back upon rhetoric's practical concern for the status of a controversy at issue, one can see that the methods of rhetoric are concerned with discovering the arguments that can enable one to achieve the purposes that are possible in a domain of discourse. Rhetoric has traditionally concerned itself with the domain of popular opinion that lies between what can be assumed and what is beyond question. Cultural studies of that domain can help us expand its critical possibilities. If we look beyond the details of traditional genres and the categories used to represent them, we can see that when rhetoric is reduced to a set of mechanical techniques such as ethical, logical, and pathetic appeals, the art is transformed into a mere *techne* or technology that is less broadly useful as a practical guide to critical thinking and deliberative action. From Aristotle and Isocrates through Cicero to the civic tradition, the topoi, maxims, and commonplaces that constitute a genre of discursive action are conceived to be its resources for collective action, its characteristic *ethos* and ethics, and its political means and ends. From a civic perspective, rhetoric is about doing and making as a means to becoming by achieving the potentials of deliberative action. The critical possibilities of traditional rhetorical techniques become evident when we consider concepts such as the enthymeme not as an informal abbreviated syllogism but as a transactional model for how audiences make sense of an argument by filling out its premises from their own experiences. Such concepts provide heuristics for thinking purposefully about the sorts of concerns identified with ethnography and other grounded modes of investigation that focus on situated cognition, enactments of shared beliefs, and interpretive frames or schema.

Rhetoric can be oriented to critical purposes by focusing on the dynamics of how disciplines and social groups construct shared knowledge through collaborative deliberations. This process begins with the historical experiences of the group, which give rise to a set of shared expectations that are codified in the norms that shape how the group acts and communicates. To help our students and colleagues think critically about the possibilities of genres, one can begin with readers' responses to texts that seem conventional or unfamiliar and work back to the sources and assumptions underlying the generic conventions. The familiar rhetorical appeals provide a useful set of heuristics for helping people examine how conventions represent experiences and shape expectations. Questions about the strategies authors use to claim ethical credibility lead into analyzing what seems logical in this genre and therefore authoritative in this domain of experience; and pathetic appeals can be viewed as attempts to identify with shared values, if we can look beyond our culture's tendency to divide human understanding into logical thinking and mere emotion. As Kinneavy and other proponents of the "new rhetoric" discussed, the ethical, logical, and pathetic appeals open up the resources of a communication situation for studies of how authors claim authority, marshal evidence from the topic at hand, and draw on their audiences' attitudes and associations. These categories are common parlance for helping students and teachers interpret a text against its context or write with an eye to their rhetorical situations. The "proofs" may well be our most familiar heuristics, but like so much of the art, we have often used them as mere techniques and failed to consider them as parts of a humanistic discipline worthy of study. This field of study can help us to redefine our work with literacy as we look beyond the literary ideologies that privileged the autonomy of individual texts and authors and expand our field of vision to include networked models of collective action.

As we expand basic composition courses into fuller programs of study, we need to step back and reevaluate the subject of rhetoric as a philosophy of social praxis. Rhetoric has the potential to become a discipline that builds on the fundamental assumption of critical pedagogy that literacy involves a dialectical interplay of action on the world and reflection on one's self (Freire 68). Our traditional engagement with learning by doing has far more power than we often recognize, because it presents a potentially radical critique of the scientism that has dominated higher education in the modern period. The research university was founded on the Enlightenment assumption that the way to know is to step back from an experience and assume a disinterested stance. The perspective of the detached observer became the disciplinary vantage point not just for those who reduced politics to a science but also for those who institutionalized a modern sense of literature as a narrow canon of nonfactual, nonutilitarian texts set apart in a privileged domain divorced from the political purposes, economic motivations, and popular uses of literacy. This perspective is collapsing in on itself because its account of how people learn is losing its value, as literacy and learning become networked, the book ceases to be the depository for all that is worth knowing, and the flow of information bursts the borders of traditional fields of study. A rhetorical perspective can help overwhelmed inquirers respond to the prevailing tendency to reduce human understanding to information processing by enabling them to realize the power of developing a shared sense of purpose, critiquing information against its contexts, and working collaboratively on problem posing and solving. By attending to the contingent and contested process of composing professional expertise, rhetoric can help us help students and colleagues think critically about how writing becomes a science or an art at the point of contact.

IS IT CRITICAL TO BE PROFESSIONAL?

To achieve such purposes, the faculties of independent writing programs have to struggle to attain the sort of professional credibility that comes naturally to those working within an established discipline. As detailed in the contributions to this collection, entrenched hierarchies stand against those who teach off the tenure track in programs that are perceived to be basic skills units. Academic disciplines are defined by the scholarship published within them, and such definitions treat much of what we do as useful but unprofessional. Faced with such hierarchies, many of the contributions included here are characterized by an understandable ambivalence about how to negotiate conflicting professional goals and institutional needs. Some of the contributors have openly expressed their sense of being torn between attending to what needs to be done and striving for professional status; and some of the programs negotiate these challenges by positioning themselves with respect to disciplinary trends, and others by reference to local needs. The disabling dichotomy between the needs of the institution and the priorities of the profession can be mediated by a civic orientation. To be persuasive, this orientation needs to be grounded in a pragmatic commitment to making colleges into institutions of public learning by fostering collaborations on teaching and writing and by extending those collaborations to involve public constituencies. It is critical to making this commitment work that we take account of how professionalism has been institutionalized within the academy in ways that foster a cosmopolitan identification with disciplines that alienates academics from becoming more actively involved in the communities in which they live and work. We all know colleagues who are more likely to read the *New Yorker* or a scholarly journal than the local paper, who are conversant with specialists around the country but have never talked to a local teacher, and who view service and teaching duties as distractions from the research needed to move up in the profession.

The tenure system channels such aspirations into professional hierarchies that systematically devalue much of the work we do. Discussions of the tenuous positions of writing instructors often focus on how the increase in nontenure-track instructors threatens the tenure system. As Murphy discusses, this system has already been so compromised by increases in part-time instructors that such defenses tend to serve to preserve the privileges of a few and thereby to limit broader-based coalitions aimed at confronting the conditions at work in colleges and universities. While faculty tend to blame corporate-minded administrators for this situation, Murphy seems to be right to focus on how tenure-track faculty have been complicit in creating this economic system, which has enabled them to download more onerous responsibilities onto those with marginal professional status. Because I have personally benefited from this professional economy, my assessments of it need to be analyzed rhetorically against the position I occupy and the purposes that it makes evident to me. While it is traditionally defended as a means to protect the freedom of speech of the professoriate, the tenure system has helped ensure that academics devote most of their critical energies to talking to themselves. Tenure criteria have systematically devalued any work done outside the profession, not just teaching and service but also publishing in popular media, collaborating with those beyond the field, and pursuing applied research to meet their needs. The tenure system upholds the general value system that has functioned within English departments to give low status to research on teaching, to distinguish literacy from literary work, and to maintain the distinction between creative and more popular and utilitarian forms of writing. In these and other ways, tenure has protected academic work, while also making its critical possibilities merely academic by containing them within specialized discourses that limit their rhetorical potentials.

While I am ambivalent about arguing that the tenure system has worked to contain the critical applications of public education within professional fields, it is clear that revising tenure and devising alternatives are crucial to broader reforms of higher education. Alternatives to tenure have been proposed in recent articles by both Murphy and Harris, and general guidelines for considering such positions can be found on the websites of professional organizations such as the American Association of University Professors and the Modern Language Association. At the University of Arizona, pedagogy has already become a well-recognized area of scholarship in the humanities, and alternatives to tenure have been developed for academic professionals of our Composition Board from models drawn from the professional staff positions held by research librarians, who participate in a review and promotion process that provides continuing status comparable to tenure. The board (which was founded upon the former University of Michigan model) oversees placement and midcareer assessments that serve almost ten thousand students a year. While students have generally been placed from writing samples (assessed in tandem with high school grades and test scores), Drs. Anne Marie Hall, Tyler Bouldin, and other members of the board have developed a portfolio initiative that brings local teachers and college instructors together to assess students' high school writing in order to place them into ESL, honors, standard, and basic course sequences. The board also manages the midcareer assessment program that supports the teaching of writing across the curriculum by bringing faculty together to discuss how they respond to writing. On the basis of their contributions to such programs, members of the Composition Board have been promoted to associate rank and given continuing status. Through our collaborations on review committees with staff and faculty from outside the program, we have developed job descriptions that establish strategic benchmarks that value the work that needs to be done if curricular reforms and instructional innovations are to be pursued in a scholarly fashion. One of our most important reforms has been to get institutional research and leadership on curricular reforms recognized as scholarly contributions comparable to published research. When written into official documents, such benchmarks can provide people with legal protections, and the process of making such assessments official can be used to articulate these assumptions through institutional channels.

On a good day, I feel that such positions can enable us to institutionalize a commitment to the work of making universities into institutions of public learning. On a bad day, I worry that we are complicit in establishing second-class faculty categories that make the teaching of writing manageable, thereby enabling research professors to continue doing what they have done without having to come to terms with changes in literacy and learning. On most days, I understand rhetoric as a means to negotiate between the pressures to get the job done and our hopes that it can be redefined to serve changing needs. If rhetoric is to become an aid in negotiating the conflicted goals of writing programs, we must expand our fields of vision to include the domains where it has practical import. Graduate and undergraduate studies of rhetoric need to include grounded research on labor organizing, social movements, state educational systems, and institutional reforms. Rhetoric and composition has been limited by its concentration on academic discourse, and we should look to rhetoric in communications for models of how to work with organizational communications, political movements, and group dynamics. Communications has been shaped by scientistic methods and functionalist orientations that need to be critiqued against more humanistic perspectives. For just this reason, communications presents a model for what may become of us if we fail to maintain a critical stance on some of the very institutional trends that are supporting the establishment of independent writing programs. The isolation of literary from literacy studies helped reduce the teaching of writing to mere mechanics concerned with utilitarian purposes, but the disabling dualism of the fine arts and the useful sciences will not be left behind by moving out from under the belletristic value system that limited English studies to a privileged canon of nonutilitarian, nonfactual texts (for a historical study of this system, see my *Formation of College English Studies*).

As we consider the broader history of the discipline and the pragmatic potentials of the alternatives that are emerging, we need to focus squarely on the teaching of writing and on teachers of writing if we are to see the power in what we do. Introductory literacy courses have the power to reinterpret prevailing assumptions against changing needs by teaching students how to make productive use of the differences they bring to the process of making knowledge. Focusing squarely on this place of power can enable us to shift our gaze from trickle-down views of change that look to elite institutions for sources of reform. Our disciplinary histories, and some of the case studies here, cite developments in prestigious private universities to explain changes in more broadly based institutions. Such an orientation is an understandable attempt to gain professional credibility by identifying with the prestige of the traditionally privileged. If we look critically at such programs, we can see that they depend upon a continuous turnover in teachers that prevents them from organizing themselves into an institutional threat to established hierarchies, even while enabling those teachers to market themselves by banking on the prestige of the institutions. Such teachers inevitably learn more from the system than its good intentions. In elite institutions as elsewhere, such systems for making the teaching of writing manageable can make it invisible, in part by keeping writing teachers moving on from institution to institution, where they become but fleeting shadows in crowded hallways who can be ignored by "regular" faculty. The invisible men and women of the profession haunt our dreams as we haunt theirs, much like Ellison's *Invisible Man,* whose main character looked to a prestigious college to gain professional standing and left with nightmares that his letter of recommendation amounted to a single line: keep this boy running. One way that the higher educational system has kept itself running is by keeping teachers of writing on the move, looking to find a place for themselves in a profession that has depended upon their absence for its sense of itself.

To achieve the possibilities posed by their often marginal situations, independent writing programs need to have a bifocal perspective that can enable them to shift their gaze back and forth from the immediate needs of teachers and students in their institutions to the disciplinary trends that are transforming literacy studies, not by the filtering down of new theories but from the generative possibilities that are rising up from work with literacy and learning. We also need to focus more on that "contact zone" that lies between the individual institution and the general profession—that civic field of vision that can enable writing programs to see ways to work through introductory literacy courses to connect with broader constituencies, especially those groups who must be brought into a public university if it is to become more than an oxymoron. Perhaps what we need is not so much a bifocal as a progressive lens, though a progressive viewpoint may too easily efface the difference between here and there. We need to attend to the boundaries that separate the positions we occupy, distorted as our sense of them may be, for it is at such borders where power is gained—and denied. Bifocals can make us aware of the spaces between us, but bifocals are really not so much about space as they are about time. Not simply the time that passes us by when we are unawares, but the time that needs to be taken to reflect upon such things. By taking the time to write this for you, I have tried to convey some of what I see in the work that we do together, while recognizing that our positions in the field may be quite different and that those differences may give you a very different perspective on what it is about, if you can make the time to think critically about it.

16

STASIS AND CHANGE
The Role of Independent Composition Programs and the Dynamic Nature of Literacy

Cynthia L. Selfe
Gail E. Hawisher
Patricia Ericsson

As a collection, the essays in *Field of Dreams* tell a compelling story about our profession's willingness to embrace change. They demonstrate, for instance, a commitment to rethinking the relationship between programs of literary studies and programs of writing studies and the role both play within twenty-first century universities. And they illustrate, as well, a recognition that writing instruction may need to be restructured to better address the needs of students and the university at large.

At the same time, however, these essays also attest to our profession's investment in stasis—most particularly, in our continued investment in, and single-minded focus on, alphabetic print, literacy. This particular investment limits our understanding of composition as practiced in many digital environments and keeps us from acknowledging the "turn to the visual" (Kress 66) that has fundamentally changed communication in contemporary settings.

Although most of the programs in this collection have been willing to reinvent themselves and their responsibilities in light of their changing relationships with traditional departments of English, they have also—for the most part—resisted the challenge of reexamining their own investment in print and of addressing the dramatic shift from the verbal to the visual. The titles of most of these programs—Technical and Professional Writing Program, the Department of Writing, Centre for Academic Writing, the Department of Writing and Linguistics—attest to the value they continue to place on conventional forms of alphabetic print literacy. Although such an investment is not problematic in and of itself, when pursued with a single-minded focus, it can result in an incomplete understanding of composition as practiced at the beginning of the twenty-first century—especially within electronic environments.

Such an investment tends to ignore the ways in which the literacies of technology are becoming inextricably linked to the literacies of print.

This chapter attempts to examine why independent programs might have subscribed to this limited perspective on written composition and how they might take the lead—in coming years—to expand our profession's understanding of composition as both a verbal *and* visual art, and, increasingly, an aural/oral art as well.

SOME HISTORICAL CONTEXT: THE PACE OF CHANGE, THE RISE OF THE INFORMATION AGE, AND THE TURN TO THE VISUAL

Manuel Castells (1996, 1997, 1998) notes that the condition of postmodernism—at a fundamental level—is a function of rapid and extensive social change: the disturbing disappearance of familiar anchoring institutions such as nation states, the dizzying global expansion and rapid multiplication of micropolitical entities, the explosive growth of alienating forces like global crime and terrorism, the undermining of authoritative systems, and the disappearance of a single version of Truth.

This rapid pace of change has been driven—at least in part—by the rise of computers and the linking of institutions, groups, and individuals through an interconnected network of communication technologies: computers, televisions, cell phones, and fax machines, among them. Importantly, these new communication technologies—scholars like Baudrillard, Castells (1996), Jameson, and Star point out—have contributed to changing not only political and social structures, but the very ways in which people understand the world, make meaning, and formulate their own individual and group identities.

Within these new electronic environments the very landscape of communication and the fundamental forms of human exchange are being altered. In particular, as Gunther Kress argues, visual forms of literacy are displacing verbal forms, and alphabetic texts are being challenged by texts comprised of visual images, multimedia elements, diagrams, photographs, sound, and animations—what we might call a multimodal approach to composition. This change is so dramatic and fundamental, Kress adds, that our conventional understanding of literacy and an "emphasis on language alone simply will no longer do" (67), especially in defining the intellectual territory of English composition programs.

Stasis and Change

Mostly, English composition programs have responded to these world-order changes by neglecting them—preferring, instead, to rely on the historical primacy of writing, as sedimented in our culture and imaginations over the past few centuries.

In many cases, programs have taken this approach because teachers of writing—educated in the age of print and invested in their own success as producers and consumers of alphabetic texts—know so little about the emerging forms of visual literacy and even less perhaps about the multimodal contexts in which these literacies are emerging. And because so few English teachers can, understandably, predict or adapt easily to the emerging power of a visual and multimodal communication, the vast majority of our profession remains unable to design and unwilling to offer instruction that goes beyond the alphabetic.

This state of affairs should not surprise us. More than twenty years ago, in her book *Culture and Commitment,* Margaret Mead (1970) argued that the pace of change in a culture determines—at least in part—the way in which information is transferred to succeeding generations, as well as the ways in which educational efforts are conducted.

In this volume, Mead describes three different cultural styles, distinguished by the ways in which children are prepared for adulthood. The first of these styles, the "postfigurative," characterizes societies in which change is largely imperceptible and the "future repeats the past." In such cultures, adults are able to pass along the necessary knowledge to children. "The essential characteristic of postfigurative cultures," Mead maintains, "is the assumption, expressed by members of the older generation in their every act, that their way of life (however many changes may, in fact, be embodied in it) is unchanging, eternally the same" (Mead, 1970,14). Education within such cultures privileges the passing down of traditional values and knowledge through an adult teacher.

The second of Mead's styles—that characterizing "cofigurative" cultures—arises when some form of disruption is experienced by a society. As Mead notes, further, such disruptions may result from the "development of new forms of technology in which the old are not expert" (39). In this kind of culture, young people look to their contemporaries for guidance in making choices rather than relying on their elders for expertise and for role models in a changing world.

A third, and final, cultural style—which Mead terms the "prefigurative"—is symptomatic of a world changing so fast that it exists "without models and without precedent." In prefigurative cultures, change is so rapid that "neither parents nor teachers, lawyers, doctors, skilled workers, inventors, preachers, or prophets" (xx) can teach children what they need to know about the world. The prefigurative cultural style, Mead argues, prevails in a world where the "past, the culture that had shaped [young adults'] understanding—their thoughts, their feelings, and their conceptions of the world—was no sure guide to the present. And the elders among them, bound to the past, [can] provide no models for the future" (70).

In the prefigurative culture of twenty-first century America, then, it is little wonder that most adults have limited success in predicting the changes happening around us, in anticipating and coping with the world as it morphs through successive and confusing new forms. Similarly, it is little wonder that English composition teachers, and most writing programs, have had limited success in predicting and understanding the importance of visual, spatial, and multimodal literacies. Nor is it surprising that so many programs offer courses on technical writing, creative writing, and professional writing, while so few offer instruction in the design of visual texts, visual argumentation, or multimedia composition.

Our single-minded focus on alphabetic literacy—and our adherence to standards for producing writing and consuming it—has had its intellectual costs. As Kress notes,

> The focus on language alone has meant a neglect, an overlooking, even suppression of the potentials of representational and communicational modes in particular cultures; an often repressive and always systematic neglect of human potentials in many of these areas; and a neglect equally, as a consequence, of the development of theoretical understandings of such modes. Semiotic modes have different potentials, so that they afford different kinds of possibilities of human expression and engagement with the world, and through this differential engagement with the world, make possible differential possibilities of development: bodily, cognitively, affectively. Or, to put it provocatively: the single, exclusive and intensive focus on written language has dampened the full development of all kinds of human potentials, through all the sensorial possibilities of human bodies, in all kinds of respects, cognitively and affectively, in two and three dimensional representation. (85)

As Kress suggests, another important reason for our adherence to alphabetic literacy has to do with our personal and professional investment—as specialists and practitioners—in writing, writing instruction and writing programs. It is much easier, given our historically determined education, abilities, experiences, and expertise, to keep reinventing a scholarly and instructional business centered on the written word than it is to undertake the difficult work of expanding our understanding of composition beyond the horizon of writing. Operating from this vantage point, we can avoid recognizing the power of new visual and multimodal literacies, dismiss these literacies as some other department's responsibility, or refuse to consider them literacies at all. This same perspective can provide newly independent writing programs, already engaged in the risky endeavor of defining their role and credibility within an institution, with a justifiable excuse to limit composition instruction to historically valorized alphabetic forms.

Unfortunately, the adherence to the status quo associated with this perspective has become increasingly inadequate as a response to the changing forms and formats of literacy, and it has limited our attempts to expand our theoretical understanding of composing as a visual and multimodal art as well as a verbal endeavor. Kress notes,

> Most obviously, if language is no longer the central semiotic mode, then theories of language can at best offer explanations for a part of the communicational landscape only. Moreover, theories of language will not serve to explain the other semiotic modes, unless one assumes, counterfactually, that they are, in every significant way like language; nor will theories of language explain and describe the *interrelations* between the different modes, language included, which are characteristically used in the multimodal semiotic objects—texts'—of the contemporary period. (82)

Hence, it is incumbent upon new freestanding composition programs to lead the way in incorporating the full range of composing strategies into their curricula, thus establishing innovative instructional models for the rest of us to follow.

Literacy is a Movie, Not a Snapshot

Contemporary scholars of literacy—among them, Street, Gee, H. J. Graff, and Brandt (1995, 1998, 1999)—have demonstrated the dynamic and culturally determined nature of literacy activities as they are practiced, valued, and situated in particular historical periods, cultural milieux, and material conditions. Brandt (1995), for instance, has noted that, with the invention of computer-based communication technologies, literacies have accumulated at the end of the twentieth century. Proliferating computer-based literacies, she notes, have imparted a "complex flavor even to elementary acts of reading and writing, . . . creating new and hybrid forms of literacy where once there might have been fewer and more circumscribed forms." This "rapid proliferation and diversification of literacy" places increasing pressure on individuals, whose ultimate success may be "best measured by a person's capacity to amalgamate new reading and writing practices in response to rapid social change" (651).

Such work suggests that forms of literacy have cultural life spans, half-lives, determined by their "fitness" with—and influence on—the "existing stock of social forces and ideas" (Deibert 31), political and economic formations, and available communication environments. Literacies accumulate most rapidly, we suspect, when a culture is undergoing a particularly dramatic or radical transition. During such a period, humans value and practice both past and present forms of literacy that exist simultaneously. Hence, in our contemporary culture, which is making a complicated and messy transition from the conditions characterizing modernism to the conditions characterizing postmodernism—along with the related transitions from a print-based culture to a digitally based culture and from a verbal culture to a visual or multimodal culture—multiple literacies accumulate and compete. In this ecology,[1] situated historically, contextualized culturally, and articulated to a specific set of material conditions in the lived experiences of individuals, we practice and value multiple forms of print and digital literacies; alphabetic literacies, visual literacies, and intertextual forms of media literacies (George and Shoos).

Eventually, however, this accumulation reaches a limit—humans can cope with only so many literacies at once and the cultural distribution of literacies takes time to unfold—and, thus, a process of selection occurs. Sets of literacy practices that fit less well with the changing cultural ecology fade, while other literacy practices that fit more robustly with that context flourish and contend with each other. Examples of emerging, competing, and fading literacies are not difficult to find. The specific literacy practices associated with letters handwritten on paper, for instance—which fit well in a culture that could depend on relatively cheap postal delivery service, a corporate sector based primarily in the United States, and an educational system that provided constant practice in cursive writing and placed a high value on a legible hand—are already fading in the United States. And email as a literacy practice—which has a robust fit with the growth of electronic networks, global markets, and international financial systems—is flourishing and now competing with the genres of both the personal letter and the business memorandum. Similarly, literacies that value extended lines of linear argument or strict adherence to forms associated with print-based essays are now emerging and contending—certainly in online settings if not in schools—with literacies that value hypertextual, web-based organization, and the visual presentation of material (Kress).

AN EXPANDED AND DYNAMIC CONCEPTION OF COMPOSITION

Especially during times of rapid and dramatic social and cultural transformation such as that characterizing the rise of this information age[2] and the turn to the visual, both traditional and independent composition programs need to be increasingly open in our intellectual understanding of composing and composition instruction, not more constrained. And both kinds of programs need to recognize, study, and address not simply a limited set of composing approaches and media— for example, those that depend solely or primarily on alphabetic systems—but, rather, a full range of composing approaches: those that may use images, animations, sounds, and multiple media; and those that represent newly emerging literacies *as well as* established literacies *and* competing literacies *and* fading literacies. Faculty in these increasingly expansive programs need to understand more about how the standards of such literacies (emerging, established, competing, *and* fading) operate to shape texts, the processes of composing, and the outcomes of composing, within specific historical periods and cultural ecologies. They need to do this work in order to help students negotiate and reconcile the contested values and practices of composing that they will encounter and produce during their lifetimes. And they need to do this work in order to help teachers of English composition negotiate these radical changes of composing practices and values.

We suggest that independent composition programs may prove to be important, and even ideal, sites for such work. Such programs, after all, often owe their genesis to departments of English, which have themselves paid the price of investing too heavily in historic forms of literacy and ignoring emerging literacies and literacy values. Thus, units like the multimedia writing and technical communication department at Arizona State University may understand better than more conventional English departments the danger of focusing so exclusively on conventional forms of print-based literacy that we ignore emerging literacy practices and values.

If independent programs—and, indeed, writing programs in general—fail to expand their understanding of composition to include visually based texts, multimedia compositions, and texts composed of animations, images, and sound, they run the risk of seeing their new departments decline in relevance to students and to the larger public and, thus, of experiencing, in relatively short order, the same fate as the English literature programs they left behind.

Reconceiving Composing Practices

How might independent programs begin such a task? Certainly, faculty can start by attending as closely to students' online literacy practices as they do to their more traditional writing practices; by listening closely, and with open minds, to what students are saying about the role of new-media compositions in the world they inhabit; and by expanding their definitions of "texts" and "composing" practices to include a range of other behaviors, among them, reading and composing images and animations; creating multimedia assemblages; combining visual elements, sounds, and language symbols into alternatively organized and presented forms of communication in digital environments.

Faculty in independent composition departments, as well as those in programs that remain situated in departments of English, can also expand their understanding of composing by studying the practices, values, and strategic approaches of other composition specialists: multimedia designers and artists, digital photographers, poets who work in multiple media, and interactive fiction authors, among others. Additionally, composition departments can hire new faculty whose expertise goes beyond print literacy to encompass some of the alternative composition approaches mentioned above.

Within independent composition departments that exist at institutions lacking both material and electronic resources (often, but not always, institutions that serve large populations of students of color or poor students), it may seem almost frivolous to focus on the kinds of new media texts we have mentioned here.[3] In fact, however, these are the very best—and most important—sites for an expanded understanding of composition and multiple literacies.

Independent composition departments in such locations should continue to fight vigorously for all students' access to electronic composing environments and for their own access to these environments. Unless we can help students of color, women, and poor students compose rhetorically effective texts in these environments and help them become critically aware of their own and others' rhetorical success in doing so, we run the risk of creating, yet again, "have nots" in a culture that associates power, increasingly, with technological reach, of being passive consumers of electronic texts, but not being able to produce these texts. Electronic composing environments are essential for all students *because* they are sites of political activism and power. As Manuel Castells explains, such environments are places within which individuals can connect with others who share their interests, values, political commitments, and experiences. It is through these electronic connections that individuals can participate in forging the new set of "codes" under which societies will be "re-thought, and re-established" during the rest of this long century (1997, 360). Hence, departments' failure to address the literacies of technology will have serious implications for the future of writing programs but, more importantly, will have enormous implications—and dangerous ones—for students. We must give the new literacies their due.

NOTES

1.   In using this ecological metaphor, we follow—at least in part—the lead of other scholars, such as Michael Deibert who uses the term to refer to the "existing stock of social forces and ideas," the current set of historic, political, and economic formations comprising the environment within which communication technologies are invented and developed (31), and Bertram Bruce and Maureen Hogan, who advocate an ecological model for studying literacy in technological environments.

The specific ecological model we construct in this paper is structured by its historical situatedness, its cultural context (including ideological, educational, political, and social formations), and the specific set of material conditions on which it is based and which it provides individuals.

We also try to suggest that this model is characterized by a complex "duality of structuring," between the historical, cultural, and material environment within which individuals develop technological literacy and their own personal values, motivations, attitudes, resources, and actions as social agents (Giddens, 1979; Manuel Castells, 1996, 1997, 1998). That is, although the ecology within which individuals develop technological literacy clearly affects individuals and their literacies, individuals are also continually involved in actively shaping the ecology through their discursive and literate practices; and according to their personal motivations, interests, and resources. In this sense, individuals often make the existing conditions of an ecology, even when they are not ideal, work for them and support their technological literacy activities in unexpected ways. These reciprocal processes have effects at multiple levels (micro, medial, and macro).

2.   A term used by Manuel Castells (1996) to describe the era generated by the "converging set of technologies in microelectronics, computing (machines and software), telecommunications/broadcasting, and optoelectronics" (30) and the "networked society" (21) that has transformed "all domains of human activity" (31).

3.   We recognize the obstacles that many departments face in enacting these changes. Admittedly, a neglect of multimodal forms of literacy is accompanied often by a scarcity of resources, even at wealthy institutions. The costs of technological change can be extraordinarily high. (See, for example, Charles Moran's "The Winds—and Costs—of Change." And we would argue that a departments' costs for technology have only risen since this article was first written in 1993.) In order to incorporate multimodal forms of composition instruction into existing programs, there must be the wherewithal not only to establish cutting-edge computer facilities but also to hire faculty and staff who demonstrate high levels of technological sophistication.

17

BIGGER THAN A DISCIPLINE?

Kurt Spellmeyer

I hesitate to call it "composition," and I'm dissatisfied with "rhetoric" as well, which has never really managed to free itself from the ponderousness of The Classics. But whatever we eventually call it, a field dedicated to the teaching and study of writing might enjoy brighter prospects now than at any time since the 1950s, when growing access to higher education made English 101 a standard feature of the undergraduate curriculum. For one thing, our society needs it. Many of my married friends have children who read less than those friends did when they were young—before computers, DVDs, CDs, and so on. And for the most part, their children not only read less, they write less comfortably and less ably as well. We need something like "comp" for other reasons, too. At the same time that the printed word has lost its former preeminence, what we refer to as "reading" and "writing" have never been more varied or more complex. Compare Jacques Derrida's encyclopedic oeuvre, which quite possibly nobody except Derrida can explain, to Northrop Frye's more modest achievement, the clear outlines of which an undergraduate could master in several diligent afternoons. Or compare Clifford Geertz's *Local Knowledge* with Margaret Mead's *Sex and Temperament,* published fifty years earlier. Or William James's accounts of pragmatism to the brain-busting difficulty of our "possible worlds" philosophers. Remember also that only a century ago, there were simply no such disciplines as microbiology or computer science or genetic engineering—no journals in those fields and no genres to go with them. And if these strange new ways of writing now proliferate like orchids in the tropics, they are not only more complex than anything before but also more divergent from each other than philosophy was from politics in the age of Aristotle or natural science from law in John Locke's time.

In place of "composition" or "rhetoric," the term that I would like to use—knowledge-ology—no one else could ever be expected to adopt, and I can hardly blame them. But my point is that something is happening to knowledge, which few of us pay much attention to, absorbed as we are individually by our own little specializations. Even prophets of the "information age" have largely overlooked the most important change: to have an "information society" is to live and work in the Tower of Babel. What has happened in the space of about a hundred years is that knowledge has gone from relative scarcity to superabundance and from relative uniformity to continuous mutation. Increasingly, our whole economy depends on the perpetual creation and circulation of new knowledge. The closest analogy to what we are living through might be the transition, which took place over many centuries and not in a matter of decades, from an economy based on jewels and gold to one that relied on paper money—except that in our case today, we no longer have a single legal tender, but employ a thousand different currencies at once. In our ever burgeoning marketplace, this person wants to buy a melon with kroner while that person tries to outbid her with a handful of yen, while another—to make matters even more complex—has just invented a fresh currency that has caught the melon grower's eye. In such a complex economy, someone has to know how to move from one tender to the next. And someone will need to track the shifting rates of exchange, if only to prevent the unsuspecting from paying fifty pounds when they really owe fifty pesos. To take my metaphor one step further, let me add that this "someone"—the knowledge broker—could be us.

The word "hermeneutics" sounds atrocious to my ears, but I cannot help but think of knowledgeology as a hermeneutic enterprise. In ancient Greece (perhaps the classics are inescapable after all), Hermes was the divine messenger, whose special task was to travel from one god's realm to another or from Mount Olympus to the earth. By making this historical allusion, which some may find pretentious and some merely banal, I am suggesting that our proper concern may lie, not with creating another discipline that can take its conventional place beside the rest, but with the task of making visible the links between one "realm" and another—not transcendent realms of timeless Being but mundane ones of transient information. It seems to me that this idea has a great deal to recommend it—and no else, so far, has taken on the job. After more than two decades of manifestos calling for "interdisciplinarity," often underwritten by the superstars of various disciplines, little has actually happened, to put it mildly. The boundaries of the disciplines as they took shape in the 1900s still determine the organization of professors—fiscally, spatially, and in terms of the microcultures each department shelters—just as these boundaries still determine the character of the knowledges these professors keep turning out. And really, who wants to see the disciplines transformed? If composition, by analogy, should get refigured in a dramatic way over the next decade or so, how do you expect that Pat Bizzell might feel, or Min Lu or Victor Villaneuva? All of them, and all us, have gambled our energies on the survival of the composition enterprise more or less as we know it now. And so it goes right across the curriculum. I suspect that most departments of English and history, as well as many in the social sciences, have already turned their backs on the kind of scholarship inaugurated by the unruly generation that came to prominence in the 1970s—the generation of Frederic Jameson, Hayden White, and James Clifford. If we can judge the shifting winds reliably from John Guillory's tortuous calls for a return to Literary studies with the capital "L" or from Clifford Geertz's trashing of James Clifford's latest book, working at the borders of different disciplines is an idea whose time has come—and gone.[1] Better for English to abide with Keats and Shelley and for fieldwork to be fieldwork than to aspire to the self-reflexive heights of phenomenology.

Until the university reimagines itself in ways that now look unlikely, the humanities and the social sciences seem determined to grind on in their deepening ruts or, if you prefer, to keep their institutional feet firmly planted on the bedrock of the past. Of course, the same does not apply to the sciences, which continue to evolve, intermingle, and expand in ways undreamed of only fifteen years ago. But whether specialized knowledge grows increasing self-contained or increasingly expansive and adventurous, the same problems face society at large. And these problems have been caused by the waning of something like a cultural common ground. I use the qualifier "something like" advisedly, since I regard as inherently repressive any effort by elite academic humanists—devotees of Karl Marx no less than those of Dr. Johnson— to create and impose on society at large a Great Tradition or National Identity or, for that matter, any Grand Narrative of Oppression and Liberation. But at the same time, it seems evident to me that our society is poorly served when college graduates cannot even start to explain how the Supreme Court and the Senate actually operate, are unaware that Islam is the faith of about a billion people, and could not, very probably, locate Indonesia or Poland if handed an unlabeled map.

The university's great strength is specialization, but specialization is its major weakness as well. Students can take courses in business or on the environment; they can study government and sociology; but very rarely—

actually, never—do they have the chance to explore at any length the connections between deforestation and international trade or between the political troubles of the Least Developed Countries and their failure to deal with problems of public health. Worse yet, our academic disciplines, like institutions of every other kind, have a vested interest in perpetuating this fragmentation long after their own day of usefulness has past. One good example is cultural anthropology. As many anthropologists are now keenly aware even if they seldom say so openly, their enterprise had an obvious urgency at the end of the 1800s, when the first stages of globalization had already started to exterminate ancient ways of life around the world. But now, when Bali has become a mecca for Australian surfer bums, when Pueblo Indians write international bestsellers and Tibetan monks perform their chants at Carnegie Hall, who really needs the cultural anthropologist to speak for the absent "native" or to commemorate his "endangered" culture? But much the same fate has overtaken English. At its inception, the purpose of English was to create a distinctly literary history for Great Britain and the United States by identifying major figures nearly lost to time and by creating reliable editions of their works. Beyond that, English professors were supposed to assist in the reception of these figures among a reading public still largely unfamiliar with the beauties of Chaucer or the charms of *Tom Jones*. Of course, no one could have foreseen that the momentous undertaking English set for itself would conclude in slightly less than sixty years. Certainly, by the Eisenhower decade, the great authors had been saved, the variorums complete, and the library shelves abundantly stocked with more books on Shakespeare and Wordsworth than even many scholars would care to read. Since then, much of what has happened in academic criticism might be understood as an increasingly desperate casting about for something else to do—a predicament made all the more desperate by the explosion of media that have now brought down the short-lived reign of the novel as the primary public forum for the vetting of ideas.[2]

Though English and cultural anthropology have run quietly dry, and probably other disciplines as well, we can scarcely expect our tenured colleagues to turn in their office keys or to close down graduate programs that continue to churn out two or three Ph.D.'s for every new job. But the death and ghostly afterlife of the disciplines still ensures that a few good minds will waste their formative years ferreting out patriarchy in the Victorian novel or learning to talk about third world women— needless to say, without meeting them—in the language of Jacques

Lacan. What does it matter, some might ask, if we expend some good minds in this harmless way or, for that matter, quite a few mediocre ones? I would respond that it matters enormously when we stop to think that more species are now vanishing from the earth than at any moment since the class Mammalia first appeared. Or that in our lifetimes we are almost certain to see human cloning, global warming, a population climbing toward the ten billion mark, and the effective breakdown of many nation states, even if the institution also sees a ghostly afterlife of its own. No prior period in human history has witnessed greater cumulative change, together with unprecedented dangers and unprecedented opportunities—not the Renaissance, the Enlightenment, the Industrial Revolution, nor the decade of my childhood in Baltimore, when I used to fall asleep visualizing the nuclear bomb that would fall on me in the night. But are matters really as precarious as I suggest? It's worth pointing out that since World War II the number of debtor nations has grown, not declined, as has the number of our fellow human beings who stagger on in abject poverty. While much of Africa and Latin America appear to have embraced democracy at last, their economies are apparently in retreat, while a whole swath of nations, reaching from Dagestan at Europe's door to the western border of China, is now spiraling into sheer anarchy.[3]

But let me give an illustration closer to home, as close as the daily paper. This morning, the *New York Times* included a report on the failure of democracy and free-market reforms to raise living standards for the poor of South America. The number of people living now in poverty on that continent has risen to 224 million, which represents the same 36 percent of total population that lived below the poverty line in 1980. Here's one part of the *New York Times*'s analysis:

> Far too often, Latin America's fledgling democracies have been too weak to effectively defend against . . . [corrupt elites]. For example, the elected governments of countries like Guatemala did little to stand in the way as the rich amassed tremendous wealth, allowing a coalition of agricultural growers and financial groups to block tax reforms. In Ecuador several years ago, so many rich people were evading income taxes that the government just abolished them, putting a tax on financial transactions instead. (DePalma 2)

The real solution, according to the analysis, does not lie in creating more of the formal institutions characteristic of democracies, but in widening access to education, which remains out of reach for millions

across the continent because of poor investment in primary and secondary schools. Typically, the largest share of education spending gets
lavished on the universities, a policy well designed to placate those
already at the top. The importance of this article seems obvious to me.
Self-absorbed and ill-informed as many North Americans are, they will
be forced to deal sooner or later with the problems of the hemisphere
on which their long-term economic future probably rests. But sadly,
most college students in the U.S. no longer read the papers from day to
day, and even fewer of them leave college with the kind of background
knowledge presupposed by a routine article in the *New York Times.*

Problems like the one outlined in the *New York Times* encourage my
strong suspicion that the academic humanities have become, if not actually pernicious, then absurdly irrelevant. In defense of this judgment,
which is bound to seem harsh to those who take on faith the importance
of what they do, let me give just one more illustration. As it happens, the
same edition of the *New York Times* also featured a review by Frank
Kermode, entitled "Cross-Examining Milton." The subject is *How Milton
Works,* a new book by Stanley Fish, showcasing an approach, "forensic
criticism," that employs tactics taken from law to establish the meaning
of literary texts. As always, Fish has managed to develop an ingenious
argument, certain to inspire its share of buzz, yet I cannot help but see
the project as fundamentally frivolous. In a court of law, inquiry typically
turns on establishing that something really happened—a breach of contract, a theft, an assault, a homicide. You may have killed your husband
or you may not have; you may have defrauded your clients or they may
now be defrauding you. Unfortunately, we never know the truth for sure,
and so the task of legal forensics is to reconstruct from the weight of evidence the most likely version of what occurred. As both text and [unwrit-
ten] precedent, the law furnishes the "ground rules" for this process of
reconstruction. But the case of meaning in literary works is hardly comparable. While lawyers argue over legal texts in much the same way that
critics argue over *Lycidas,* the interpretation of law serves a purpose
beyond interpretation itself—and that is the discovery of what really happened and, more broadly, the preservation of justice in the conduct of
social life. But literary interpretation has no purpose beyond itself: it is as
though lawyers gathered in the courtroom simply to defeat one another
in exegesis and then to take pleasure in the brilliance of it all.

While Kermode would surely greet my line of reasoning with scorn,
his review makes it clear that Fish's critical innovation has produced few

real gains in understanding. He finds Fish's reading of *Paradise Lost* to be "faulty" and alleges that Fish "appears to misunderstand" *Samson Agonistes* "even more completely." Kermode lists other objections as well:

> In the course of his [book] Fish does some close analysis of particular texts, sometimes brilliantly, sometimes far-fetchedly, as when he wants the word "raised" in "Paradise Lost" to mean not only what it seems to mean but also its opposite, "razed"; or when he finds, in Milton's account of the war in heaven, too unwieldy a bundle of sexual puns. (In his quest for puns he incorrectly glosses the phrase "propounded terms/Of composition" in the same passage.) And why should he find evidence of evil in the ambiguities of Satan when, on his own account, the good guys also use them? (3)

Given these objections, we might expect that Kermode would wrap up his review by damning Fish's enterprise, but in fact he could end with scarcely higher praise. "Fish's forensic cogency," Kermode writes, is "almost always a delight, even when overingenious or wanton. 'How Milton Works' is a very distinguished book, and it should restore Milton to the center of critical interest" (3). Such a laudatory judgment may seem puzzling until we understand what both Kermode and Fish already recognize—that criticism has one purpose beyond itself, notwithstanding what I claimed a page ago. And that purpose, finally, is not to establish literary truth, whatever literary truth might be, or even to forge connections between literature and law, but simply to keep English studies alive. And Kermode says as much: the key word in his last assessment is "distinguished," which signals that Fish has succeeded in shoring up the prestige of his profession, even by concocting arguments that are absurd on their face or outright wrong, as Kermode acknowledges.

But is it really such a triumph? "Raised" and "razed," sexual puns, the ethics of ambiguity—could anything be more threadbare, immature, and insignificant? I do not mean to suggest that reading Milton is a waste of time, nor do I believe that social justice should be our sole concern. Nevertheless, as inhabitants of a knowledge society—a society where knowledge keeps developing, often in unforeseen directions—we need to exercise *some* principle of selection. Given that almost any human activity can be made into the object of specialized study and can be studied literally without end, we might do well to ask which forms of knowledge matter most in our time—that is, which forms of knowledge touch most consequentially on our lives and which ones are most important for our future as individuals and as a society? I cannot in good conscience

argue that the forensic criticism of *Paradise Lost* deserves equal time with
global warming or the disappearance of species. Even if my rhetoric of
crisis turns out to be hyperbolic and even if the future should prove
more utopian than anyone now anticipates, does it not stand to reason
all the same that our society would benefit more substantially from people who know something of world trade and string theory than from people who have read *Areopagitica?* Of course, English does not bear all the
responsibility for the university's failure to prepare its graduates for the
life of their own times. With every field struggling to prepare hyperspe-
cialists while carving out its slice of resources, the logic of the disciplines
as a whole strongly gravitates against the general knowledge I see as the
potential ground of composition. Nor are all the disciplines alike in their
capacity to address the problem. With technology developing so rapidly,
I cannot imagine that programs in computer science or genetic engineering would tack on substantial new requirements in, say, the social
consequences of the web or the economics underlying genetic engineering. The social sciences and humanities, by contrast, might play a more
syncretic role, but they show few signs of doing so to date.

For those of us who wish to step into the breach, perhaps the major
challenge lies in freeing ourselves from the conceptual legacy of our
training in English studies. If some compositionists have at last turned
their backs on "Young Goodman Brown" and "The Lottery," many continue to conceive their proper task as the teaching of "the text," be it the
cultural text, the social text, or merely the old-fashioned five-paragraph
theme. In other words, we show our bastard origins most clearly when we
begin by divorcing knowledge from the contexts in which that knowledge serves some real-world purpose—the contexts I would like to call
"action horizons." Instead of starting with the primacy of action, we continue to treat language as a subject in itself, just as we were trained to do
in reading poetry, where language has no context other than the class
and no purpose other than to be read. But there are alternatives: for
example, we might think of reading and writing as modes of involvement
with the lived world. In a first-year composition class, students might
learn something, say, about the environmentalists' notion of "carrying
capacity," instead of wasting time deconstructing some poor author's
"representations" of nature. I suppose most of us could benefit, as well,
from learning more about stem-cell technology, instead of inducing our
students to critique the "discourse" of Monsanto's advertising. By the
same token, we might actually study international trade, although to do

so we will probably need to set aside the Rube Goldberg paradigms con-
cocted by the superstars of postcolonial studies. I will even go so far here
as to propose that the whole enterprise of treating knowledge as a "text"
is the sheerest pseudoscience, on a par with phrenology or astrology—
also disciplines whose subjects are purely fanciful.

We make a serious mistake—and, for our profession, a fatal one—
when we take literary language as the starting point of our considerations, because literary language is unique in its purely fictive character,
its lack of any action horizon or determinate real-world reference. In
fact, it is the pressure of facticity—the pressure brought to bear on us by
a world that typically resists us and by people who often see that world in
ways very different from our own—that the ideology of "text" ignores. If
we set aside the case of literary language, then, reading and writing
stand revealed as inseparably linked to the asking of questions about the
world for the purposes of action in concert with others. But the attempt
to teach writing in the name of "textuality" is no less absurd and fruitless
than the attempt to teach science without actually doing science—without actually engaging in a range of practices from which scientific
knowledge arises. Of course, this desire to invent a knowledge that can
stand above or outside of action is just what theorists of science like
Donna Haraway have undertaken; but then, no one ever came away
from her massive tomes with a working knowledge of cybernetics or
oncology or anything else. The crude truth is that people cannot learn
to paint simply by explicating paintings; they cannot learn to play an
instrument by criticizing musicians. The kind of "science studies"
Donna Haraway exemplifies has created the illusion of knowledge, a
knowledge ostensibly superior to science itself when in practice it is
utterly autistic. No less than deconstruction and cultural studies, it disguises its paralysis by evoking grand political change, but these evoca-
tions are also chimerical, since critique is no substitute for a genuine,
real-world politics, which very few of our luminaries dare to offer us.

I am not suggesting that we should abandon the desire to think critically about the consequences of projects like genetic engineering. In fact,
I believe that writing courses are the one place in the curriculum where
consequences and connections might be explored, but I feel that there
can be no methodology or paradigm that tells us in advance which consequences we should discover or which connections we should trace out.
The belief in an all-purpose system of inquiry is the El Dorado of cultural
conservatives and also of the marxist left: for the former, truth already

waits for us somewhere in the past; for the latter, it already waits for us in the revolution to come. But I believe that our profession's legitimate interest lies with the contingencies of the present moment, and in this spirit I would say that the search for consequences and connections must begin with pragmatic information, not with philosophic or ideological truth. What this means for us as compositionists is that the teaching of writing unconditionally demands a working knowledge of economics, science, politics, history, and any other disciplines impinging on matters of broad public concern. This working knowledge might be gained from formal study, and we might also pick it up on the fly. But an hour with Benjamin Barber or Susan Blackmore is, in my view, time far better spent than a decade with Quintilian or James Berlin.[4] If we know something real about something real, then our colleagues might at least respect us, an improvement in our current situation that neither the Great Rhetor of ancient Rome nor his Great Successor of Purdue, Indiana, can bring about.

I fully recognize how unnerving—even deeply shocking—this argument might strike people in our field, especially when our struggle for respect has often prompted us to ally ourselves with "theory," which we have tacitly and correctly recognized as the most prestigious form of knowledge in English studies. The success of the move strikes me as debatable, however; I can't imagine that most literary theorists would ever return the favor by citing colleagues in composition. In fact, our effort to dignify ourselves by drawing on literary theory serves only to reinstate the whole hierarchy that has for so long kept us in our place. We need instead to create an alternative way of thinking that privileges our specific situation and our particular needs. It does us no good if we blithely celebrate the "production" of knowledge over "consumption" and then turn once again to epistemology. We need, in other words, an approach that starts with the synthetic activity from which knowledge arises. If our training in English taught us anything, however, it has taught us to view such an approach as "instrumentalist"—as the philosophical equivalent of a frontal lobotomy.[5] This contempt for working knowledge and the horizon of real-world engagement has an august lineage. For Plato, as for most of the Athenian elites, work was the curse of slaves; practical knowledge by its very nature dulled the mind and prevented ascent to higher levels of understanding. The carriage maker might know how to fasten wheels to the axle; the potter might know how properly to prepare the clay; but the knowledge of the philosopher was different in kind and not simply in degree. The goal of philosophy was truth and beauty and wisdom: strictly speaking, the philosopher had no interest in what we today would call knowledge—finance, chemistry, medicine, and so on. But for the modern humanities, the major exponent of this otherworldliness was Matthew Arnold. In *The Function of Criticism* and *Culture and Anarchy* Arnold rescued the arts and letters by celebrating what amounts to their uselessness. To the "philistines" he relegated the work of creating railroads and discovering the cures for typhoid fever. Precisely because the man of letters knew nothing about these ordinary things, he could offer the higher, more encompassing, and more critical vision. Like the speaker in the poem *Dover Beach,* the critic alone surveyed the "darkling plain" while "ignorant armies" went on struggling below.

Although our marxists are usually quite ready to proclaim the decisive importance of "materiality," together with the human labor that has given human life its shape, neither Marx nor his epigones in composition have managed to renounce altogether the idealist legacy that inspired Arnold. While Marx imagined that he had built his philosophy on the foundations laid down by Darwin, modern Darwinists understand what modern marxists do not: there is no evolutionary telos, no direction to history. The only truth of evolution is that species evolve under the pressures of natural selection. These species may become more complex over time, or they may become less complex; more social, or less; more intelligent, or less. What this means for humankind is not simply that there are no guarantees, but also that the perpetual remaking of our lives is fundamentally experimental. Only after the fact can we ever know if our activity has brought us greater happiness or has plunged us into deeper misery. The spread of globalization may look like an utter disaster, but it probably explains why the U.S. and China have not already launched a new Cold War. And it has probably helped to break the stranglehold of the *Partido Revolucionacio Institucional* (PRI) in Mexico. While I admit that globalization holds the possibility of undermining the lives of working people around the world, hastening the death of the environment as well, I want to study the issue in its real complexity, instead of using every shred of evidence to confirm a view I already hold.

What might this all mean, in a practical sense, for those of us who teach writing? On my desk right now I have letter from the mayor of Somerville, New Jersey, and in it he tells the story of a Rutgers undergraduate who completed a planning document as her research project for one of our courses in "Writing for Business and the Professions." After submitting the paper, she sent a copy to the city's Planning Board, and then to her surprise they incorporated it into their own documents. At the same time, they offered her a job after graduation. I have received letters like this one on other occasions as well: from students who wrote grant proposals that went on to get funded; from the editors of various law reviews; and even from the dean of a medical school commending the "Writing in the Sciences" course his daughter took last year. About three weeks ago I received an email with the heading "just to keep in touch," from a former student in our internship program, who now writes for Fox 5 Television in New York. Openly or otherwise, many of my colleagues in English have turned up their noses at achievements like these, while the marxists in my own field have denounced me as the tool of an oppressive economic regime. What good does it do, they might remonstrate, to add a few acres of open space to a midsized bedroom community, when the change we really need is a total transformation— the complete overthrow of capitalist patriarchy and advent of heaven on earth. Of course, our marxists have no idea how such a change might actually happen, other than through the practice of continuous critique. Nor can they say what their paradise will look like specifically. (Will there be representative government? Will people still have money? Will people still get married and have last names? Will the state raise the children? Will kids still get an allowance?) In my view, no one benefits from this sort of absurdly long-range dreaming, just as no one eats in the long term, but only meal by meal. How concretely to revise land-use policies qualifies as genuine knowledge in my instrumentalist book. By contrast, how to tease out suppressed class conflict in a beer commercial is not just a waste of time but a destructive fraud, since it encourages the unwitting to suppose that they actually know something or have really made some kind of difference in the world, when all they have done is to watch TV and whine about it. And, of course, they still drink the beer.

Following the course I have charted out would probably entail that we relinquish forever our hopes for the status of a discipline on the model of English, with a canon of our own and so forth. But I believe that disciplinarity is not what we need now. The great repressed of the humanities is the transience of knowledge. Yes, everyone recognizes that *The Canterbury Tales* and Shakespeare will live forever, but who reads, or even remembers, Charles Hall Grandgent or E. M. W. Tillyard—the first, a leading Dante scholar of his day; the second, *the* authority on the Renaissance? Somewhere, even now, a Ph.D. candidate has on her desk a copy of Tillyard's tiny opus *The Elizabethan World*

Picture or Grandgent's massive study *Dante Alighieri,* but these scholars, and the works of countless scholars just like them, are nothing more than antiquarian curiosities. This is the fate that awaits all scholarship. The day may not be far off when Frederic Jameson is as forgotten as Granville Hicks, his marxist counterpart half a century earlier. Our historians of criticism may already have started penning their sprawling chapters on "The Age of Derrida," yet increasingly it seems that this great man is destined to occupy, not a large, enduring place in our hearts and minds, but a two-foot expanse on the library shelf, after Henri Bergson and before Jean-Paul Sartre, also leading lights of French philosophy in their time.

If you don't believe me, you might conduct a brief experiment for yourself. Go to your nearest library and find an anthology of criticism published before 1970. For the sake of honesty, I just now pulled one at random from the stacks where I often work, *Contemporary American Literary Criticism,* a collection "selected and arranged" by James Cloyd Bowman, A.M., Litt. D., and published in 1926 by Henry Holt. Here are the names of the critics featured: James Russell Lowell, Walt Whitman, J. E. Spinarn, H. L. Mencken, W. C. Brownell, Irving Babbitt, Grant Showerman, Stuart P. Sherman. Percy H. Boynton, Van Wyck Brooks, Sherwood Anderson, Robert Morss Lovett, Carl Van Doren, Irwin Edman, Llewellyn Jones, Theodore Maynard, William McFee, John Macy, Henry Seidel Canby, Amy Lowell, Conrad Aiken, Fred Lewis Pattee, George Woodberry. Setting aside the canonical authors included in the collection to lend authority to the rest, ask yourself how many of these scholars have you ever heard of and how many, or how few, have you actually read.

I don't mean to suggest that these essays are not *worth* reading; I assume that many of the writers in the collection have something important to say and say it with intelligence, skill, and conviction. But the fact remains that the one inescapable mission of the university is the continuous production of new knowledge, and this requires, in turn, the continuous displacement of knowledge no longer new. I understand, of course, that this claim runs counter to much of the explicit ideology underlying archival disciplines such as literary studies, which has consistently claimed to preserve the heritage of the past. These claims notwithstanding, the persistence of a canon or of quasi-permanent categories, such as genre and historical periods, should not mislead us into believing that all scholarship up to the present day tells a coherent, collective story in which the hero is "the profession" or "criticism" or, simply, "the advancement of learning." I suggest instead that academic knowledge does not evolve organically and incrementally like a conversation among leisured interlocutors, but is driven forward haphazardly by a complex manifold of forces.

It is these forces that we must understand better than we do, not only if we want to teach writing in the way I have suggested—in conjunction with real-world social practices—but also if we want the teaching of writing to continue as a quasi-autonomous enterprise. Chris Anson's narrative should remind us that the growing desperation of English studies may end with the historical tragedy of our reabsorption in the tradition of belles lettres. Anson's account is important not least of all because it shows the naivety of all our talk about discourse communities, professionalism, and so on. It seems to me that Anson did everything a person in his position could do. He published voluminously; he won numerous awards for teaching and administration; he earned a national reputation. All of these achievements should have invested him with institutional power—at least if we accept the conventional thinking about the university and the disciplines. But they didn't, and instead of wringing our hands as compositionists often do (though not Anson himself, I'm glad to see), we need to think again about the politics of knowledge. I would like to close with a few speculations on that subject—as prolegomena to future research.

First, disciplines exist with a system of disciplines. Within that system, prestige and power get distributed hierarchically, although prestige and power may not always go hand in hand. Cosmology, for instance, enjoys great prestige, but its power depends on its continued relevance to technological innovation. At many universities, for this reason, medical schools are among the most prestigious and protected units, precisely because they can draw into their orbits enormous amounts of funding, federal and private alike. Genetic engineering, biochemistry, pharmacology, and computer science—these disciplines sit atop the pyramid because of the revenues they generate. Although many observers of the academy deplore this "commercialization," power and prestige have always followed from the capacity to make change or else to prevent it. The difference between the humanities and the sciences is not that one has become commercialized while the other has not, but that the humanities have typically drawn their power and prestige from an avowed ability to slow down the pace of change or to arrest certain changes altogether. It was politically expedient, for example, for Americans in the years after World War II to think of England as the

Mother Country and of Europe as the land where our cousins live.[6] Now that these alliances have come less important, Anglo-Saxon attitudes may be on the wane, and as the pace of change continues to accelerate, Americans may feel much less acutely the need to put on the brakes.

My point is not only that the various disciplines are inherently unequal, but that the prestige and power of a discipline may have little to do with the numbers of articles published or titled chairs occupied or journals linked to national organizations. The decline of English ought to disabuse us of this fantasy. More archival research on Fred Newton Scott will not increase our chances of survival in the academic struggle for resources. Our best chance lies, instead, with getting closer to the funding that sustains the academy's most prominent players. This means linking our courses to medical education, to schools of engineering, and to programs in management and business. Call me vulgar if you must, but I see medicine, the sciences, and so on, as the principal levers of social change, for good or for ill, for better or for worse, as our society decides. Turning our backs on commercialization won't give us a moral advantage; it will simply leave us all the more powerless. Please consider also that alliances with medical schools and with business and the sciences—especially alliances that entail the sharing of financial resources—would give us powerful assistance when we need it the most, on that crucial summer weekend when some part-time dean (who may or may not be sleeping with the local Donne scholar) decides to take out the axe. Of course, we can forge other alliances as well. Where I teach, for example, about a third of all our teaching assistants come from departments other than English, and these departments have so far been strong enough en bloc to foil English in its periodic forays on our territory.

We should remember, too, that the standing of the disciplines depends on public perception to some extent. Even in its moribund condition, English benefits from the persistence of a long-lived propaganda machine. Why is it, after all, that Fish's 600-page discussion of Milton has made the pages of the nation's largest paper? Is it because more people are actually reading the 1645 *Poems of Mr. John Milton*? Is it because Stanley Fish has played a crucial part in shaping the temper of our times? Obviously not. But English, over more than a century, has created a network of quasi-popular venues in the form of book reviews and topical essays. Kermode writes for the *New York Times*, Louis Menand for the *New Yorker*, Mark Edmundson for the *Atlantic Monthly*. Needless to say, composition enjoys nothing like a comparable network. Mike Rose and William

Lutz stand virtually alone as our only truly public voices. If we want to survive, this situation has to change. Instead of grooming all our graduate students for careers publishing in *Philosophy and Rhetoric* and *CCC* (not to disparage these excellent journals), we might try to prepare a few of them for a different audience. If students can be taught to write like Habermas, they can be taught to write like Bill McKibben. And if they have a working knowledge of a field that people respect—let's say business, urban planning, or bioengineering—then they will be prepared to take up Hermes' role, connecting our various specialists to a public often desperately in need of explanation. Of course, such writers already exist—but they tend to teach in schools of journalism, when they teach at all. Still, matters might be different. Should the day arrive when our graduates can write for truly public readerships, English might conceivably begin to fret about the prospects of *our* absorbing *them*.

NOTES

1. See Geertz's "Deep Hanging Out" and John Guillory's *Cultural Capital.*

2. For one of many doleful reports on the current state of English, see Andrew Delbanco. Delbanco begins his discussion by citing Carol Christ, a provost at Berkeley, who had recently written, "On every campus there is one department whose name need only be mentioned to make people laugh; you don't want that department to be yours." On most campuses, Delbanco suggests, that department will be English (32). His idea, however, is that English return to what it used to be. Anthropology, to its credit, has been somewhat more constructive and forward-looking in its reflections. See Grimshaw and Hart.

3. As Armando Bravo Martinez points out, "With the exception of about ten countries (the so-called Big Emerging Markets), the majority of Africa, South Asia, and Latin America has experienced mostly economic decline in the past 30 years" (70). The World Bank's own statistics indicate that the absolute number of poor people increased over the last twenty years (World Bank). These figures, of course, are likely to downplay the depth of the failures. According to the Global Policy Forum, the number of poor grew by 17 percent between 1970 and 1985 (Gates).

4. Barber is a major political theorist, Blackmore a psychologist. See Barber and Blackmore.

5. I am well aware that my argument is at odds with the broad sweep of academic thought since Horkheimer and Adorno, whose influence I regard as a disaster for the left. For them, instrumentalism meant submission to a soulless, mechanical regimen. Critical thought was supposed to begin, by contrast, with the repudiation of means-ends rationality: instead of asking "how," the practitioner of critical theory must ask "why." But my objection is that without a knowledge of the "how," discussions of the "why" become silly, arcane, and ineffectual. See Horkheimer and Adorno, *Dialectic of Enlightenment,* and Max Horkheimer, *Critique of Instrumental Reason.*

6. For an elaboration of this argument, see Bill Readings, *The University in Ruins.* Actually, Readings should have entitled his book *Literary Studies in Ruins.*

AFTERWORD
Countering the Naysayers—Independent Writing Programs
as Successful Experiments in American Education

Larry W. Burton

ONE

We are conditioned by countless negative perspectives on American education, on the corrupt nature of our political institutions, on the bleak future for individual consciousness, on the failed experiment in nation-building that began a relatively brief two hundred years ago. Poets, novelists, historians, philosophers, literary critics, educators, and many others have passed judgment on these situations as if they are permanent facts of existence without the possibility of improving themselves. For these critics, pessimism outweighs optimism. In almost any direction we turn, we hear voices of doom, none more gloomy than Allen Ginsberg's. Writing in 1959, for example, he opens an essay with this assessment:

> Recent history is the record of a vast conspiracy to impose one level of mechanical consciousness on mankind and exterminate all manifestations of that unique part of human sentience, identical in all men, which the individual shares with his Creator. The suppression of contemplative life is nearly complete. (3)

For Ginsberg, poetry is not only the refuge for "contemplative life," but it is also a place beckoning "those who've entered the world of the spirit." It is an escape from deadening and corrupting modern life for the artist.

Rather than cite examples of negative perspectives *ad nauseam* on various American institutions, this essay will focus instead on something positive—namely, independent writing programs as successful experiments in higher education. Many readers already know the arguments against these programs, ranging from the position that the costs are prohibitive, that faculty are either untrained or lack appropriate professional credentials, to the position that freestanding departments deprive students of exposure to the liberal arts, most notably to literature. Readers of this book can see these perspectives at work in Chris Anson's story about the independent program at the University of Minnesota that was dissolved, despite evidence supporting its effectiveness. In Section Two of *A Field of Dreams: Independent Writing Programs and the Future of Composition Studies*, Anson speculates that the reasons for this dismantling were not only financial but also something that Barry Maid calls Academic Fundamentalism. As explanation, Anson offers an argument from one of the English professors that quite possibly alarmed university administration into shutting down the writing program.

> The field of composition is likely to lose its heritage in the tradition of rhetorical studies that evolved into literary criticism and to lose touch with the finer workings of our language by which even the earliest groping efforts are tuned. (Do you know what happens to people who spend most of their reading time between the language of "remedial" students and the language of irremediable behavioral scientists?' (Manning, qtd in Anson 165)

Anson reasons that Manning's text was "less a plea for keeping composition allied with literary study than a rejection of the very questions that composition scholars and teachers continue to ask in their professional work, chief among them how to help struggling writers, those 'remedial students' whose writing no good literary specialist wants to read" (165).

Rather than simply go along with the way in which pessimism has answered optimism about this experiment at Minnesota, it seems more useful to lend one's problem-solving abilities to working on our educational institutions, specifically to the universities that are experimenting with independent programs as a way of educating students in the fundamentally important skill of writing. Experiments do not always succeed, nor do they always fail. But what they do is presuppose a critique of the status quo. As I hope to suggest, *A Field of Dreams: Independent Writing Programs and the Future of Composition Studies* contributes information, along with vital perspectives toward the experiment in progress in American education, particularly with reference to independent writing programs as a logical home for writing education in postsecondary education today. Both the ongoing development of our political institutions and the fact that several educational institutions have changed their stance on where writing should be taught has emboldened me to ask: "Why not have more and more independent departments and programs of writing in the United States?"

TWO

A Field of Dreams: Independent Writing Programs and the Future of Composition Studies is not deliberately controversial. Its purpose is not to plot a course for the development of independent writing programs, nor is it to malign English departments to make ourselves look good in comparison. (What would make this book "upsetting" would be a critique of "dependent" writing programs. Critiques of English studies exist, and one can find them without any trouble in bookstores and libraries.) Our book looks elsewhere. We had a different reason for putting together this book, and we wanted a chance to speak our minds about our freestanding department at Georgia Southern University, where we remain optimistic about the unit's future. Today, as was true five years ago, we are optimistic because the department has the sanction and ongoing support of the university (the university would not have created the department of Writing and Linguistics in order to see it fail), and while the unit was in its early years, it made sense for us to see who else was in our situation. It seemed natural to look outward for signs of similar forms of life. We wondered if we were by ourselves, so to speak.

In short, *A Field of Dreams* is not a book that attacks English departments, communication arts departments, academic success centers, developmental studies departments, or any other sites where students take writing courses. But it is ambitious. This book is about problems that face those of us who belong to independent programs. Even departments that run smoothly had their share of problems along the way, bumps in the road, unforeseen "things," most of which they overcame, worked around or through (e.g., Harvard, Hampden-Sydney, Winnipeg).

More to the point, this book is ambitious because of what it implies about the future. The time may be coming when high school students make their college choices on the basis of the first-year writing program, the usefulness of the writing minor, the attractiveness of courses required for the writing major, the reputations of the writing faculty, the resources for writing students (e.g., "smart" classrooms, laptop access, writing scholarships, internships, opportunities for interdisciplinary concentrations that feature writing courses, to name a few). The time will come when "writing" courses will look completely different from the way that they look today. Independent departments have already given faculty a fresh way of thinking about what it means to teach writing, and they have given students increased opportunities for developing themselves as writers. These are implications that need underscoring. They constitute perhaps the major argument for supporting independent departments of writing. The goal of producing excellent writers within independent departments means that the department can plan a curriculum that aims at putting students through writing and rhetoric courses that round them out as writers. This goal presupposes a writing curriculum that exists in few, if any, English departments. In addition to rhetorical knowledge and skills courses in professional and technical writing, the courses for writing students include electives from many departments. Writers need the freedom to read what interests them and what serves their desires as emerging intellectuals, whether the reading comes from literature, history, art, art history, psychology, anthropology, sociology, business, or health and professional fields.

THREE

Only because they are in their infancy, independent departments are in the experimental stage at Georgia Southern University, Grand Valley State University, San Diego State University, the University of Arkansas at Little Rock, and Arizona State University East. The Ph.D. program in rhetoric and composition at Syracuse University is in its teens. Hampden-Sydney's program is a kid, too, in comparison with Harvard's Expository Writing Program, which is probably the oldest continuing program in the United States. (Harvard's program underwent a significant transformation in the late 1980's, which changed the one-course requirement into a thematic offering that allowed teachers freedom within general constraints. According to Nancy Sommers, the program's director, the changes have met with enthusiasm by all parties, including upper administration.)

Certainly, the mentality in an independent department is different from what one will find in many English departments. One reason for the difference is the make-up of faculty—i.e., independent departments like Grand Valley's or Georgia Southern's have created a community of scholars in writing studies bolstered by hires with Ph.D.'s in rhetoric and composition. In the 1990's, for example, Grand Valley State hired eight tenure-track faculty in rhetoric and composition. Between 1997 and 2002, Georgia Southern University hired thirteen assistant professors, ten of whom hold Ph.D.'s in rhetoric and composition. Syracuse University boasts ten tenure-track faculty in rhetoric and composition.

A second reason for the different mentality has to do with departmental autonomy. Independent writing programs write their own policy manuals, including tenure and promotion guidelines. They develop curricula, design courses, and build up areas of faculty expertise that most likely would not enjoy support in English departments. The Department of Writing and Linguistics at Georgia Southern University, for example, has hired two faculty in technical and professional writing, one in computers and writing, one in gender studies and identity issues, one in cultural studies, one in minority studies and writing, one in the history of rhetoric and composition, one in assessment, one in creative writing, one in writing center administration, and two in linguistics. What English department would hire in all of these areas? What English department would share the same vision of the future in writing studies or uphold the same values when it comes to putting "writing" on equal footing with "literature"? Following this train of thought, what English department would not perceive itself threatened when it witnessed an independent department of writing growing and garnering support from the university administration? In time, independent departments of writing will declare that their majors and their "writers" are different from majors and "writers" produced within English departments. The time will come when independent departments will assert that their writers are not only different, but that they are "better" than writers produced within English departments. One has only to read Turner and Kearns's article in this collection to understand how independent writing programs could profit from aligning themselves with the concept of the "civic rhetorician," who is not only guided by rhetoric's "internal standards of completion and perfection," but who also "practices his art responsibly, aware that his rhetorical choices will have consequences not only for himself but also for his auditors and for the community they both inhabit" (this volume, 90). In other words, the "experiment" in independent programs might well focus on the public rhetor as its identity for the future.

FOUR

At this moment in the history of American education, it is hard to imagine contributors to this book—at least those who are from independent units—asserting that independent programs produce better writers than English departments. To the best of my knowledge, none of the independent departments represented in *A Field of Dreams* makes this claim to superiority. But perhaps they should. Perhaps the time has come to ask where students should go to reach their potential as writers, and while we are asking the question of "where" students should go, we should also ask questions about our definition of good writing and good writers.

In separate articles within this volume, Jane Hindman and Angela Crow identify three requirements that must be met before independent departments can focus without distractions on their work as writing teachers in independent departments. The first requirement has to do with labor issues, more specifically with who teaches writing, what their qualifications are for teaching writing, and how these faculty will be held accountable for the writing instruction they have been charged to deliver in different areas of writing, which include creative writing, writing in the workplace, journalism, academic writing, and rhetoric. The second requirement is resources (money for travel, supplies, equipment, books, to name a few) that speak loudly on behalf of a commitment from the institution for instruction in writing. Finally, the third requirement is leadership. Independent departments need visionaries who are willing to call for changes that will improve upon what constitutes a top-notch writing education. When these requirements have been met, independent departments will be able to proclaim that they serve a purpose different from that of English departments. Then independent departments can say that they give students and teachers the freedom needed to foreground writing practices that are either housed in or identified with centers, degree programs, concentrations, clusters, minors, interdisciplinary alliances, teacher development, and classrooms. When all requirements have been met, members of independent departments of writing will have discovered a new mentality–a refreshing mentality—out of which they conduct their professional lives. Who is to say that this new mentality is not already making a positive difference in the lives of students and teachers?

REFERENCES

Altieri, Charles. 1983. The ADE and Institutional Politics: The Examples of Tenure and Composition. *ADE Bulletin* 17: 24–27.

Amorose, Thomas. 2000. WPA Work at the Small College or University: Re-Imagining Power and Making the Small School Visible. *Writing Program Administration* 23:3 (Spring):85–103.

Anderson, Joel. 18 Mar 1993. Where Do We Go From Here. Memo to Department of English. University of Arkansas Little Rock.

Anson, Chris M. 19 July 1997. (Re)locating Literacy: Reflections on the Place of Writing Programs in Higher Education. Annual Conference of the Council of Writing Program Administrators, Houghton, MI.

———. 2002. Figuring It Out: Writing Programs in the Context of University Budgets. Enos and Brown: 233–52.

———. 6 Nov 1996. Administration. Online posting to WPA-L. Archived at http://lists.asu.edu/archives/wpa-l.html.

Anson, Chris M. and Carol Rutz. 1998. Graduate Students, Writing Programs, and Consensus-Based Management: Collaboration in the Face of Disciplinary Ideology. *Writing Program Administration* 21(2/3): 106–120.

Anson, Chris M. and Richard Beach. 1999. Journeys in Journaling. Bishop: 20–29.

Anson, Chris M., and Robert L. Brown, Jr. 1999. Subject to Interpretation: Researching the Textual Representation of Writing Programs and Its Effects on the Politics of Administration. Rose and Weiser: 141–52.

Anson, Chris M. and Richard Jewell. 2000. Shadows of the Mountain. Schell and Stock: 47– 75.

Appleby, Bruce C. and John C. Brereton. 1990. Review of Freshman Composition Program, University of Arkansas Little Rock. Report for Council of Writing Program Administrators.

Association of American University Professors. 1940. Statement of Principles on Academic Freedom and Tenure With 1970 Interpretive Comments. http://www.aaup.org/1940stat.htm. Accessed 27 Mar 2001.

Ball, Stephen. 1987. *The Micropolitics of the School.* London: Methuen.

Barber, Benjamin. 1998. *A Place for Us: How to Make Civil Society and Democracy Strong.* New York: Hill and Wang.

Baudrillard, Jean. 1983. *Simulations.* Translated by Paul Foss, Paul Patton, and Philip Beitchman. New York: Semiotext(e).

Bender, John and David E. Wellbery. 1990. Rhetoricality: On the Modernist Return of Rhetoric. Bender and Wellerby: 3–39.

Bender, John and David E. Wellbery, eds. 1990. *The Ends of Rhetoric: History, Theory, Practice.* Stanford, CA: Stanford University Press.

Bender, Thomas. 1993. *Intellect and Public Life, Essays on the Social History of Academic Intellectuals in the United States.* Baltimore: Johns Hopkins University Press.

Benjamin, Ernst. 1995. A Faculty Response to the Fiscal Crisis: From Defense to Offense. Bérubé and Nelson: 52–72.

Benjamin, Lloyd. 17 Mar 1993. Current Events. Memo to Department of English. University of Arkansas Little Rock.

———. 6 May 1993. Futures. Memo to Department of English. University of Arkansas Little Rock.

Bergonzi, Bernard. 1990. *Exploding English: Criticism, Theory, Culture.* Oxford: Clareden Press.

Bérubé, Michael. 1994. *Public Access: Literary Theory and American Cultural Politics.* New York: Verso.

———. 1998. *The Employment of English: Theory, Jobs, and the Future of Literary Studies.* New York: NY University Press.

Bérubé, Michael, and Cary Nelson, eds. 1995. *Higher Education Under Fire: Politics, Economics, and the Crisis of the Humanities.* New York: Routledge.

Bishop, Wendy, ed. 1999. *The Subject is Writing* 2nd ed. Portsmouth, NH: Heinemann.

Bishop, Wendy and Gay Lynn Crossley. 1993. Doing the Hokey Pokey: Why Writing Program Administrators' Job Conditions Don't Seem to Be Improving. *Composition Studies/Freshman English News* 21.2: 46–59.

———. 1996. How to Tell a Story of Stopping: The Complexities of Narrating a WPA's Experiences. *Writing Program Administration* 19.3 (Spring): 70–79.

Bizzell, Patricia. 1986. Composing Processes: An Overview. Petroskey and Bartholomae: 49–70.

Blackmore, Susan. 2000. *The Meme Machine.* New York: Oxford University Press.

Bloom, Lynn Z., Donald Daiker, and Edward M. White, eds. 1996. *Composition in the Twenty-First Century: Crisis and Change.* Carbondale: Southern Illinois University Press.

Boland, Mary. 2001. *Academic Freedom and the Struggle for the Subject of Composition.* Ph.D. diss., University of Rochester.

Boyer, Ernest. 1990. *Scholarship Reconsidered: Priorities of the Professoriate.* Princeton: Carnegie Foundation for the Advancement of Teaching.

Brandt, Deborah. 1999. Literacy Learning and Economic Change. *Harvard Educational Review* 69: 373–394.

———. 1995. Accumulating Literacy: Writing and Learning to Write in the Twentieth Century. *College English* 57: 649–68.

———. 1998. Sponsors of Literacy. *College Composition and Communication* 49: 165–85.

Braxton, John M. and Joseph B. Berger. 1999. How Disiplinary Consensus Affects Faculty. Menges et al.: 243–67.

Brown, Stuart, Rebecca Jackson, and Theresa Enos. 2000. The Arrival of Rhetoric in the Twenty-First Century: The 1999 Survey of Doctoral Programs in Rhetoric. *Rhetoric Review* 18: 233–42.

Bruce, Bertram and Hogan, Maureen P. 1998. The Disappearance of Technology: Toward an Ecological Model of Literacy. Reinking: 269–81.

Bullock, Richard and John Trimbur, eds. 1991. *The Politics of Writing Instruction: Postsecondary*. Portsmouth, NH: Boynton/Cook Publishers, Heinemann.

Case Study. Spring 1993. *ADE Bulletin* 104: 56.

Castells, Manuel. 1996. *The Rise of the Network Society*. The Information Age: Economy, Society, and Culture, vol. 1. Malden, MA: Blackwell.

———. 1997. *The Power of Identity*. The Information Age: Economy, Society, and Culture, vol. 2. Malden, MA: Blackwell.

———. 1998. *End of the Millennium*. The Information Age: Economy, Society, and Culture, vol 3. Malden, MA: Blackwell.

Coalition on the Academic Workforce. 1999. Who Is Teaching in U.S. College Classrooms? A Collaborative Study of Undergraduate Faculty, Fall 1999. Press release. American Historical Association. Accessed 8 Feb 2001. http://www.theaha.org/caw/pressrelease.htm.

Condon, Bill. 1 Dec 2000. Job Opportunity. (Posting for Victor Villanueva). Online post to WPA-L. Archived at http://lists.asu.edu/archives/wpa-l.html.

Conference on College Composition and Communication. 1989. Statement of Principles and Standards for the Postsecondary Teaching of Writing. *College Composition and Communication* 40: 329–36.

———. 1998. CCCC Promotion and Tenure Guidelines for Work with Technology. Accessed 22 Dec 2000. Available http://www.ncte.org/positions/4c-tp-tech.html

Connolly, Paul and Teresa Vivaldi, eds. 1986 *New Methods in College Writing Programs: Theory and Practice*. New York: MLA.

Connors, Robert J. 1994. Crisis and Panacea in Composition Studies: A History. Winterowd and Gillespie: 86–109.

———. 1999. Composition History and Disciplinarity. Rosner, Boehm and Journet: 3–22.

———. 6 Nov 1996. Administration. Online posting to the WPA-L. Archived at http://lists.asu.edu/archives/wpa-l.html.

Consortium on Negotiation and Conflict Resolution. Feb and Mar 2000. Executive Summary of An Organizational Development Process for the Department of Writing and Linguistics, Georgia Southern University. Georgia State University.

Corbett, Edward P. J. 1992. The Shame of the Current Standards for Promotion and Tenure. *Journal of Advanced Composition* 12: 111–16.

Council of Writing Program Administrators. 1999. WPA Outcomes Statement for First-Year Composition. *WPA: Writing Program Administration* 23.1/2: 59–66. Available at: http://www.cas.ilstu.edu/English/Hesse/outcomes.html.

Crowley, Sharon. 1998. *Composition in the University: Historical and Polemical Essays.* Pittsburgh: University of Pittsburgh Press.

Deibert, Ronald. 1997. *Parchment, Printing, and Hypermedia: Communication in World Order Transformation.* New York: Columbia University Press.

Delbanco, Andrew. 4 Nov 1999. The Decline and Fall of Literature. *New York Review of Books:* 32–38.

DeLong, Linwood et al. 1993. The Report of the Internal Committee to Review the Writing Program. Winnipeg.

DePalma, Anthony. 24 June 2001. Latin America's Poor Survive It All. Even Boom Times. *New York Times on the Web.* Available at http://www.nytimes.com/2001/06/24/ weekinreview/24DEPA.html.

Department of English and Philosophy, Georgia Southern University. 4 Oct 1996 through 23 May 1997. Minutes.

Diamond, Robert M. 1994. *Serving on Promotion and Tenure Committees: A Faculty Guide.* Bolton: Anker.

Donovan, Timothy. 1991. Professing Composition in the Academic Marketplace. Bullock and Trimbur: 171–178.

Eagleton, Terry. 1983. *Literary Theory: An Introduction.* Minneapolis: Minnesota University Press.

Elbow, Peter and Pat Belanoff. 1986. State University of New York: Portfolio-Based Evaluation Program. Connolly and Vivaldi: 95–105.

———. 1989. *A Community of Writers: A Workshop Course in Writing.* New York: Random House.

Enos, Theresa. 1996. *Gender Roles and Faculty Lives in Rhetoric and Composition.* Carbondale, IL: Southern Illinois University Press.

Enos, Theresa and Stuart Brown, eds. 2002. *The Writing Program Administrator's Sourcebook: A Guide to Reflective Institutional Practice.* Hillsdale, NJ: Erlbaum.

Farris, Christine and Chris M. Anson, eds. 1998. *Under Construction: Working at the Intersections of Composition Theory, Research, and Practice.* Logan, UT: Utah State University Press.

Finkin, Matthew W., ed. 1996. *The Case for Tenure.* Ithaca: Cornell University Press.

Fish, Stanley. 1980. *Is There a Text in this Class? The Authority of Interpretive Communities.* Cambridge: Harvard University Press.

———. 1995. *Professional Correctness.* Cambridge: Harvard University Press.

———. 2000. Nice Work If You Can Get Them to Do It. *MLA Profession 2000:* 109–114.

Flash, Pamela. 1999. Personal communication.

Fleishman, Avrom. 1995. The Condition of English: Taking Stock in a Time of Culture Wars. *College English* 57: 807–22.

Fleming, David. 1998. Rhetoric as a Course of Study. *College English* 61: 169–191.

Fontaine, Sheryl and Susan Hunter, eds. 1993. *Writing Ourselves into the Story: Unheard Voices from Composition Studies.* Carbondale IL: Southern Illinois University Press.

Freire, Paulo. 1970. *Pedagogy of the Oppressed.* New York: Continuum Press.

Fulwiler, Toby and Art Young. 1990. *Programs that Work: Models and Methods for Writing Across the Curriculum.* Portsmouth, NH: Boynton Cook/Heinemann.

Garver, Eugene. 1994. *Aristotle's Rhetoric: An Art of Character.* Chicago: University of Chicago Press.

Gates, Jeff. May 1999. Statistics on Poverty and Inequality. *Global Policy Forum.* http://www.igc.org/globalpolicy/socecon/inequal/gates99.htm

Gebhardt, Richard C.1997. Evolving Approaches to Scholarship, Promotion and Tenure in Composition Studies. Gebhardt and Gebhardt: 1–20.

Gebhardt, Richard C. and Barbara Genelle Smith Gebhardt, eds. 1997. *Academic Advancement in Composition Studies Scholarship, Publication, Promotion, Tenure.* Mahwah NJ: Erlbaum.

Gee, James. 1990. *Social Linguistics and Literacies: Ideology in Discourses.* Brighton, GB: Falmer Press.

Geertz, Clifford. 22 Oct 1998. Deep Hanging Out. *New York Review of Books.* http://www.nybooks.com/nyrev/WWWarchdisplay.cgi?19981022069R.

Geisler, Eliezer. 1997. *Managing the Aftermath of Radical Corporate Change: Re-engineering, Restructuring and Reinvention.* Westport CT: Quorum Books.

George, Diana and Diane Shoos. 1999. Dropping Bread Crumbs in the Intertextual Forest: Critical Literacy in a Postmodern Age or: We Should Have Brought a Compass. Hawisher and Selfe: 115–26.

Giddens, Anthony. 1979. *Central Problems in Social Theory: Action, Structure and Contradiction in Social Analysis.* Berkeley and Los Angeles: University of California Press.

Ginsberg, Allen. 2000. Poetry, Violence, and the Trembling Lambs. *Deliberate Prose: Selected Essays 1952–1995.* New York: HarperCollins.

Glassick, Charles E., Mary Taylor Huber, and Gene I. Maeroff. 1997. *Scholarship Assessed: Evaluation of the Professoriate.* San Francisco: Jossey-Bass.

Goggin, Maureen Daly. 1995. The Disciplinary Instability of Composition. Petraglia: 27–48.

Gottschalk, Katherine K. 1995. The Writing Program in the University. *ADE Bulletin* 112: 1–6.

———. 30 Jan 2001. Re: The politics of changing requirements. Online posting WPA-L. http://lists.asu.edu/archives/wpa-l.html.

Graff, Gerald. 1987. *Professing Literature: An Institutional History.* Chicago: University of Chicago Press.

———. 1992. *Beyond the Culture Wars.* New York: Norton.

Graff, H. J. 1987. *The Legacy of Literacy: Continuities and Contradictions in Western Culture and Society.* Bloomington, IN: Indiana University Press.

Graubard, Stephen R. 1997. Preface to the Issue: American Academic Culture in Transformation: Fifty Years, Four Disciplines. *Daedalus* 126.1: i–x.

Greenblatt, Stephen and Giles Gunn, eds. 1992. *Redrawing the Boundaries: The Transformation of English and American Literary Studies.* New York: MLA.

Grimshaw, Anna and Keith Hart. Anthropology and the Crisis of the Intellectuals. *Critique of Anthropology* 14.3: 227–61.

Guillory, John. 1993. *Cultural Capital: the Problem of Literary Canon Formation.* Chicago: University of Chicago Press.

Gunner, Jeanne. 1993. The Fate of the Wyoming Resolution. Fontaine and Hunter: 107–22.

Hairston, Maxine. 1985. Breaking Our Bonds and Reaffirming Our Connections. *College Composition and Communication* 36: 272–82.

———. 1992. Diversity, Ideology, and Teaching Writing. *College Composition and Communication* 43: 179–95.

Harris, Joseph. 2000. Meet the New Boss, Same as the Old Boss: Class Consciousness in Composition. *College Composition and Communication* 52: 43–68.

Hartzog, Carol P. 1986. *Composition and the Academy: A Study of Writing Program Administration.* New York: MLA.

Harvard Expository Writing Program. n.d. *Expository Writing at Harvard.* Pamphlet. Cambridge, MA: Harvard University.

———. 2000. Harvard Study of Undergraduate Writing. *Expos.* Harvard University. Accessed 15 Dec 2000. http://www.fas.harvard.edu/~expos/studyinfo.html.

———. 2000. Harvard Writing Project. *Expos.* Harvard University. Accessed 15 Dec. 2000. http://www.fas.harvard.edu/~expos/hwp.

Haswell, Richard and Min-Zahn Lu. 2000. *Comptales.* NY: Longman.

Hawisher, Gail and Cynthia Selfe, eds. 1999. *Passions, Pedagogies, and 21ˢᵗ Century Technologies.* Logan, UT: Utah State University Press.

Herrington, Anne and Charles Moran, eds. 1992. *Writing, Teaching, and Learning in the Disciplines.* New York: MLA.

Hindman, Jane E. 2002. Writing An Important Body of Scholarship: A Proposal for an Embodied Rhetoric of Professional Practice. *Journal of Advanced Composition.* In press.

Horkheimer, Max. 1974. *Critique of Instrumental Reason.* New York: Seabury.

Horkheimer, Max and T. W. Adorno. 1972. *Dialectic of Enlightenment.* New York: Herder and Herder.

Horner, Bruce. 2000. *Terms of Work for Composition: A Materialist Critique.* Albany: SUNY Press.

Howard, Rebecca Moore. 30 Jan 2001. Re: The politics of changing requirements. Online posting WPA-L. Archived at http://lists.asu.edu/archives/wpa-l.html.

Iser, Wolfgang. 1993. *The Fictive and the Imaginary: Charting Literary Anthropology.* Baltimore: Johns Hopkins University Press.

Jameson, Frederic. 1991. *Postmodernism or the Cultural Logic of Late Capitalism.* Durham, NC: Duke University Press.

Jauss, Hans Robert. 1982. *Aesthetic Experience and Literary Hermeneutic.* Trans. Michael Show. Minneapolis: University of Minnesota Press.

Johns, Ann and Carol Sweedler-Brown. Oct 1999. DRWS: A Short History. *1999 Academic Program Review Self-Study: Department of Rhetoric and Writing Studies San Diego State University.* 17–21.

Kearns, Judith and Brian Turner. 1997. Negotiated Independence: How a Canadian Writing Program Became a Centre. *Writing Program Administration* 21: 31–43.

Kermode, Frank. 24 June 2001. Cross-Examining Milton. Rev. of *How Milton Works* by Stanley Fish. *New York Times on the Web*. http://www.nytimes.com/books/01/06/24/ reviews/010624.24kermodt.html.

Kernan, Alvin, ed. 1997. *What's Happened to the Humanities?* Princeton, NJ: Princeton University Press.

Kinneavy, James. 1980. *A Theory of Discourse.* New York: Norton.

Kitzhaber, Alfred R. 1990. *Rhetoric in American Colleges: 1850–1900.* Dallas: Southern Methodist University Press.

Kolln, Martha. 1999. *Rhetorical Grammar: Grammatical Choices, Rhetorical Effects.* 3rd ed. Boston: Allyn and Bacon.

Kress, Gunther. 1999. 'English' at the Crossroads: Rethinking Curricula of Communication in the Context of the Turn to the Visual. Hawisher and Selfe: 66–88.

Lambert, L., and Tice, S., eds. 1993. *Preparing Graduate Students to Teach: A Guide to Programs that Improve Undergraduate Education and Develop Tomorrow's Faculty.* Washington, D.C.: American Association For Higher Education.

Lang, Susan, Janice Walker and Keith Dorwick, eds. 2000. Special Issue: Tenure 2000. *Computers and Composition* 17.1.

Leverenz, Carrie. 2000. Tenure and Promotion in Rhetoric and Composition. *College Composition and Communication* 52: 143–147.

Little, Sherry et al. Mar 1993. A Proposal for Establishing a New Department of Rhetoric and Writing Studies. San Diego State University.

Lindemann, Erika and Gary Tate, eds. 1991. *An Introduction to Composition Studies.* New York: Oxford University Press.

Luhmann, Niklas. 2000. Why Does Society Describe Itself as Postmodern? Rasch and Wolfe: 35–49.

Lunsford, Andrea, Helene Moglen, and James F. Slevin, eds. 1989. *The Future of Doctoral Studies in English.* New York: MLA.

Maclean's. 9 Nov 1992. 105.45: 78.

Mahala, Daniel, and Jody Swilky. 1997. Remapping the Geography of Service in English. *College English* 59: 625–646.

Maid, Barry. 23 Mar 1993. Another Program in Crisis. Online posting WPA-L. Archived at http://lists.asu.edu/archives/wpa-l.html.

———. 7 May 1993. YES!!! Online post WPA-L. Archived at http://lists.asu.edu/archives/wpa-l.html.

———. 14 April 1993. The Decision. Memo to Joel Anderson and Lloyd Benjamin. University of Arkansas Little Rock.

———. 19 April 1993. Some Final Reflections. Memo to Lloyd Benjamin and Joel Anderson. University of Arkansas Little Rock.

Mailloux, Stephen. 1998. *Reception Histories: Rhetoric, Pragmatism, and American Cultural Politics.* Ithaca: Cornell University Press.

Malchup, Fritz. 1996. In Defense of Academic Tenure. Finkin: 9–25.

Manning, Sylvia. 1986. Reflections on Having Separated Freshman Writing from the English Department. *ADE Bulletin* 73: 22–25.

Martinez, Armando Bravo. 1999. The New World Order and What We Make of It. *World Policy Journal* 16.3: 69–78.

Massy, William, Andrea Wilger and Carol Colbeck. 1994. Overcoming "Hollowed" Collegiality. *Change* July/August: 11–20.

McCarthy, E. Doyle. 1996. *Knowledge as Culture: The New Sociology of Knowledge.* London: Routledge.

McKenzie, Onie. 1998. College Experience Satisfaction Questionnaire: Summary Report of 1998 Survey Results. Hampden-Sydney College.

McQuade, Donald. 1992. Composition and Literary Studies. Greenblatt and Gunn: 482–519.

Mead, Margaret. 1970. *Culture and Commitment: The New Relationships between the Generations in the 1970s.* New York: Doubleday.

Menges, Robert J. et al., eds. 1999. *Faculty in New Jobs: A Guide to Settling In, Becoming Established, and Building Institutional Support.* San Francisco: Jossey-Bass.

Miller, J. Hillis. 1997. Foreword. Olson and Taylor: xi–1.

Miller, Richard E. 1994. Composing English Studies: Towards a Social History of the Discipline. *College Composition and Communication* 45: 164–179.

———. 1998. *As If Learning Mattered: Reforming Higher Education.* Ithaca, NY: Cornell University Press.

———. 1999. 'Let's Do the Numbers': Comp Droids and the Prophets of Doom. *MLA Profession*: 96–105.

Miller, Richard I. 1987. *Evaluating Faculty for Promotion and Tenure.* San Francisco: Jossey-Bass.

Miller, Susan. 1991. The Feminization of Composition. Bullock and Trimbur: 39–53.

Miller, Thomas. 28 Jan 2001. The politics of changing requirements. Online post, WPA-L. Archived at http://lists.asu.edu/archives/wpa-l.html.

———. 1997. *The Formation of College English: Rhetoric and Belles Lettres in the British Cultural Provinces.* Pittsburgh: University of Pittsburgh Press.

Modern Language Association (MLA). Fall 1999. Survey of Staffing in English and Foreign Language Departments. Available at http://www.mla.org.

MLA Commission on Professional Service. 1996. Making Faculty Work Visible: Reinterpreting Professional Service, Teaching, and Research in the Field of Language and Literature. *MLA Profession:* 161–216.

MLA Committee on Professional Employment. 1997. *Final Report.* New York: MLA.

Moran, Charles. 1993. The Winds—and Costs—of Change. *Computers and Composition* 9: 35–44.

Murphy, Michael. 2000. New Faculty for a New University: Toward a Full-Time Teaching Intensive Faculty Track in Composition. *College Composition and Communication* 52: 14–42.

Myers-Breslin, Linda, ed. 1999. *Administrative Problem-Solving for Writing Programs and Writing Centers*. Urbana: National Council of Teachers of English.

North, Stephen M. 1987. Research in Writing, Departments of English, and the Problem of Method. *ADE Bulletin* 88: 13–20.

North, Stephen M. et al. 2000. *Refiguring the Ph.D. in English Studies: Writing, Doctoral Education and the Fusion-Based Curriculum*. Urbana, IL: National Coucil of Teachers of English.

Odell, Lee. 1986. Diversity and Change: Toward a Maturing Discipline. *College Composition and Communication* 37: 395–401.

Olson, Gary A. and Todd W. Taylor, eds. 1997. *Publishing in Rhetoric and Composition*. New York: SUNY University Press.

Paré, Anthony and Judy Z. Segal.1993. University of Winnipeg Writing Program External Review Report. Winnipeg.

Parks, Steve and Eli Goldblatt. 2000. Writing beyond the Curriculum: Fostering New Collaborations on Literacy. *College English* 62: 584–606.

Petraglia, Joseph, ed. 1995. *Reconceiving Writing, Rethinking Writing Instruction*. Mahwah, NJ: Lawrence Erlbaum.

Petrosky, Anthony and David Bartholomae, eds. 1986. *The Teaching of Writing*. Chicago: NSSE.

Poovey, Mary. 1999. Beyond the Current Impasse in English Studies. *American Literary History* 11: 354–7.

Poston, Lawrence. 1986. Putting Literacy at the Center. *ADE Bulletin* 85: 13–20.

Rasch, William and Cary Wolfe, eds. 2000. *Observing Complexity: Systems Theory and Postmodernity*. Minnesota: Minnesota Press University Press.

Readings, Bill. 1996. *The University in Ruins*. Cambridge, MA: Harvard University Press.

Redirection Committee. 1996–1997. Recommendation Document. Department of English and Philosophy, Georgia Southern University.

Reinking, David, ed. 1998. *Handbook of Literacy and Technology: Transformations in a Post-Typographic World*. Mahwah, NJ: Erlbaum.

Roen, Duane, Stuart C. Brown, and Theresa Enos, eds. 1999. *Living Rhetoric and Composition: Stories of the Discipline*. Mahwah, NJ: Lawrence Erlbaum.

Rose, Shirley K. and Irwin Weiser, eds. 1999. *The Writing Program Administrator as Researcher: Inquiry in Action and Reflection*. Portsmouth, NH: Heinemann.

Rosner, Mary, Beth Boehm and Debra Journet, eds. 1999. *History, Reflection and Narrative: The Professionalization of Composition, 1963–1983*. Stamford, CT: Ablex.

Royster, Jaqueline Jones. 2000. Shifting the Paradigms of English Studies: Continuity and Change. *PMLA* 115.3: 1222–28.

Russell, David R. 1991. *Writing in the Academic Disciplines: 1870–1990: A Curricular History*. Carbondale: Southern Illinois University Press.

———. 1992. American Origins of the Writing Across the Curriculum Movement. Herrington and Moran: 22–42.

Schell, Eileen E. and Patricia Stock, eds. 2000. *Moving a Mountain: Improving the Working Conditions of Adjunct Writing Faculty.* Urbana, IL: National Council of Teachers of English.

Schoenfield, Clay A. and Robert Magnum. 1994. *Mentor in a Manual: Climbing the Academic Ladder to Tenure.* 2nd ed. Madison: Magna Publications.

Scholes, Robert. 1998. *The Rise and Fall of English: Reconstructing English as a Discipline.* New Haven: Yale University Press.

Schulz, Max, and Michael Holzman. 1981. English Departments—Writing Programs: Marriage or Divorce? *ADE Bulletin* 70: 26–29.

Schuster, Charles I. 1991. The Politics of Promotion. Bullock and Trimbur: 85–95.

———. 1991. Theory and Practice. Lindeman and Tate: 33–48.

———. 1996. Seeking a Disciplinary Reformation. Bloom, Daiker and White: 146–149.

Scott, Joyce and Nancy Bereman. 1992. Competition and Collegiality. *Journal of Higher Education* 63: 684–698.

Shamoon, Linda K. et al. 1995. New Rhetoric Courses in Writing Programs: A Report for New England Writing Program Administrators. *Writing Program Administration* 18: 7–25.

Shor, Ira. 26 Nov 1996. Minnesota. Online posting WPA-L. Archived at http://lists.asu.edu/archives/wpa-l.html.

———. 19 Jul 1997. Not Minnesota: What Writing Programs Can Be. Plenary Address. Annual Conference of the Council of Writing Program Administrators. Houghton, MI.

Sledd, James. 1991. Why the Wyoming Resolution Had to Be Emasculated: A History and a Quixotism. *Journal of Advanced Composition* 11: 269–81.

———. 2000. Return to Service. *Composition Studies* 28: 11–32.

Slevin, James. 1991. Depoliticizing and Politicizing Composition Studies. Bullock and Trimbur: 1–21.

———. 1991. The Politics of the Profession. Lindemann and Tate: 135–59.

Soley, Lawrence. 1995. *Leasing the Ivory Tower: The Corporate Takeover of Academia.* Boston: South End Press.

Spellmeyer, Kurt. 1998. Marginal Prospects. *Writing Program Administration* 21: 162–182.

Star, Susan Leigh, ed. 1995. *The Cultures of Computing.* Cambridge: Blackwell.

Stewart, Donald. 1992. Harvard's Influence on English Studies: Perceptions from Three Universities in the Early Twentieth Century. *College Composition and Communication* 43: 455– 471.

Stewart, James and Rhonda Spence. 1996. A New Look at Factors Related to College Faculty Morale. *Educational Research Quarterly* 20: 29–41.

Strain, Margaret. 1999. "Whispering Between the Lines": An Interview with Andrea Abernathy Lunsford. *Composition Forum* 10.1: 54–68.

Street, Brian V. 1995. *Social Literacies: Critical Approaches to Literacy in Development, Ethnography, and Education.* London: Longman.

Sullivan, Francis J. et al. 1997. Student Needs and Strong Composition: The Dialectics of Writing Program Reform. *College Composition and Communication* 48: 372–391.

Thaiss, Christopher et al. 1990. George Mason University. Fulwiler and Young: 221–242.

Tierney, William G. and Robert A. Rhoads. 1993. *Enhancing Promotion, Tenure and Beyond: Faculty Socialization as a Cultural Process*. ASHE-ERIC Higher Education Report No. 93–6. Washington: George Washington University.

Trimbur, John. 1999. The Problem of Freshman English (Only): Towards Programs of Study in Writing. *Writing Program Administration* 22.3: 9–30.

Tucker, Wayne. 1979. Rhetoric Reborn: A Theme with Commentary. *The Record of Hampden-Sydney College* 55 (Winter):19–22.

Tudor, Thomas R. and Randall Sleeth. 1997. Using Communication Consultants to Rightsize Successfully. *Journal of Technical Writing and Communication* 27: 87–93.

Van Alstyne, William. 1996. Tenure: A Summary, Explanation, and `Defense.' Finkin: 3–8.

White, Edward. 16 Oct 2000. Re: Need Info re Separate Writing Departments. Online posting WPA-L. Archived at http://lists.asu.edu/archives/wpa-l.html.

———. 1985. *Teaching and Assessing Writing*. San Francisco: Jossey-Bass.

———. 1989. *Developing Successful College Writing Programs*. San Francisco: Jossey-Bass.

Wilson, Robin. 1 Aug 1997. Universities Turn to Psychologists to Help Dysfunctional Departments. *Chronicle of Higher Education* 43:47: A10–11.

Winterowd, Ross W. and Vincent Gillespie, eds. 1994. *Composition in Context: Essays in Honor of Donald C. Stewart*. Carbondale: Southern Illinois University Press.

World Bank. May 2001. Income Poverty: The Latest Global Numbers. *Poverty Trends and Voices of the Poor.* http://worldbank.org/poverty/data/trends/income.htm

WPA Executive Committee. 1996. Evaluating the Intellectual Work of Writing Program Administrators: A Draft. *Writing Program Administration* 20: 92–103.

Young, Art and Toby Fulwiler. 1986. *Writing Across the Disciplines: Research into Practice*. Portsmouth, NH: Boynton-Cook.

NOTES ON CONTRIBUTORS

ELEANOR AGNEW is an associate professor in the Department of Writing and Linguistics at Georgia Southern University. She teaches first-year writing, Writing in the Workplace, Advanced Composition, and Linguistics and Grammar for Teachers. She has published articles in *Journal of Basic Writing, Assessing Writing, TESOL,* and in the anthology *Grading in the Post-Process Classroom.*

CHRIS ANSON is Professor of English and Director of the Campus Writing and Speaking Program at North Carolina State University, where he helps faculty in nine colleges to use writing and speaking in the service of students' learning and improved communication. He has written or edited twelve books and has published over fifty articles.

ANNE ARONSON is an associate professor in the Writing Department at Metropolitan State University in St. Paul, Minnesota. She teaches courses in composition, women's studies, professional writing, and rhetorical theory. Her research interests include the writing of adult students, feminist approaches to composition, and the intersections of professional and creative writing. She has been co-chair of Metropolitan State's Writing Department for nine years.

WENDY BISHOP, Kellogg W. Hunt Professor of English, teaches writing at Florida State University. She is the author or editor of sixteen books, including *Ethnographic Writing Research; Teaching Lives: Essays and Stories; Thirteen Ways of Looking for a Poem; Metro; The Subject Is Research; In Praise of Pedagogy: Poems and Flash Fiction on Teaching; The Writing Process Reader* and several chapbooks of poetry.

LARRY W. BURTON is Chair of the Department of Writing and Linguistics at Georgia Southern University. Writing and Linguistics includes first-year composition, creative writing, technical and professional writing, linguistics, the English Language Program, the University Writing Program, and the Georgia Southern University Writing Project. Larry's most recent publication is *The Language of Argument* (with Dan McDonald), 10th edition, Longman Publishers.

ANGELA CROW is an assistant professor at Georgia Southern University. In her research, she often addresses issues related to university living. In addition, she publishes on aging and literacy and on kinship practices in genre studies. Her writings have been published in a variety of venues–from *Teaching English in the Two-Year College* to *Kairos* to *Computers and Composition.*

PHYLLIS SURRENCY DALLAS is an Assistant Professor in the Department of Writing and Linguistics at Georgia Southern University. Despite having a Ph.D. in American literature, she was among the literature faculty placed in the new writing department. She has published articles on composition taught via distance technology and has regularly presented at CCCC.

THERESA ENOS is Professor of English and Director of the Rhetoric, Composition, and the Teaching of English Graduate program at the University of Arizona. Founder and editor of *Rhetoric Review,* she teaches both graduate and undergraduate courses in writing and rhetoric. She has numerous publications on rhetorical theory and issues in writing. She is the author of *Gender Roles and Faculty Lives in Rhetoric and Composition* (1996) and a past president of the National Council of Writing Program Administrators.

PATRICIA ERICSSON is currently a Ph.D. candidate in Rhetoric and Technical Communication at Michigan Technological University and formerly Director of Writing at Dakota State University. She has published articles in *Computers and Composition, Kairos, ACE Journal, Text Technology* and chapters in several books. She received the 2001 Kairos/Lore Computers and Writing Award for Scholarship.

CRAIG HANSEN is co-chair of the Writing Department at Metropolitan State University and director of the Technical Communication program. He has published a variety of articles and book chapters in the areas of technical communication, business communication, and composition and is the author, with Ann Hill Duin, of *Nonacademic Writing: Social Theory and Technology* (Lawrence Erlbaum, 1996).

GAIL E. HAWISHER is Professor of English and founding Director of the Center for Writing Studies at the University of Illinois, Urbana-Champaign, where she teaches graduate and undergraduate courses in writing studies. She has primarily published in literacy and technology studies, and her work has appeared in journals, such as *College English, Written Communication,* and *College Composition and Communication.* She and Cynthia Selfe continue to edit *Computers and Composition* (Elsevier) and also have co-edited several books, including *Passions, Pedagogies, and 21st Century Technologies* (Utah State University Press, 1999).

JANE E. HINDMAN is an associate professor in the Department of Rhetoric and Writing Studies at San Diego State University. Her work has appeared in *College English, JAC, Pre/Text, Journal of Basic Writing, Writing Program Administrator, LIT,* and other venues. She has edited a special issue of *College English* on the place of the personal in academic discourse and is completing a book on the same subject.

JUDITH KEARNS is an associate professor, Acting Dean of Humanities, and former Director of the Centre for Academic Writing at the University of Winnipeg. Her research interests include the rhetoric of inquiry and Renaissance women's writing. She has published articles in *Inkshed, Journal of Teaching Writing, WPA: Writing Program Administration,* and *Textual Studies in Canada.*

BARRY M. MAID is Professor and Head Faculty of Technical Communication at Arizona State University East where he recently led the development of a new program in Multimedia Writing and Technical Communication. Before moving to ASU in January 2000, he spent nineteen years at the University of Arkansas, Little Rock where, among other duties, he directed the Writing Center and the First-Year Composition Program, chaired the Department of English, and helped in the creation of the Department of Rhetoric and Writing.

THOMAS P. MILLER teaches in the English Department at the University of Arizona. While director of the writing program, he won a university-wide award for his service to graduate students in 1999. His research examines the history of college English from its origins in more broad-based institutions in the eighteenth-century British cultural provinces. The first volume of *The Formation of College English Studies* received the MLA's Mina Shaughnessy Award in 1998.

PEGGY O'NEILL began her career in the Writing and Linguistics Department at Georgia Southern University. She has since moved to the Communication Department at Loyola College, Maryland, where she teaches writing and directs the composition program. Her scholarship, which includes writing assessment and composition pedagogy, has appeared in journals such as *College Composition and Communication, Composition Studies,* and *Assessing Writing* as well as several edited collections. She also has a co-edited volume, *Practice in Context: Situating the Work of Writing Teachers,* forthcoming from NCTE.

LOUISE REHLING directs the Technical & Professional Writing Program at San Francisco State University, where she is an Associate Professor. Previously, she taught at the University of Utah, Westminster College, and Salt Lake Community College. Dr. Rehling also has over 15 years of industry experience, as a writer, editor, trainer, consultant, and manager. Her Ph.D., A.M., and A.B. degrees are in English Language & Literature from the University of Michigan, Ann Arbor.

DANIEL J. ROYER and ROGER GILLES are associate professors of Writing at Grand Valley State University. While directing the composition program, they developed a course-wide, team-based portfolio grading system and instituted directed self-placement. In 1998, they and their colleagues began working toward an independent Writing department, which became official in July of 2001. Royer and Gilles are co-editors of *Directed Self-Placement: Principles and Practices* (forthcoming from Hampton Press).

CYNTHIA L. SELFE is Professor of Humanities in the Humanities Department at Michigan Technological University, and the founder (with Kathleen Kiefer) and co-editor (with Gail Hawisher) of *Computers and Composition: An International Journal for Teachers of Writing.* Recipient of many awards for innovative computer use in higher education, Selfe has also served as the Chair of the Conference on College Composition and Communication and the Chair of the College Section of the National Council of Teachers of English.

ELLEN SCHENDEL teaches academic and professional writing courses in the Writing Department at Grand Valley State University. Her research focuses on writing assessment and has been published in *WPA: Writing Program Administration* and *Assessing Writing*, among other places.

KURT SPELLMEYER is the Director of the Faculty of Arts and Sciences Writing Program at Rutgers University in New Brunswick, New Jersey, a program that serves about 11,000 students each year. He is the author of *Common Ground: Dialogue, Understanding, and the Teaching of Composition*, and *Arts of Living: Reinventing the Humanities for the Twenty-first Century*, (forthcoming). With Richard Miller, he is the editor of *The New Humanities Reader* (forthcoming).

BRIAN TURNER is an associate professor in the Centre for Academic Writing, University of Winnipeg, where he teaches composition, rhetorical criticism, modern rhetorical theory, and rhetoric in the disciplines. His articles have appeared in such journals as *Teaching English in the Two-Year College, Journal of Teaching Writing, Rhetoric Review*, and *Textual Studies in Canada*. He is currently working on a book about *ethos* in American nature writing.

JESSICA YOOD is an assistant professor of English at Lehman College, City University of New York. She teaches undergraduate and graduate courses in literary genres, literary and rhetorical theory, and composition and co-directs the Writing Across the Curriculum Program.

INDEX